D0379620

Growing Through the Pain

GROWING THROUGH THE PAIN

The Incest Survivor's Companion

Catherine Bronson

PRENTICE
H A L L
PARKSIDE

A Prentice Hall/Parkside Recovery Book

New York   London   Toronto   Sydney   Tokyo   Singapore

Parkside Medical Services Corporation is a full-service
provider of treatment for alcoholism, other drug addiction,
eating disorders, and psychiatric illness.

Parkside Medical Services Corporation
205 West Touhy Avenue
Park Ridge, IL 60068
1-800-PARKSIDE

 PRENTICE HALL PRESS
15 Columbus Circle
New York, NY 10023

PRENTICE HALL PRESS and colophons are registered trademarks
of Simon & Schuster, Inc.

PRENTICE HALL/PARKSIDE™ is a trademark
of Simon & Schuster, Inc.

Library of Congress Cataloging-in-Publication Data
Anonymous.
    Growing through the pain : the incest survivor's companion /
Catherine Bronson
      p.   cm.
    ISBN 0-13-366915-7
    1. Incest victims—United States—Psychology—Case studies.
2. Incest victims—United States—Family relationships—Case
studies.   3. Adult child sexual abuse victims—United States—
Psychology—Case studies.   I. Title.
HQ72.U53A66   1990
362.7'6—dc20   89-77778
                                                                   CIP

Manufactured in the United States of America

10 9 8 7 6 5 4 3 2 1

First Prentice Hall Press Edition

Dedication

To all the children who survived,
but most of all
To those who didn't.
"May flights of angels sing thee to thy rest."

ACKNOWLEDGMENTS

My thanks to the women who contributed to this book in terms of their courage and their determination to have a quality life. They hope that by telling their story they would cut short the pain of other survivors, and would help them get beyond this pain. People should remember that we're not just our past and our dysfunction. Although we don't often express it, we too are developing a more meaningful life.

My thanks to The Women's Center of Northern Virginia for its commitment to helping women not only survive, but grow.

My thanks to (in alphabetical order): Lorraine Beaulieu, M.Ed (C.Ed), Northern Virginia Counseling and Consulting Associates of Springfield, Virginia; Mark Binderman, Ph.D., Vienna Family Therapy Clinic of Falls Church, Virginia; Jean Thurow, Psy.D., Woodstock, Illinois; for your support and for your professional criticisms of the manuscript.

My thanks to John Small, Jr., Director of Parkside Publishing, for encouraging and supporting the book; to Terry Spohn for his editorial patience and perseverence; to Ellie Cerniglia, Pat Martindale, and Georgeanne Glennon for transcribing and manuscript preparation; to Nancy Ethiel for sensitive copyediting; to Janet Plant for editorial proofreading; and to Sharon W. Pepping for text design.

To my husband and children for reminding me that life has to go on.

TABLE OF CONTENTS

> The Medusa; Denial and Isolation: The Enemies of Recovery; Three Elements of Recovery; Recovery: Where You Get Better; Guilt; Denial; Loss of Self-Possession; Take Possession of Yourself; Accept Our Powerlessness; Listen to Yourself; Inventory the Parts; A Place of Your Own; Take This Friend on Your Journey Through Incest; An Intellectual Approach Is Not Enough; Write Your Way Through.

Introduction to Chapter 2

> What Is Incest?; Incidence; The Victims; All Methods of Obtaining Compliance Are Violent; Characteristics of Abusers; Alcoholism and Incest; Commonalities of Incest Survivors and Adult Children; Specific Effects of Incest; Post-Traumatic Stress Disorder; Prevalence of Incest in Treatment Populations; Disguised Presentation; Three Long-Term Effects Emerge With "Developmental Triggers"; Chronic Traumatic Neuroses—Denial and Recurrences; Parentification—Relational Imbalance in the Family; The Intergenerational Risk of Incest; Incest Recognition Profile; Hallucinations in a Nonpsychotic Person; Veterans of Another Kind of Violence.

Chapter 3—"Who Are We and What Happened?"

Introduction to Chapter 3

Chapter 6—Specific Effects of Incest Trauma: "Am I Crazy or Does Everybody See Lizards Dining Out in Washington, D.C.?"

Introduction to Chapter 6

Chapter 7—Therapy: A Series of Small Nuclear Explosions 222

Introduction to Chapter 7

Problems; My Therapist Kept Falling Asleep; I Think My New Therapist Is Disgusted With Me; Therapy Issues; The Pain of a Newborn Baby.

Introduction

This book is written for incest survivors. It is about incest as it is *experienced* from the inside, rather than incest analyzed objectively from the outside. The value of this book is in its simple sharing of experience by six incest survivors. It can be a helpful companion for the incest survivor on the journey through recovery. It validates a survivor's experience, while offering companionship and hope. It says to the reader, "You are not alone in this, and you will get through it."

Isolation is one of the most painful parts of the incest experience. For the survivor who is ready to receive them, this book offers six new friends who speak from many different levels of recovery. Some of it is painful, some of it is confusing, some disturbing, but all of it is an honest and accurate account of how it feels to grow through the pain from incest victim, to incest survivor, to freedom from incest.

Although most of the material is experiential, some analytical and theoretical material is necessary to an understanding of the incest experience. This is, however, kept at a simple and basic level. The book has also undergone several reviews by experienced, credentialed practitioners who have worked for years with incest survivors. The book is not meant to be a scholarly or theoretical work, though professionals will find the stories to be valuable case histories. It was not written to advance research or explore the latest clinical techniques. It does not try to say everything that can be said about incest trauma. The goal of the book is to bring companionship, hope, and validation to the incest survivor. It says to the reader, "We do get through the pain, and life can be good. Recovery is possible. We know, we are doing it."

1

We Are Survivors

We are survivors, not victims. We were victims when, as trusting and dependent children, someone we loved and believed in used us for his own devices. First, we felt our bodies were taken from us. Then, when our pain and anguish were met with denial, we felt our minds were taken:[1] "No, that never happened. How dare you say such a thing about your father (or brother, or uncle, or grandfather)!" "That's disgusting—I don't want to hear it!" "Forget about it. It's not important." So we gave up possession of our thoughts and feelings to others.

In the end, we may lose our souls to alcohol, drugs, damaging relationships, or other destructive behavior, unless we get angry enough to say, "Enough." Sometimes we have to reach the bottom of the pit of despair to realize that our pain will be infinite unless we grab it, turn it around, and face it. We are victims while we endure it. We are survivors when we face it.

And we *can* face it. In the process of recovery, we face the "monster." We examine it, we come to terms with it, and we dispose of it once and for all. We regain our self-possession and we are free, no longer victims, no longer survivors, just ourselves at last.

THE MEDUSA

How did we get stuck with our monster to begin with? In Greek mythology, there is a story about the Medusa, a creature so horrible to look upon that it turned the viewer to stone. So the Medusa was locked away, and the world was warned, "Do not look upon this thing."

Those of us who have suffered incest have been made to feel that we carry the Medusa within. We are the keepers of the monster. We have suffered not only the pain of the crime against us, but the pain

3

of the aftermath—the cold rejection and denial of our suffering. The message to us from our families, from society, even from the mental health profession has been, "Do not look upon this hideous thing." So we have carried the monster around alone, protecting others from it, keeping up appearances while we suffered within. And always, we got the message from others, "Don't look, don't make us see." Until we defy that message and face the monster, it will dominate our lives.

Many of us have become consummate actresses. We have jobs, marriages, friends, and families. We get up in the morning, dress with care, put on our faces, and smile. We go to parties and talk to other people about everyday things. We listen sympathetically to our friends' problems with their boyfriends, their jobs, their cars, their children. Sometimes we might do this with the help of alcohol or another drug that numbs our own inner pain a little.

We often feel vulnerable inside. The hard, brittle, "normal" world other people seem to live in can cut through our defensive facade. The stress of maintaining our defenses exhausts us when we're with other people for too long. We have to retreat to the safe place within where we're alone with our monster and we don't have to pretend. We can cry, be hurt, and grieve. And nobody can know. Many of us find that we only feel safe when we are alone. Nobody can hurt us then. Only when we're alone can we be ourselves, because only when we're alone can we have those forbidden feelings.

It feels crazy to have this world within that doesn't fit the world without. We think sometimes, "One of them must not be real!" Some of us may doubt the reality of our experience with incest. "Maybe it was a dream?" *"Did I make it all up?"* "Am I making a big deal out of nothing?" In this way, our minds are taken from us.

But by insisting on the truth, we can change that. Even though it may seem impossible when you are stuck in it, you will emerge from the pain and dispossession of incest to claim your life again.

Denial and Isolation: The Enemies of Recovery

Traditional Freudian psychology has helped to perpetuate the refusal to accept the truth about incest. When Sigmund Freud, the father of modern psychology, first started hearing well-bred young Viennese girls talk about having been sexually abused by their fathers and other male relatives, he was stunned. Being male, and having a professional investment in protecting the stereotypes of masculinity, he decided not to believe that big strong men could victimize helpless female children. So he constructed an elaborate explanation of their stories: They were fantasies arising from the girls' own sexual desires for their fathers.

As a result of this myth, abusers were protected and incest victims devastated for almost a century. In combination with the denial within our families, the denial of the mental health profession reinforced societal denial and effectively prevented us from getting treatment for our injuries and our pain. In the last ten years, Freud's error has been exposed, and the mental health field has begun to recognize the pervasiveness of incest and to develop a sane, compassionate response. But the societal denial all of us suffer on a daily basis persists.

When I told acquaintances I was writing this book, their responses illustrate the extent of our isolation:

> "Isn't incest over-reported? I mean, isn't most of it just a fantasy they make up to explain their problems?"

> "It's not really incest unless it's forcible rape."

> "Oh." (End of conversation.)

> "Let me tell you about *those people*—it's the hill people and it's part of their culture. It's better just to leave them alone." (This from a former social worker.)

> "Insects? You mean—bugs?"

And these were all well-educated, intelligent, and urbane people. We've all been hurt by attitudes like those. But we don't have to be.

Three Elements of Recovery

Denial and isolation hurt us. Facing our pain together helps us to recover. The process of recovery is long and arduous. It should not be undertaken alone. You will need three things:

1. A good therapist, one who is familiar with the long-term negative effects of incest and who has experience in working with it.
2. A support group or therapy group of other incest survivors.
3. A commitment to recovery. You will need to feel that you can't go on anymore with things the way they are, because once you confront what's inside of you, you can't ever again return to ignorance. There will be times when the process is so painful that you will wish you could turn back. But you can't.

RECOVERY: WHERE YOU GET BETTER

Guilt

In the process of recovery, we overcome guilt and denial to heal the pain of incest.

Three things to remember always are:

1. It's not your fault.
2. It's not your fault.
3. It's not your fault.

Years and years of denial have made many of us feel that somehow the responsibility for incest is ours. The burden of coping with the Medusa has been placed on us when it should have been placed on the perpetrators. Nevertheless, we feel guilt and shame for carrying the monster that everyone hates so much they won't even recognize its existence.

To feel better about ourselves, we have to work on remembering that the thing that happened to us was *not our fault.* We didn't do it to ourselves. We have to insist that the primary assumption must always be that *when there is any sexual activity between an adult and a child, the adult is responsible.* If you were not abused by an adult, but by a sibling or a related peer, remember that *you were a victim of a power imbalance, and the more powerful party is always responsible!*

Another thing to remember is that incest is inherently violent.[2] Many abusers dismiss their behavior by saying, "I never hurt her." Maybe we weren't beaten or tied up or threatened with a weapon. Maybe we were seduced and compliant. No matter how willing we were to do what we were told, we were victims of violence. We were overwhelmed by the real or perceived power of our abuser. That is violence. It feels like violence and it is violence. We were not accomplices; we were victims of violence. When we start to feel guilty, we must remember that.

Denial

The inability of others[3] to deal with incest comes from their feelings of horror toward the crime. Because, as victims, we embody the crime, horror gets directed at us. People don't like victims because they don't know how to act or what to say. They feel they should respond, but can't find a response. So they often become inept and say things that hurt. The most common response is to deny our experience in some way.

We need to remember that their inability to face us, their inability to respond, is *their* shortcoming, not ours. It doesn't mean we are horrible, or that they are horrible. It means sometimes people don't know what to do or how to act appropriately.

How are we to respond to the denial of others? It is a difficult problem for us and one we, as survivors, must continually address. This question is explored in more detail in another chapter. But one very basic concept that must be established is how denial affects our self-possession.

We lose our self-possession through denial.[4] Denial has two parts— the denial of others and our own denial. Denial on the part of others is an attempt to reject something that is real because they don't know how to respond to it. When the reality of our incest experience or its effects is denied when we are children, we incorporate that denial into ourselves.

The formation of our own denial started when we were children and was reinforced as we grew up. Generally, we came from families in which the perceptions and needs of children were not validated very well to begin with. When we were abused, we looked to those around us for a response, to validate our feelings. Like all children, we relied heavily on our environment for a model on which to base our own responses.

The first thing we learned was that incest was "bad." The next thing we learned was that it didn't really happen, or if it did, it wasn't really important, or it was our own fault. The abuser is usually the first and most damaging source of this denial, telling us, "It's just a game; I didn't hurt you. You know you like it; this is our special secret." As we grew older, our denial was continually reinforced as we failed to get a validating response to our trauma.

But the trauma was still there. It didn't go away. Painfully, we tried to incorporate another version of reality, but it never really fit because we still had our inner experience of pain, hurt, and anger that never quite went away. But since we got the message that the incest wasn't "real" or wasn't "important," we were made to feel that our inner experience of it must be *something we invented, something we were doing to ourselves*. We were forced to blame ourselves for our own traumas. When we felt grief, pain, anger, fear, our response became, "There must be something wrong with me. I shouldn't feel this way." The connection with the original trauma was lost, and so were we.

The ultimate effect was to place the "badness" of incest on us. The abuser was forgotten. We were made responsible first for his crime, then for its effect on us. The responsibility was wrongly placed on us first by our abusers, then by our families, society, and in many cases, by incompetent psychology. We are given the "badness" of incest, and we acquired guilt and shame in taking responsibility for this thing.

Loss of Self-Possession

The next step is our loss of self-possession. Denial teaches us that our feelings, thoughts, and perceptions are not true. Our families tended to do that a lot when we were children. We never had the experience of knowing what we knew or feeling what we felt. As a result, we never learned to trust our own perceptions. We grew up without developing an internal mechanism for self-validation. Even in adulthood, we continue to give ourselves to sources outside ourselves for validation, as children do.

As adults we are vulnerable to self-definition by sources outside ourselves. Other people can take possession of our identities, dictate our self-esteem. To some degree we can be told what to think and who we are. Thus the final, ultimate violation of incest is not only that we feel our bodies are taken away from us, but that we feel our minds are taken from us. We don't feel what we feel, and we don't know what we know, and we always have to adjust to imposed feelings and knowledge from outside ourselves. We don't possess ourselves.

This process occurs to some degree in all of us, with great variation. How many of us have spent our lives trying to be someone else? Changed our names? Depended too much on a relationship, our achievements, our jobs, our church, or some other external source for our identity and our self-esteem?

Take Possession of Yourself

Our first act in recovery is to take possession of ourselves. Claim your experience, your thoughts, and feelings for yourself. Respect them, even love them. Protect them from the ignorant and unenlightened. Choose your friends carefully, select your therapist with care, treat yourself very protectively. Love and hold the child within who was hurt. Believe in her and defend her. She is part of you. Tell her every day:

"It wasn't your fault."

"You have been very hurt and now I will take care of you and make it better."

"You are a good person, and I love you."

Let her cry, be hurt, be angry, and grieve. And all the while, hold her tight.

Accept Our Powerlessness

For many of us, this is a hard thing to do. Many of us cannot face that child within. We might even hate her (which is to hate ourselves) for "letting" the incest happen. If we are ever to possess ourselves again, we must accept something that at first feels overwhelming and degrading:

We were powerless over our abuser.

We really were victims.

It is hard to accept this, because it violates one of our most cherished illusions, that we are always in control. Admitting we were powerless feels threatening to the "Big I" within that insists, "*I* was never powerless. *I* am in control."

There is a fear that if we admit we were powerless, our whole image of ourselves as strong and powerful adults will collapse, and we will be helpless and vulnerable again. We are afraid of humiliation.

So, we hold responsible the abused child that we were. But in doing that, we face the ramifications: If she is responsible, we have to reject her. If we reject her, we reject ourselves, we lose our self-possession. Ironically, by insisting we are always in control, we ultimately lose ourselves.

Listen to Yourself

An effective technique for taking possession of yourself again is to keep a journal. After years of losing ourselves to denial, sometimes it's hard to find ourselves. Writing a journal daily is a good way to get back to yourself. It must be a completely confidential record of whatever is on your mind for that day. It is important that you make it totally confidential, because if you know that someone else might read it sometime, you'll find yourself distorting, denying, and dressing things up. By writing just for yourself, you can gradually find that voice inside that is totally, honestly yours. It may be a screaming, angry, hurt voice, but it's all yours. You will begin to have confidence in that voice. You can begin to possess yourself again.

Inventory the Parts

The other step necessary for taking possession of yourself is to identify, through therapy, which parts of your thoughts and feelings were forced on you by abuse and denial. These are the parts that hurt you. These are the parts you can cast away to make room for yourself. But you have to confront everything if you want to do this.

Imagine a room crammed so full of junk and debris that you have very little or no space to live in it or to arrange in it the things that you need and like. After years of exhausting maneuvering through all the useless junk and debris to get to the few things that are yours, you decide to take an inventory. Piece by piece, you get to know every item in the room. You try it out, and if it doesn't fit, you cast it out. Finally you begin to clear a space for yourself, and you find the things that are yours.

A Place of Your Own

When you are in possession of yourself, you finally will have a solid place inside to stand. At the beginning it may be just a tiny spot and you might feel sometimes that you wish it were a better spot. But hold onto that spot and respect it. The denial that made you believe that being yourself was shameful will not work so well anymore when you have your own spot to stand on. Your guilt and shame will start to go away as you confront the abuse that was forced on you and place the responsibility on the abuser, where it belongs. Your pain will gradually diminish, and you will find that you can experience it without being destroyed by it.

Instead of shamefully "hiding" your experience from others, you will be taking care of yourself by refusing to subject yourself to the ordinary limitations of other people. "Hiding" and "protecting" are two different things and feel quite different. We have to "hide" when we allow denial to tell us that the abuse is all ours. It becomes our Medusa, and we respond to the demand, "Do not look upon this thing."

As we confront our abuse, after a while, we won't be afraid of the Medusa. As we recognize ourselves and claim the thoughts, feelings, and experiences that are ours, the Medusa will be transformed. What you will find inside is not a terrifying monster, but YOURSELF. You will have possession of yourself.

You will not have to hide. Instead, you will protect, you will nurture, and you will begin to heal.

Take This Friend on Your Journey Through Incest

This book is for incest survivors who want to face the Medusa, who want to possess themselves again. It has been written to be a companion in the process. Nobody should do it alone. It helps to have the companionship and compassion of others who are going our way. The loneliness of incest is indescribable. I always felt like a child alone in the cold dark, watching through a window at other people celebrating Christmas. This book is a sharing and caring friend for all the children of incest. You won't be alone in the dark anymore.

The following chapters will help you understand what has happened to you, and what it feels like to go through the process of confronting and healing. Chapter 2 provides a typical clinical, theoretical picture of incest and its aftermath. This is a theoretical framework used by therapists, and it is useful in that it provides general classifications and terms for our experience. In this chapter, we are described by the language of psychology. This is a reductionist approach: Complex and various experiences are reduced to a single term such as "dissociation." In reading this chapter, you will be looking at incest through the eyes of a therapist.

An Intellectual Approach Is Not Enough

Many of us feel that we are more in control of our experience when we can look at it with this sort of objectivity. It makes us feel secure to place labels and classifications on our behavior—as if we could construct a cage of words to contain the monster. This is often a way of avoiding the emotional realities within and would ultimately prevent us from coming to terms with those emotions if we let it. Although the clinical literature can help us understand ourselves and gives us a terminology, it is no substitute for the process of letting ourselves experience our feelings. An intellectual understanding of incest is not enough. We have to feel the pain of what happened to us and grieve for ourselves before we can get better. Healing happens when we find our wounds and dress them. That process can take many years. Although it is often exhilarating, it can be lonely and frightening.

That is why most of this book is devoted to communicating the experiences of other survivors as they make their way through the process. Each chapter addresses some component of the clinical picture presented in Chapter 2, but from the point of view of people who are experiencing it in their daily lives. It helps to know that other victims have passed this way before, and they survived it to go on to happier, healthier lives.

Reading about others will not diminish your pain, but will diminish your fear of it. I found that the fear I had of my intense and disrupting emotions made them much worse. I needed to know, at all times, that I was not the only person to go through it and that others with the same experiences had come through it to feel stronger and happier.

I needed help to keep from being swallowed up by my feelings. I needed hope to overcome feelings of despair and helplessness. I needed validation of thoughts and feelings that had been denied all my life. The following chapters were written for those purposes.

Write Your Way Through

As suggested earlier, a journal is a good way to start getting in touch with ourselves. That kind of writing is free form and associative. It helps us to find thoughts and feelings we had not allowed ourselves to recognize.

Another therapeutic use of writing is to take a more structured approach. In addition to the journal, try to write your own story. Writing our own stories can be highly therapeutic, but it can also be overwhelming. This book provides guidance and structure with a therapeutic format for you to follow. As you read each section, try to write your own story for that part. The topical divisions of the book will help you to focus on specific subject areas. You will be able to make sense of your experience. Those of us who contributed our stories to this book found that in the end we knew more than when we started.

> *"We shall not cease from exploration*
> *And the end of all our exploring*
> *will be to arrive where we started*
> *And know the place for the first time."*

> T.S. Eliot
> "Little Gidding"
> *The Four Quartets*

CHAPTER 1—FOOTNOTES

1. The concept of feeling that our bodies, then our minds were taken from us was first presented to me in a group meeting conducted by Lorraine Beaulieu, M.Ed., C. Ed.
2. "Coercion, manipulation, force, and violation are inherent any time an adult sexually abuses a child. To regard the weak, inadequate men who

abuse children as nonviolent is to fail to see these offenders as their victims see them—as big and powerful adults." (Conte, Jon R., "Progress in Treating the Sexual Abuse of Children," *Social Work* (May-June 1984) 260).

3. When I refer to "others" here, I am excluding the perpetrators. Their denial is another matter altogether.
4. Denial, validation, and self-possession are discussed in greater detail in Chapters 4 and 5.

2

A Clinical View of Incest—Tools for Thought

This chapter is meant to give you the basic concepts and terminology needed to understand incest on an intellectual level. You may find yourself described here, but not in the way you experience yourself. The chapters following this one will take parts of this clinical description and tell you what a number of survivors feel like on the inside. Attaching concepts and terms to these feelings and experiences allows us to organize in our minds what may feel initially like a jumbled mass of overwhelming emotions.

In showing how incest survivors are described in the clinical literature, from the outside, I have depended heavily on an article by Denise J. Gelinas. This is one of the most comprehensive descriptions I have found and also the most accessible to the average reader. I have used other sources as well to show some of the variety of thinking on this subject. This chapter is not meant to be original or scholarly work, but simply a typical example of the way we look to mental health professionals from the theoretical point of view.

This chapter is not an exhaustive discussion of incest, nor is it meant to be. That would be far beyond the scope of this book, which is an experiential view of incest. Even since this book was started, more developments in theory and clinical practice have been published. For those who are interested in the latest research and a more thorough theoretical discussion of incest, I suggest you survey professional journals for articles and bibliographies on the subject written for mental health practitioners.

As you read this chapter, remember that it is to provide you with tools you can use to work on your feelings—work that must be done if you are to recover. An intellectual understanding of incest is enough for a practitioner to help us recover, but it is not enough for us. For us, recovery comes with working through the pain.

WHAT IS INCEST?

What is Incest? Legal definitions vary, and many of them rely on physical evidence that is rarely available, especially in very young victims. For clinical purposes, incest is commonly defined as sexual contact between an adult and child with an established familial relationship. This definition is not broad enough, however, to include sibling incest. A more accurate definition would include two crucial components in the relationship that would extend it to cover sibling and surrogate parent incest: imputed trust and a power imbalance. In this more inclusive definition, the more powerful party (father, mother, cousin, brother, stepfather) abuses the real or imputed familial trust of the less powerful party for sexual purposes. "Imputed trust" is important to the definition, because it makes clear that regardless of whether the less powerful party actually trusted the more powerful party, there was a legitimate *expectation* of trust inherent in the familial relationship.

"Sexual contact" includes all forms of sexual behavior, ranging from autoerotic displays, to fondling of genitals, to oral-genital contact, and both anal and vaginal intercourse.

Incidence

Although it is speculated that the incidence of incest is as great for males as for females, available data shows that 80 to 90 percent of reported victims are female, and approximately 90 percent of offenders are male.[1] Prevalence of incest among the general female population has been estimated in a recent study to be as high as 16 percent.[2] Data on prevalence of sexual abuse in general is more abundant than that on incest alone, and guesses at what percentage of reported sexual abuse may be incest vary from 10 percent to 50 percent.[3]

This may reflect a bias in the clinical population upon which reported data is based. As MacFarlane, Waterman, et al., point out, the clinical population represents victims who have problems of an order of magnitude that require treatment, and may therefore include a higher proportion of incest, which is generally recognized to be more damaging than other forms of sexual abuse, than in the general population.[4]

The Victims

There is a great variation in the ages of victims. Gelinas cites studies that report the most usual ages to be between 4 and 12 years old, with most frequent occurrence at ages 4 and 9.[5] Forward cites other studies that place the average age between 11 to 13 years, although Forward herself reports an average age of 7 or 8.[6]

Duration of incest also varies widely and appears to have no correlation to the severity of trauma. The victim's age does determine to some extent the type of sexual activity and methods of obtaining compliance. Sexual intercourse is generally too difficult with small children, although anal intercourse is somewhat easier to achieve. Consequently, other, less physically detectable forms of sexual activity are preferred until the child reaches adolescence, when intercourse becomes more common.

All Methods of Obtaining Compliance Are Violent

Methods of obtaining compliance become more threatening and violent as the age of the victim increases. Very young children are easily seduced, having no basis for evaluating the sexual requests made of them. Force is usually unnecessary since the child ordinarily trusts the abuser and may crave the special attention offered, even though the sexual acts themselves may be frightening. However, it is important to remember, as Conte points out, "Coercion, manipulation, force, and violation are inherent any time an adult sexually abuses a child . . . To minimize what has happened to a child who has been abused by suggesting that there has been no violence done is to tolerate the abuse of power and the use of force."[7] Secrecy is often secured by telling the child that disclosure would result in imprisonment or death of the perpetrator or with threats of punishment. Since the perpetrator is usually a male relative known and possibly loved by the child, such threats are usually effective.

An adolescent or older child, however, is commonly persuaded to comply and keep silent through her sense of guilt, responsibility for her family, and threats of violence. Abusers often tell older victims that disclosure would destroy the family, or that the victim herself is to blame for the act, so the children are reluctant to report. Another threat that occurs frequently in the abuse of older children is that if they fail to comply, the abuser will victimize younger sisters.

Characteristics of Abusers

As a group, incest offenders are heterogeneous. An abuser can be anyone. No particular ethnic group or social class is disproportionately represented. A few characteristics do stand out, however. Catholics have, in one study, comprised as much as 44 percent of the offenders and victims.[8] Although this particular study identifies Catholics, it is likely that any religious denominations characterized by rigid dogma may be disproportionately represented. Religious prohibitions against going outside the family to meet needs may be one of the factors contributing to the abusers turning to other family members when the marriage fails to provide what the abuser regards to be necessary nurturing. Another explanation may be that incest occurs within a context of serious family dysfunction, one characteristic of which is the rigidity and inflexible coping mechanisms associated with an equally rigid religious structure. Regardless of the causes, strict religious affiliations occur frequently among incestuous families. Ironically, many victims report that a religious taboo against any discussion of sexual information within the family actually facilitated the mystification and sexual abuse of the children.

Alcoholism and Incest

Another characteristic that emerges among paternal incest offenders is alcoholism. Alcohol has been reported as a factor in up to 90 percent of child abuse cases.[9] In one program for incest treatment, 75 percent of the families reported alcohol problems, and a prison research study reported that 46 percent of incest offenders had alcohol problems.[10]

Offenders often blame the disinhibiting effects of alcohol for their incestuous behavior. However, incest is usually premeditated. The abuser carefully chooses the time, place, and type of sexual behavior with the deliberate intent of commission and concealment. It is, therefore, more likely that abusers use alcohol deliberately as a facilitator.[11]

In some psychological models, the alcoholic is, like the incest offender, characterized by a primary narcissistic defect and exhibits profound psychosexual immaturity.[12] Other studies show that both alcoholics and incest abusers are highly symbiotic. These are more convincing links between alcoholism and incest than the simplistic belief that alcohol use resulted in episodes of poor impulse control.

The immaturity and narcissism of the offender is just one similarity between alcoholic families and incestuous families. Both kinds of families are remarkably similar in that both family systems are constructed around a family secret. Much of the current literature describing alcoholic families applies to incestuous families. Both are characterized by denial, inadequate boundaries, rigid and inappropriate coping mechanisms, parentification of children, marital and sexual dysfunction, social isolation, physical and psychological abuse of children and spouses, lack of nurturing, and emotional deprivation.

Commonalities of Incest Survivors and Adult Children

Long-term effects characteristic of adult children of alcoholics (referred to as "adult children") and common to incest survivors are best described by Claudia Black in *It Will Never Happen to Me:*

> "Adult children of alcoholics often have difficulties identifying and expressing feelings. They become very rigid and controlling. Some find themselves overly dependent on others; they feel no sense of power of choice in the way they live. A pervasive sense of fear and guilt often exists in their lives. Many experience depression and frequently do not have the ability to feel close or to be intimate with another human being." (pp. 4–5.)

Janet Woititz, in her book *Adult Children of Alcoholics* (1983, 23–54), lists some of the characteristics of adult children that will be very familiar to incest survivors, or any other person from a dysfunctional family built upon a secret: no concept of normal behavior; difficulty following through on projects; habitual dishonesty; hyper-self-criticism; inability to "play" because of overdeveloped self-vigilance; inability to maintain intimacy; constant approval-seeking behavior; over-responsible or irresponsible; impulsive; inappropriate or undeserved loyalty.

SPECIFIC EFFECTS OF INCEST

In families where the child is subjected to both parental alcoholism and incest, it may be particularly difficult to make a distinction between the effects of the dysfunctional family system and the effects of the incest. However, while family dysfunction alone may produce the complications described by Black and Woititz, other effects are attributable exclusively to incest. Gelinas defines these as "traumatic neurosis and its related elements, [such as] confusion, repetition, compulsion, flashbacks, repressed memories, and affect."[13] As Gelinas explains, "Exposure of the child to chronic marital estrangement, inadequate parenting and role reversal with the mother is obviously not optimal and can lead to some negative effects later in life. But such exposure will not produce a traumatic neurosis. Sex with a parent usually will."[14] "Sex with a parent" can be extended to the more generic definition of incest that includes siblings, surrogate parents, and other related parties.

Post-Traumatic Stress Disorder

Kovach has similarly identified "Post-Traumatic Stress Disorder (PTSD)" among 50 percent of alcoholic women who experienced father-figure incest, finding that PTSD is the major distinction between alcoholic women and alcoholic women who are also childhood incest victims. PTSD is another term for what Gelinas first identified as traumatic neuroses in incest victims.[15] It is noteworthy that incest victims have been found in disproportionate numbers in alcohol treatment populations. Kovach reported 29 out of 117 participants in one AA group were incest victims.[16] A comparative study of alcoholic versus non-alcoholic women reported that among the alcoholic women, 74 percent had experienced sexual abuse as opposed to 50 percent within the non-alcoholic population.[17] It is not known whether the higher number of incest survivors in alcoholic treatment populations is a result of the incest or a result of alcoholism in the family of origin, or a combination of both.

Prevalence of Incest in Treatment Populations

Among female psychiatric patients, prevalence of incest has been reported as varying from 8 percent to 13.4 percent in inpatient populations.[18] Outpatient populations have presented with prevalence rates as high as 33 percent.[19] One study of 188 psychiatric patients reported that almost half had been physically or sexually abused, and of those, 90 percent had been abused by family members.[20] According to MacFarlane, Waterman, et al., "It is unclear how frequently psychopathology results in child victims of sexual abuse; estimates range from about 20 percent to 50 percent of victims. However, it appears that gross psychopathology and/or social impairment is the exception rather than the rule as a long-term consequence of sexual abuse."[21]

Disguised Presentation

Gelinas suggests that incest may be present but undisclosed in a large portion of the clinical treatment population.[22] It is not surprising that "disguised presentation" appears to be a chronic problem in the clinical experience of incest.[23] As noted previously, incest victims originate in a dysfunctional family system to which much of the typical presenting symptom picture can be attributed. When victims seek treatment, according to Gelinas, if it is not for alcohol or other substance abuse, it is often for marital or job difficulties, sexual dysfunction, depression, anxiety, fears, and low self-esteem (associated with suicidal ideation or intent). Without knowledge of the incest, the clinician would treat the disguised presentation without any progress.

Three Long-Term Effects Emerge With "Developmental Triggers"

However, Gelinas identifies the symptoms that send victims to treatment as merely a presenting part of the long-term negative effects of incest. The long-term effects often emerge as a result of what she terms a "developmental trigger," which is described as any new developmental stage involving some functional area that has been damaged by the incest.[24] Gelinas offers a most comprehensive and accurate clinical description of the long-term negative effects of incest in her article "The Persisting Negative Effects of Incest" (*Psychiatry* 46, November 1983). She identifies three effects that, with their "secondary elaborations," compose an exhaustive clinical description of the devastation of incest. They are: (1) chronic traumatic neuroses, (2) relational imbalances, and (3) the intergenerational risk of incest. As she says, "These effects are so persistent they can emerge many years after cessation of abuse, and so pervasive they can blight the victim's past, present and future."[25]

Chronic Traumatic Neuroses—Denial and Recurrences

The following is a summary of the three long-term negative effects of incest as described by Gelinas. To paraphrase Gelinas, chronic traumatic neuroses with "secondary elaborations" resulting from lack of treatment are characterized first by denial, with "repetitive intrusions" of certain elements of the trauma. Total denial about the occurrence of the event is infrequent and associated with abuse in a very young (preschool) child.

Total denial or inability to remember the incest is associated with more extreme and disrupting intrusions of the repressed trauma later in the victim's life. Because the victim has no memory of the incest, the recurrences of elements of the incest trauma are experienced as "crazy," weird, and frightening unexplained events wreaking havoc in the victim's adult life.

Most common is denial of the significance of the event.[26] Victims will report that they know something is wrong with their lives, and they are aware that some sexual activity occurred, but they do not connect the two. It is also common to repress elements associated with the experience, such as the time period, the emotional content, or the place.

The "repetitive intrusions" are the recurrence of some aspect of the repressed trauma.[27] The recurrences may be cognitive, such as nightmares, hallucinations, recurrent images, or obsessive ideas. Or they may be emotional, such as uncontrollable weeping, fear, or panic without any awareness of the relationship between the event and the trauma. The recurrence could also be behavioral, such as compulsive talking about the trauma, bodily reenactments, or artistic renderings.[28]

When repetitive intrusions occur, Gelinas warns, "The individual's memory and affect relation to the original trauma may be so vivid, intense, and unmodified as to constitute flashbacks, and they can be triggered by circumstances similar to the original trauma or by therapy itself."[29]

Gelinas notes that dissociation is another characteristic of traumatic neuroses often found in incest victims.[30] Many victims will report the use of dissociation as a defense at the time the incest occurred. Unfortunately, dissociation often continues to occur involuntarily in stressful situations long after the incest stops. This may be reported as episodes of confusion, disorientation, "freezing" of thought processes, or total amnesia.[31]

Once the incest is disclosed, the traumatic neurosis will become evident and available for the therapeutic process.[32] Gelinas warns, however, that discussion of the incest is usually accompanied by very intense emotions as the repressed memories are released. She goes further to say, "The intensity of the affect during this process can be disconcerting for both patient and therapist, and it can easily be mistaken as psychotic decompensation, which it is not."[33] She also suggests that the therapist help pace the process so that the intense affect can be released gradually with control. A storm-trooper assault on the memory is not advised.

Parentification—Relational Imbalance in the Family

The second long-term negative effect of incest identified by Gelinas is "relational imbalance with secondary elaborations."[34] As previously noted, this is also a common characteristic of other dysfunctional families and highly prevalent in alcoholic families. Gelinas observes that, "Incest victims also show the effects of the relational imbalances within the family that allowed the incest to occur in the first place, to continue and to remain undisclosed and untreated."[35] It is important to remember that incest is no isolated event. It occurs within the context of family dysfunction, and it is that continuing dysfunction that compounds the negative effects of the incest, creating a large part of the damage. The effects of the relational imbalances are usually the symptoms that compel the victim to seek treatment.

The most typical pattern of imbalance in the incest family, as in the alcoholic family, is what Gelinas calls the "parentification" of children.[36] This phenomenon is also well documented and described in the clinical literature of adult children of alcoholics. It is a term for the process whereby a child takes over the functions of the parent. Gelinas makes the important distinction between children *helping* with adult functions, and children becoming *responsible* for them. Helping is appropriate; carrying full responsibility is not.

Another critical distinction is that of appropriateness. While it may be appropriate for a three-year-old to help Mommy put napkins on the table, it is not appropriate for the mother to depend on the three-year-old to remember to set the entire table for dinner and to punish her for not doing the job. In dysfunctional families where the process of parentification occurs, the child will take responsibility for the household, for cooking, cleaning, laundry, child care, arbitrating the parents' disputes, listening to the parents' problems, and trying to take care of everyone.

The child learns to take care of everyone but herself. She is the caretaker and nurturer, and as Gelinas points out, "She begins to form her self-identity around the notion that she has responsibility for caring for people, but they have no responsibility to care for her in return."[37]

In adulthood, the parentified child will not know how to get her needs met and will not even be able to recognize her needs. At work, she may assume more responsibility than she is equipped to deal with and will not know how to tell her employer when her work load is too great. She therefore adjusts readily to an exploitative job and may typically be underpaid and overworked. Ironically, she may find herself fired when, after taking on too much work, she is unable to perform at the level of expectation she herself established.

She will most likely enter into a marital relationship that has a potential for incest to develop. Gelinas describes the process well. The man she will attract will be narcissistic, immature, insecure, and dependent. He may have experienced emotional deprivation himself as a child. Together, the parentified female and narcissistic, symbiotic male form the nucleus of a potentially incestuous family. The potential explodes with the birth of the first child.

Suddenly, the husband is deprived of the nurturing, caretaking mother-wife and may resent the child. The wife will feel "emotionally depleted and exhausted," having been a surrogate mother to everyone and having no reserves for herself.[38] She may for the first time begin to turn to her husband for help or support, exactly at the time that he feels betrayed and abandoned by her focus on the child. He may increase his demands, thereby increasing her sense of depletion and bitterness.

As the family grows, she will turn increasingly to the children for help, making them responsible for functions that she is too depleted to perform. This will include not only household tasks, but emotional and relational functions as well. A second generation of parentification begins.

The father, feeling abandoned and neglected by his wife, will turn to others for the caretaking he feels he deserves. If he does not go outside the family, he may easily find it inside the family in the form of a parentified female child, suffering from the neglect of her mother and eager for the attention of her father.

Gelinas suggests that this is the typical context in which incest occurs.[39] The potential is especially acute if alcohol is present. Another contributing factor may be the father's loss of a job or a parent, a serious illness in the mother, or the birth of another child. Gelinas takes the position that most incest offenders are not pedophiles.[40] She suggests that incest is rather the result of the offender's need for nurturing. Because his sexual development may be arrested at the pre-oedipal stage, he easily confuses sexual contact with nurturance, and the parentified child is a trusting and susceptible victim. Conte disputes this position, pointing out that there is not enough evidence to determine whether the sexual behavior of an incest offender differs pathologically from other child sexual offenders.[41]

Clearly, family circumstances play a role in the occurrence of incest. However, it is not possible to say that the abuser would not have committed child sexual abuse in the absence of those circumstances. Nor is it possible to say the abuser would not commit child sexual abuse outside the family. Given these limitations, we can assume family dynamics contribute to but are not an exhaustive causal explanation of the occurrence of incest. Gelinas describes the pervasiveness of the family dynamics as they extend into the next generation. For the victim, the long-term effects of incest and relational imbalance together do most of the damage. First, she never has a childhood, so she has an overdeveloped sense of responsibility for others and an underdeveloped sense of self. She will be markedly lacking in self-esteem, having grown up without the concept of self-rights. In particular, she will have been taught that she must not have needs.

To have them was a major threat to the family, so even a perception of a need is accompanied by a great deal of fear and guilt.[42]

Guilt is an important feature in her psychological landscape. Victims feel responsible for the incest and blame themselves. The degree of guilt is related to the degree of parentification, in which she was taught that she was responsible for everything. It is also magnified by the victim's awareness that she may have loved her abuser, enjoyed the special attention, and may have experienced sexual arousal.[43]

Victims of relational imbalance will have serious trouble in all other relationships, because they do not know how to balance "obligation and entitlement."[44] Friendships will be difficult, and in sexual relationships these women will be exploited. They will repeat their mother's pattern and enter into relationships that will be abusive or exploitative because that will be what feels familiar and comfortable to them. They will not know how to have another kind of relationship and will feel unbearable anxiety if they attempt a relationship with a more mature, giving, emotionally accessible male.

As parents they, too, will feel depleted and overwhelmed. They will not know how to establish boundaries, set limits, provide structure, administer meaningful discipline, or nurture beyond the biological level. They will withdraw from their children, who may then begin to misbehave for attention. This will compound the mothers' feelings of depletion and they will withdraw even more from their children. Parentification of their own children will begin. Marital estrangement will follow the same pattern as in the family of origin, and in this scenario, the victim's daughter is now at risk for incest.[45]

The Intergenerational Risk of Incest

Gelinas thereby explains how relational imbalances lead directly to the third persistent negative effect of incest: the intergenerational risk of incest. Within this context, both parental and sibling incest are a risk. Further, Gelinas makes the point that with an untreated traumatic neurosis, the victim-mother is even less likely to notice the incest. She will subconsciously block any reminders of her own trauma.[46] In her depleted condition, she may also be susceptible to abusing her own children physically and emotionally.

The secondary elaborations of relational imbalances push victims into treatment more often than does chronic traumatic neurosis. Victims will report family and marital problems, sexual dysfunction, ask for help in dealing with disobedient children, talk about depression, and discuss suicide. The incest may not be mentioned unless the therapist can see through the disguised presentation.[47]

INCEST RECOGNITION PROFILE

Disguised presentation, Gelinas points out, is a problem for both the therapist and the victim. The victim is at the mercy of ingrained denial and will not be able to break through it without therapy. But therapy will not be available until the incest is disclosed. The incest will not be disclosed because of denial. Gelinas offers an Incest Recognition Profile (IRP) that alerts the therapist to the disguised presentations most typical of incest, thereby enabling the therapist to make the inquiry and treat the real problem.[48]

IRP

Presenting Problem

Chronic Depression With Recent Exacerbation.   Depressed mood and affect, very low self-esteem, guilt, and needy depressiveness.
Complications of a Chronic Mood Disorder.   Substance abuse, self-injurious or suicidal behavior, impaired judgment, difficulty in parenting, poor relationships, sexual dysfunctions.

Atypical Elements

Dissociative Elements.   Complaints of "confusion" from a nonpsychotic person, recurrent nightmares, unpleasant memories or reactions precipitated by an event or person, episodes of depersonalization.
Impulsive Elements.   Running away, seriously impulsive eating, drinking, or spending, promiscuity, auto accidents, child abuse.

Personal History

History of Parentification.   Premature and heavy financial, housekeeping, or child care responsibilities as a child or adolescent, pseudomaturity.

Hallucinations in a Nonpsychotic Person

Another presenting symptom of untreated incest that is not included in Gelinas' Incest Recognition Profile is hallucinations in a nonpsy-

chotic person. This is a contradiction to classical theory, which recog
nizes hallucinations only as a manifestation of psychosis. It is becoming evident that presenting symptoms of untreated incest (such as
dissociation and hallucinations) that were traditionally considered to
be psychotic are not psychotic. They don't originate as a thought disorder within the victim. They are not pathological. They are rather
the responses of a healthy mind to a trauma imposed from without.
Neither psychotic nor neurotic, they defy classification in traditional
psychological theory.

Veterans of Another Kind of Violence

Gelinas presents one of the most thorough and optimistic clinical pictures I have seen of the diagnosis and treatment of the long-term negative effects of incest in the adult. She addresses the problem of diagnosis and treatment very honestly and effectively. The truth is most
incest survivors have not been competently diagnosed and treated.

As Gelinas notes, "The often painful details of the abuse and its aftereffects can test both the therapist's ability to handle such material
and therapeutic conviction that is essential and curative to do so.
Many therapists have perhaps understandably shied away from this
disturbing and painful material and have preferred not to treat these
issues."[49] Many therapists are not trained or prepared for this type of
patient. A perfunctory review of textbooks used ten years ago will re-
veal no mention of incest and its long-term elaborations in the adult
survivor. Chronic traumatic neurosis (or Post-Traumatic Stress Disorder) has been recognized, as Gelinas notes, predominately in war
veterans. It is only recently that the profession has begun to recognize another type of veteran of another kind of violence, one that has
been hidden within us for a long, long time.

CHAPTER 2—FOOTNOTES

1. Gelinas, Denise J., "The Persisting Negative Effects of Incest,"
   Psychiatry 46 (November 1983): 313. Gelinas originally reported a
   rate of 97–98 percent male offenders, but since then she has seen an
   increase in the number of female offenders.
2. Russell, Diana E.H., *The Secret Trauma: Incest in the Lives of Girls and
   Women,* Basic Books, Inc., New York, 1986, 60.
3. MacFarlane, Kee, and Waterman, Jill, *Sexual Abuse of Young Children,*
   The Guilford Press, New York, 1986, 8.
4. Ibid.

5. Gelinas, 313.
6. Forward, Susan, and Buck, Craig, *Betrayal of Innocence*, Penguin Books Ltd., New York, 1983, 20.
7. Conte, Jon, "Progress in Treating the Sexual Abuse of Children," *Social Work* (May–June 1984), 260.
8. Ibid., 32.
9. Lovingfosse, M., "Incest Connection," *Alcoholism, The National Magazine* 5 (1984) 2:51.
10. Burns, L., "Fathers and Daughters: A Hidden Hangover," *Magazine of the Texas Commission on Alcoholism* 8 (1982) 304:8–9.
11. Covington, S.S., "Alcohol and Family Violence," (Paper delivered at the Ninth Annual California Conference on Alcohol Problems: New Waves of Knowledge, '84, San Mateo, California) 17–21 September 1984, 9–20.
12. Noiville, P., "L'alcoolique, le sexe et l'alcool," *Haut Comite d'etude et d'information sur l'alcoolisme: Serie Documents* (Paris: *La Documentation Francaise,* 1981).
13. Gelinas, 330.
14. Ibid.
15. Kovach, J.A., "Incest as a Treatment Issue for Alcoholic Women," *Alcoholism Treatment Quarterly* 3 (1986) 1:1–15.
16. Ibid.
17. Covington, S.S., "Facing the Clinical Challenges of Women Alcoholics: Physical, Emotional and Sexual Abuse," *Focus on Family* 9 (1986) 3:10–11, 37, 42–44.
18. Gelinas, 313.
19. Ibid.
20. Carmen, E.H., Rieker, P.P., and Mills, T., "Victims of Violence and Psychiatric Illness," *American Journal of Psychiatry* 141 (1984) 3:378–383.
21. MacFarlane, Waterman, 107–108.
22. Gelinas, 313.
23. Ibid, 326.
24. Ibid, 317.
25. Ibid, 315.
26. Ibid, 316.
27. Ibid, 317.
28. Ibid.
29. Ibid, 319.
30. Ibid, 316.
31. Ibid.
32. Ibid, 315.
33. Ibid.
34. Ibid, 319.
35. Ibid.
36. Ibid.

37. Ibid, 320.
38. Ibid.
39. Ibid, 320–321.
40. Ibid, 321.
41. Conte, Jon., "Sexual Abuse of Children," *Social Work* (May-June 1984), 259.
42. Ibid, 322.
43. Ibid, 322–323.
44. Ibid, 323.
45. Ibid, 323–325.
46. Ibid, 325.
47. Ibid, 325–326.
48. Ibid, 326.
49. Ibid, 330.

3

"Who Are We and What Happened?"

"Incest is commonly defined as sexual contact between an adult and child with an established familial relationship . . . Two crucial components that extend it to sibling and surrogate parent incest [are] imputed trust and a power imbalance . . . Sexual contact includes all forms of sexual behavior . . . 80 to 90 percent of reported victims are female and approximately 90 percent of offenders are male[1] . . . There is great variation in the ages of victims . . . The victim's age does determine to some extent the type of sexual activity and methods of obtaining compliance . . . As a group, incest offenders are heterogeneous . . . An abuser can be anyone . . . Strict religious affinities occur frequently among incestuous families . . . Another characteristic that emerges among paternal incest offenders is alcoholism . . . Incest is often associated with a crisis such as a death of a parent or spouse, loss of a job, a serious illness in the mother, the birth of another child . . . Offenders often blame the disinhibiting effects of alcohol for their incestuous behavior; however, incest is usually premeditated . . . It may be particularly difficult to make a distinction between the effect of the dysfunctional family system and the effects of the incest."

In this section, we will meet six incest survivors who will introduce themselves, briefly describe what happened to them, and give us a general idea of the context in which incest occurred in their lives. In this section, you will find that incest victims and incest offenders do not fall into any neat ethnic or socioeconomic categories. It should shatter any stereotyped images.

As you read these introductory passages and the sections that follow, be aware that each person's story is presented to you as it was told. If there are parts that are unclear or confusing, it is because those parts are still unclear or confusing to the survivor. There may be gaps or inconsistencies in each person's story, or you may find interpretations of events that seem distorted or confusing. This is because each person is giving an account of their lives as they experienced them, interpreted only to the extent that they understood it at the time the story was recorded. Each story is a sort of psychological snapshot, recording a life as it is comprehended at a specific point in time. As such, it will reflect all the limitations of each person's understanding at that time.

As you yourself progress in your recovery, you will find that each time you read this book, you will find something in it you never saw before, and you will find things in yourself that you never knew were there. And those insights will help you to develop yet a deeper understanding of yourself.

In succeeding sections, we will examine each person's experience more closely to develop a thorough understanding of the long-term effects of incest. This book is designed to be read in two ways. You can read the book topically, section by section, reading every story in each section as an example of that particular topic. For example, if you are troubled by your past behavior and wonder how incest may have influenced it, Chapter 4 will address the period in our lives where most of us had "stuffed" the incest away and had little awareness of what was happening to us. Or, you may be troubled by recurrent episodes of anger, crying, or nightmares—the subject of Chapter 6 on recurrences.

Another way to read the book is to go through it reading one history at a time. If one person in particular seems to share your experience very closely, you can read her story straight through. But don't skip the chapter introductions—they provide the conceptual framework needed to understand the material presented.

Either way, this book is written specifically to meet the needs of the adult survivor. In it you will find a friend to take with you on your journey through recovery.

Noelle
Financial Planner
Age 39
Married twice; two children.
Paternal incest; didn't remember until age 36.
Nine years of therapy with intermittent breaks.
Alcoholic father.

Noelle gives a detailed account of what it feels like to not remember the incest trauma, but to have it intrude destructively throughout her life.

Sexually abused by her alcoholic father at age three, Noelle forgot. Because the trauma was totally repressed, its expression in her life was directed through other channels rather than conscious memories.

The incest trauma recurred over and over again in the form of unexplained episodes of fear, phobias, panic, anger and weeping, fainting, recurring nightmares and hallucinations, dissociation, and inappropriate sexual relationships. These are what we call "recurrences."

Noelle's story is of special value in showing us what a recurrence is and what it feels like (Chapter 6). It also is especially useful in that she will take us through the mechanics of remembering (Chapter 7). Noelle had a problem with denial and a long battle to piece together the incest puzzle from dreams, emotional recurrences, behavioral recurrences, and, finally, a few fragments of memories.

Noelle also shares the difficulties of trying to be a parent and seeing her own emotional disruption reflected in her children (Chapter 5). Children bring another dimension to the problems of incest survivors as they go through the process of recovery.

Noelle and others who didn't remember seem to feel more "craziness" than those who have clear memories of their abuse. This may be a product of years of unexplained episodes of extreme behavior, labelled as crazy by others and eventually by themselves. It is difficult for them to connect their recurrences to the incest trauma when they remember little or nothing at all about it. They need extensive, competent therapeutic support in this process, which can be lengthy.

For those who don't remember, Noelle, and later Ellen, will be particularly useful in validating experience and overcoming the tenacious grip of denial.

I Don't Look Like an Incest Victim

I don't think anybody meeting me for the first time, or even people who know me very well, would ever guess what happened to me. There is a perception that incest is such a horrible thing that people who have experienced it must be readily identifiable, that somehow we should look different, be obviously identifiable in a group. That just isn't true. In a way, that's one of the problems I have, this feeling that I'm not ever really all there for the people who know me, because there is this chunk of my experience they don't know about. But, it's also kind of reassuring, because it means that in terms of my whole life, the incest is just a small part. It wasn't always that way, but it is now, now that it is being put in its proper place.

I did not remember the incest until I was 36 years old. Even though I did not remember it, it was there, buried inside, distorting my behavior and devastating my life, and I didn't even know what was happening to me. I couldn't do anything to help myself because I had no idea what it was. I just knew that sometimes I felt and did things I knew were "crazy" but I couldn't seem to stop.

I'm almost forty; I have a husband I love and two children I adore. I have a home I like. I've had a successful career and I've achieved prominence in my field. Well, incest victims are supposed to be really screwed up, you know—drug addicts, prostitutes, runaways. Scott Fitzgerald wrote *Tender Is the Night* and made Nicole Diver into a hopeless schizophrenic, a psychotic.

That's not necessarily true. I think I'm a fairly normal person to all appearances. I look all right. I get up in the morning. I do all the normal things people do. I clean my house; I take care of my children. I work. I do most of my business at home; I run a national consulting business out of my home. I have a lot of interests. You'd never notice me in a crowd.

Alcoholic Father

I was born in a small town in New England. My family is prominent in this town. Not wealthy, but they've lived there a long time, an old name in town. And even when I go back there, which I rarely do, people know me, they recognize that name.

When I was born my father was a lawyer, but he was also an alcoholic, and that changed everything. My mother had been a war bride. She was from France; she had been trained as an artist. She taught art when we were little to keep us alive, because my father's drinking was so bad at that time we had no money; we were really destitute. My mother, who was a lost soul in this country and alone, had nowhere to go, just had to find some way to feed us, and that's how she did it.

My early childhood was very difficult. In fact, my whole childhood was difficult and traumatic until I left home, because my father was very abusive. To him, children were either objects of gratification or to be ignored. I grew up feeling I was there either to do his bidding or to disappear. He made me feel I had no right to exist, except as I pleased him. We were *allowed* to grow up in his home.

My Mother, Imperfect But Important

My mother, from an old-world culture, was a poor, pathetic slave to my father, and I didn't even think of her as an adult. To me she was just another abused child. She was a very loving and tender woman and I know she loved me. She would hold me on her lap, and I remember touching her hair and face and saying, "Mommy, please don't ever die." She was the source of tenderness and comfort in my life. She didn't make me feel safe, she could not make me feel safe because she was scared to death herself, but she did love me. And she still does. I still cherish my relationship with my mother, imperfect but important.

My father was terrifying. He quit drinking when I was about five years old, but it really didn't make any difference. He quit drinking, but he did not change. It meant he didn't get drunk, but instead he would come home and have uncontrollable rages. My brother and I used to say he was a mad dog. It really didn't matter what we did, somehow he was going to nail somebody and that person was going to get nailed bad. So, it was real chaotic, there wasn't any rhyme or reason to his rages or who he chose to victimize. We were just his whipping boys.

Isolated With the Abuser

I suppose I am glad he quit drinking, but he did not stay active in AA so he never really went into recovery. He was an alcoholic who became a workaholic. He was a terribly ambitious man and he gained some prominence in international trade, so we traveled quite a bit and lived in other countries, wherever his clients were. We lived in the Middle East, and in several countries in Europe while I was growing up.

The traveling made things even worse, because we were so isolated. Here I was, in this terribly abusive situation, and I was isolated with the abuser. There was no extended family, nobody to help me. My parents had no friends, no community, they were very isolated people. No one was there for me and I was terrified most of the time. I was very withdrawn.

Incest Is Part of a Continuum

The reason I'm establishing all this about the ordinary garden variety of abuse is because it is so important for people to realize incest is just part of a continuum of abusive behavior. It's not like you have a normal, ordinary mom and dad, and one day Dad gets an impulse and he follows through on it and he abuses you sexually, and then after a while maybe it stops and things go back to normal. It isn't like that at all. The incest is part of a continuum of abusive behavior, and my father's incestuous behavior was just part of his narcissism and inability to love his children for themselves. It's a part of my mother's helplessness and her inability to protect us; it was part of her dysfunction as well. It was part of the whole family system. It wasn't an inevitable part though—a lot of families are like that and incest doesn't happen. The incest was my father's responsibility entirely.

All the Risk Factors Occurred Together

It happened when I was three years old. It was a very bad time in our family. My father's mother had died, and it was a real shock. She died suddenly. Things had been bad before she died, but at least my parents had her there. My dad adored his mother, and my mom felt as though her mother-in-law was her own real mother. My mom really depended on her. When she died the family was devastated.

Then my mother got very sick; she had to be hospitalized. After that she wasn't well for a long time, but she still struggled to work. It must have been a frightening time for her. My father was drinking very heavily, having blackouts, disappearing. Sometimes she had no money for food. Once she stole food from a neighbor because we were hungry.

I see myself when I was three, very scared, very desolate. I wanted my mommy. I was cold and sick that Christmas. My nose was chapped. I hate Christmas now, when I think of that Christmas. I don't let myself think of it, if I can help it.

I Blocked Out the Memory Until My Daughter Was Born

We lived in a very old New England farmhouse. It was a historical relic, in fact. All the plumbing was in the basement, which was where the toilet was. My father found he could catch me downstairs when I was in the basement going to the bathroom, and that's where he abused me. It was pretty terrifying because I was very little. I blocked it out completely until I was 36. Even though everything about my life just fits beautifully with the profile of an incest victim, I didn't remember, and I understand that's not unusual for children who are abused at a preschool age.

I started to remember the abuse when my daughter was born. That is one of the developmental triggers commonly associated with the emergence of memories. The way I remembered was in a dream. It was quite unlike any ordinary dream.

That's really important because there was to me a qualitative difference between this dream, which replayed something that really happened, versus dreams that were just symbolic. When I had my memory dream, which I still remember in exact detail, with complete clarity, I woke up screaming and crying. I could not stop crying for about six hours. The release of emotions was so intense that it totally disrupted my life for days. It was like I was thrown back in time thirty-some years. It was very disorienting and humiliating. I could not get hold of myself. I had all the intense feelings of a three-year-old being sexually abused again. Here I was 36, and I had a baby, and I had a really hard time. I knew the dream was real; I knew it was real.

Then gradually, little by little, more memories came back to me. And each time a memory came back, it came wrapped in the intense emotions associated with the event. Each time I felt like I was shot back in time more than 30 years, reexperiencing the emotions of a three-year-old being abused by her father. Each time it was horribly disrupting, but also very relieving; there was a relief. It was almost like the pressure inside me was released a little every time. And I was so grateful to be able to get it out, in spite of the craziness, the feeling of unreality that came with it. I used to pray for a dream to come so I could be free of it all!

I Loved My Daddy

From what I can piece together, from what I remember, he came to me in the basement. He was not drunk; he was very nervous. I could tell it in his tone of voice and his gestures and the way he talked to me and the way he touched me; he was real nervous. He kept saying, "It's all right, it's just a game. It's all right. Don't worry, it's all right." He had me sit sideways on the toilet, positioning me in such a way that he could watch the top of the stairs, so he could see if anyone was coming. This was all premeditated; he was very careful. He knew exactly what he was doing; he was not drunk. He attempted intercourse, which was unsuccessful, so he had me perform oral sex, which he also did to me. He told me that if I told anyone, they would come and take him away and kill him, and I loved my daddy, I loved him deeply, I adored him.

That was one of the things that just shocked me to death when I had my first memory. You see, all my life the love I had for my father has been tainted by anger and fear and hatred and even some pity. Then when I had this first dream, the overwhelming emotion with it, aside from the fear and aside from the grief, was this uncontaminated feeling of love. I couldn't believe that feeling of love I had never loved anyone like that. That must have been the way I felt when I was three. It was that complete love I had for him that enabled him to do what he did to me. When I had that first dream, I had great fear that something was going to happen to my daddy and they were going to take him away, and I had to protect him. Along with my grief and fear at what he was doing, I had enormous love for him. The only other times in my life I ever had anything close to that feeling of love have been when I first meet and fall in love with someone, before they hurt me or disappoint me.

I Felt I Had No Right to Be Alive

Well, that's what happened, and I'm not sure if it persisted until we moved, and he quit drinking. We moved to a new house where it was harder for him to get to me—the bathroom wasn't isolated. Like I said, he was a very smart man. He knew what he was doing, and he didn't want to be caught. He was very careful to cover up for himself. I don't think my mother ever found out about it. He also quit drinking. I think the alcoholism played a key part in his behavior, but I don't think I can attribute the abuse to some sort of drunken, out-of-control binge. He was just not drunk; he was not drunk.

Anyway, after that, he quit and he withdrew from me. I think he still loved me, but he didn't know how to interact with me. You can imagine how he must have felt. He could not allow the admission of imperfection in his life, and there I was, a living example of his imperfection. So you can imagine how uncomfortable he was with me, and he made me feel I had no right to be alive. He withdrew from me, and I think part of it was to protect me from himself, too. I think he did love me.

Growing Up With Problems

In my teen years there was an awful lot of acting out behavior. I got into serious trouble with the authorities. I was sexually abused by every boy I went with, because that's what felt inevitable to me, even though at the time I couldn't understand it. Somehow, I was able to get control of my life at age sixteen, and eventually I put myself through undergraduate school and got two graduate degrees.

My first marriage after college was a ten-year failure. I went into therapy after my first marriage because I knew something was awfully wrong with me, even though I was a compulsive overachiever. By then I had two advanced degrees, I was doing very well career-wise, thanks to my work compulsion. I appeared to be a very successful person, but something was terribly wrong. I went into therapy, and after five years I finally remembered the incest. After that my therapy really accelerated and I got much, much better. And I feel like I'm almost over it. I feel like I'm on the downside of the recovery curve; I'm almost there, almost there.

The Vestiges of Incest

But the vestiges of the incest and the abuse still haunt my life. It's hard for me to have relationships with other people. In some ways I'm too easy to know and other ways I'm not possible to know. I don't know how to act around people. I always have this awareness of being different. I literally sweat when I have to deal with people, even on the phone. I can soak my shirt in a fifteen-minute conversation. I feel most comfortable and safe when I'm alone, and I like to be alone. I do have friends I care for tremendously and I like to have them around me sometimes, but I like it best when I'm alone.

I love my children, but I've had an awful lot of trouble raising them, and that's another vestige of my abusive family. I work very hard at trying to learn normal, healthy parenting techniques, because it doesn't come naturally. I hate the way my children have suffered because of my heritage, but I'm doing so much better than my own parents did. I have to accept some credit for the fact that I've overcome the worst of what they did. I'll never do to my children what my parents did to me.

Parents—The Fantasy Father

The memories I have of my parents are mixed. Although I remember nothing but unrelenting emotional abuse and neglect from my dad, I know he loved me. This may be because my mother was always telling me, "You don't know your father. He really does love you." I knew that in a real crisis, he would save me. Otherwise, stay out of his way. The crisis never came, either. Actually, the crisis came in the basement, but he wasn't able to save me then.

The really peculiar thing to me is how I built up this fantasy father who coexisted with the abusive father. I am aware of how I exaggerated his positive traits until he took on godlike proportions in my fantasy. I saw him as a superman, a man of grand ideals and integrity against a corrupt and dirty world. I saw him as a great intellect. I felt this fantasy father was lurking somewhere inside him, and I used him to excuse the abuse of the real father. I can hear my mother's words even now, and I know she promoted this fantasy image of him.

"Your father is very sensitive, he's a wonderful man. You just don't get to see that because he's so overworked and can't relax."

This fantasy father lived in my imagination until I went away to college. Then a strange thing happened. Without realizing it, I talked about him all the time. In every situation, every conversation, I referred back to my fantasy father. He was my frame of reference. I didn't realize this until one day when a friend of mine said, "Get off it, Noelle. Isn't it about time you broke away from 'Daddy'?" I was shocked to hear this. I remember telling her in shock, "I hate him! He's the meanest man I ever knew!" I'd had no awareness of how contradictory my behavior had been, or how the fantasy father had become the frame of reference in place of my real father. From that day on, I began a real effort to see my father as he was. Not the unreal monster, and not the godlike superman, but as a real, imperfect human being. It took years to do that. Now I realize the real man is pretty small. I don't know him, and he is not accessible to me. But that is his problem, not mine. I love him, and I feel the sadness of his loss, but I no longer take responsibility for him.

A Loving and Ineffective Mother

My mother has been more of a consistent image to me. She has always been childlike, ineffective, and very loving. I've gone through periods of anger, when I resented her because she loved me but could not take care of me. I now feel she did the best she could, given her own programming. She is a real victim. Actually, when I was little, her helplessness was real. She went to heroic lengths to do what she could with what little resources she had. The one thing she needed to do was to leave my dad, which she could not do. She was trapped by her own sense of helplessness. Plus, back then, given her circumstances, there really was no escape for her. She couldn't support us, she was alone in a strange country. I can see how trapped she was.

Later, from about ages 5 to 11, we lived overseas and she was very sick all the time. She was hospitalized for years. We had a maid to take care of us. I did not see her much. When she was not sick, she had a social life that took her away. She also had a prolonged affair, about which I know little. Was it a last attempt to escape my dad?

Then there was the period from sixth grade through my first two years in high school when there was a financial crisis in our family and she had to go out to work. That was when my feelings of her as a slave, a victim, really peaked. I see her as ill, totally exhausted and depleted, unable to take care of herself. I felt very depressed about her. I tried to take care of her. I remember assuming responsibility for household chores. I also used to make her little presents and write her little notes. I felt sorry for her and cried for her.

Two Kids Growing Up Alone

Then, as I progressed in my teens, I became more and more detached from my parents. They had never been able to help me anyway. They became irrelevant except for the trouble they occasionally caused me. When I look back, I see them as two people caught up in their own problems and unable to do anything for me. I see myself as someone who just struggled alone to grow up in their house. I had to invent myself as I went along, from books, from other people, from movies, from fantasies. My parents were not there. They were just not there.

I realize I've put little or nothing about my brother into this material. This is because in our family we were all involved in a struggle to survive and we were on our own. There was no chance for a sibling relationship. That was a luxury. He was there, but we grew up separately in the same house. I have a relationship with him, but none of my issues are recognized. He had a totally different life, with different problems. He is far away from me. I love him, but there are gaps I can never bridge because he cannot accept the truth. He has invested in the family denial. There is nothing I can do.

Rewriting History

My parents have decided nothing was ever very badly wrong with our family. Any problems I or my brother have have nothing to do with them, and any claims to the contrary are just incorrect. And they don't want to hear about my therapy or my brother's problems because to them it implies they did something wrong, and they have decided they didn't. My father says I was totally sheltered from his drinking, that life at home during that time was actually very happy, and that I was "Daddy's Special Girl."

They have a lovely facade. They have joined a strict fundamentalist church in which my father holds an exalted position. I mean, he is very close to God, and everybody thinks they're just about perfect. They live in a perfect house, and they have a perfect image. People who know my father think he is perfect.

It is true that my dad is an idealist and has done many admirable things in his life. I actually had to go to some sort of award ceremony once and hear a man say that, to his knowledge, my father has never made a mistake and he can't imagine my father making mistakes—

and I had to sit there and listen to it. So, anybody meeting them would think, "Wonderful people, wonderful people."

It's so important for this to be on record, because it shows how incest is such an insidious thing. Most family dysfunction is so insidious, you just can't tell from appearances unless you are trained to see certain patterns of behavior.

Persisting Parental Denial

I have never confronted my parents about the incest. They do know I'm in therapy because of some problems relating to the past. I even went so far as to say it had to do with a family dysfunction, that it had to do with my father's drinking, and that I was sexually molested. My father's reaction to this was not, "Oh, I'm so sorry you are in such pain. Is there anything I can do?" No. His reaction was, "Well, how do you think this makes me feel? What kind of reflection is this on me?" Well, for the record, I have to tell you, he said, "Let's make it perfectly clear that our family just wasn't that bad. My drinking was never that bad. My behavior was never that bad." That was his reaction. They are both in total denial.

They are old now, and I'm convinced my father has completely rewritten history. He may have convinced himself that what he did never happened. In fact, I think it's entirely possible, because he is good at denial, not honest with himself. So any type of confrontation between me and my parents is out of the question. I think I'm finally at the stage now where it would not be destructive to me, but it wouldn't help, and it certainly would make no difference to them. It would not change them or enlighten them, it would just make it impossible for me to have any type of relationship with them.

I do want to maintain some kind of relationship with them. I want my children to have grandparents, and I also want my mother in my life. She was a weak woman but she loved me, and if it weren't for her, my life would probably not be salvageable. Her love, I think, gave me just enough of a foundation to recover from the abuse, so I do want a relationship with her. And I do not want to hurt my father any more. He does a good enough job of hurting himself. So meet me, meet my family, and we all look just fine. And if you saw us, or met us, you would think, "How lucky these people are. I'm sure they don't have any problems."

I Didn't Think I Could Feel This Happiness

After years of therapy, I can say things are all right now, they are all right. I never thought they could be. I didn't think I could feel this contentment. I didn't think I could feel this happiness I didn't know it was there, but I've found it, and every day, every day is part of the process of just getting a little bit better. I am still very fearful, still feel very threatened and vulnerable. Some days are worse, some days are great. You go back and forth a little, but every day I feel I'm taking one more step toward getting better. It can be done. I just wish that . . . I want very much for other people to know that there is a chance for happiness, there really is.

Megan
Management Specialist
Age 36
Single
Sibling incest.
Eight years of therapy.
Alcoholic mother.

"We were the picture-perfect family" is the way Megan describes it. Then she tells how eight years of therapy has helped her reach an understanding of the family dynamics associated with her rape at age 10 by her 14-year-old brother.

In Megan's story we find many of the family characteristics associated with incest—strict religious affiliation, maternal depletion, parentification of children, serious illness in a parent, immature and narcissistic abuser, and denial of the trauma. In her story we also find one of the characteristics of sibling incest—physical violence occurs more often when there is a significant disparity in the ages of the victim and sibling.

Megan herself exhibits the time bomb effect of incest, particularly when there are repressed memories. She forgot the rape until age 35, and thought her brother had "only" molested her, that it hadn't affected her, and that everything was fine—except for fear of men, fear of sex, fear of intimacy, debilitating depressions, and suicidal episodes, all of which intensified as she reached adulthood. Then the time bomb went off.

Megan was lucky. She found a good therapist quickly and began to confront the incest in spite of her disguised presentation. She went into therapy talking about depression, which she attributed to the recent deaths of her mother and father, providing more than enough material for any therapist. Fortunately, her therapist responded when she mentioned her brother's "molestation" in passing.

As you read through Megan's story, notice how her sexual behavior was distorted by the incest. Whereas Noelle compulsively sought out sexual relationships, hoping they would meet her overwhelming needs, Megan withdrew from sexual involvement, afraid of her overwhelming needs. They are both manifestations of the same problem—a distorted model of love and sex. Sometimes we experience both types of behavior in the form of on again/off again sexual activity. As you read about Megan and Noelle, you may be able to identify which form your own sexual dysfunction may have taken.

A Picture-Perfect Family

I'm thirty-six, I grew up in a suburb of a midwestern city. I'm trying to think of a way to describe it. It was like when Erma Bombeck talks about the invasion of the city people to the suburbs after World War II—that was my family. My family was one of those that made the migration from the city. I'm the sixth out of eight children, four boys and four girls. I came from a very Irish-Catholic family. Both parents were very, very, very devout Catholics, and on the surface, we were the picture-perfect family.

My father was an engineer with a college degree, and my mother had been a legal secretary before they married. Then she was a full-time mom and stayed home with us. They sent us all to Catholic schools, from kindergarten through senior year of college, and five of the eight finished college. I always looked fine on the surface—I was an above-average student, responsible, never got involved in drugs or too much alcohol, had lots of girlfriends, starting working part-time at 16. So, from the outside, everyone appears to be self-sufficient adults and taking care of themselves, with the exception of one sister.

She has been the one surface exception that would indicate something was wrong in the family. She is 47 now, and I haven't communicated with her in three years. I don't know if anyone has in the last year. She is divorced, and she gave custody of her children to her husband. She has worked as a waitress for the last 20 years, and she's got a college degree and postgraduate degree, so she is very bright, but she is literally just dropping out. She started to drop out about when my mother died. That is when she divorced her husband, so it has been 15 years now. She is the one surface exception to that picture-perfect family.

My Mother Screamed and Yelled

What was it like inside the family? You know, it's so hard in some ways to describe it, but I finally am getting more objective. Up until I started therapy, and in the first year, I always told my therapist I came from this wonderful family and I had two parents who loved me, they liked each other, and all that neat kind of stuff. That was actually the first thing I said when I was in therapy. As I progressed, it became obvious it wasn't a picture-perfect family in any shape or form.

My mother screamed and yelled. She didn't really physically hit, but boy, she had such a screaming voice that, to this day, if anyone raises her voice I get sick to my stomach and I have to leave the room. I get chilled dealing with anger.

She screamed at us from the time we woke up until we went to bed, for anything and everything we did. If you didn't make your bed, you didn't eat your breakfast, you didn't do what she asked you to do when she asked you to do it, she would let loose. Actually she didn't yell at me so much because of my behavior. The way I coped with things was to be bound and determined to be perfect so she wouldn't scream. I wanted to make everything right for her.

My brother Kevin, the one who abused me, is 4 years older than I am, was always the juvenile delinquent of the family, always in trouble. He cut school, he didn't go to Mass on Sundays. He signed up for violin lessons and quit going, meanwhile pretending to my parents that he continued going. I wasn't going to be like him. I never wanted to give her a reason to yell.

The Worst Mother in the World

I just couldn't live with it when she started screaming, I thought she had to be the worst mother in the entire world. I can remember standing in our driveway once when I was about five or six. It was during the summer and all the windows were open in the house. She was yelling at somebody for something. I remember standing there thinking, just hating her for being such a horrible mother and being embarrassed that someone could hear her screaming because it was carrying out through the windows. My father usually wasn't home; she only behaved like that when she was with all of us during the day. When he came home at night, it was relatively quiet. She was a little bit more calm.

After my younger brother was born, she started drinking martinis. She and my dad would have two martinis at the end of the day when he came home from work. She told my aunt once that she had found this neat new drink, and my aunt said, "What is it?" and she said, "It's a martini." My aunt said, "Maureen, that's all alcohol." My mother said, "Yeah, but two of them and you really don't care how much noise the children make." She had about seven kids then and was about 40.

A Strict Catholic Family

Another thing, too, that is a real important clue about our family is that the incidence of incest is disproportionately high in Catholic families. Even for a Catholic family, my parents were extraordinarily Victorian and prudish in the way they handled sex. The most affectionate they ever were in front of us was when my father would always kiss my mother before he left for work in the morning or when he came home. But, even after 30 years of marriage and children, my mother would still blush if she realized any one of the eight of us observed this.

They also ruled that you could not leave your bedroom unless you were fully dressed or, if in pajamas, you had to be wearing your bathrobe and slippers.

Sex was never discussed, never acknowledged. My older sister was 16 when the youngest was born. And they told my older sister what they told everyone else in the family, "Your mother and I have gone to the hospital and picked out a new baby sister for you." Pregnancy was never acknowledged; we never even used the word "pregnant." I heard my mother utter the word once in her travel when she was talking about someone else. So sex didn't exist, you weren't supposed to talk about it. It wasn't part of life.

The other rule they had, which is interesting in light of what happened to me, is that the boys must never touch us girls. With eight kids, there was a lot of physical fighting between us, and that was the rule, that the boys were absolutely, positively not to touch us girls.

Mother Needed Me After Dad Died

My mother did not have a close relationship with her children. The only closeness that came out was after my father's death. The year after he died was the only time in my life that I can say I got to know her as someone other than a mother. I got to know her personality. It was as if she had let her hair down and allowed us to get close to her, and we came through. She hadn't much choice, because my father had died.

My mother and father were very close. The one positive thing about them is they did care for each other. It may have not been the most healthy marriage, in that she did not ever show anger with my father. That was the unhealthy part, but I don't know whether it was because my father couldn't handle it, or whether she was unable to do it. That part is very unclear.

I just remembered something about my mother. Some of this has changed so much, it's hard to put myself back to how I felt. But I just remembered the way I related to my mother. I became her sounding board, in some ways, after my father died. She needed someone to talk to and I seemed to be the one she turned to. I got to know her for the first time, just a little. But when I was younger and I was hurt, or when I cried, I couldn't go to her. I went to a brother or sister.

I Thought She Did Not Care

Years later when I was in therapy and remembered the incest, I felt such hatred for her that she had not protected me, that she always yelled at us and never told us she loved us, and that she let herself die of cancer less than 2 years after my father's death. It seemed obvious to me that she did not love us, she did not love me, and I cried to know that I had a mother who did not care.

Once, when I was about 15, I asked her if she had wanted eight children, and her answer was that she was 24 when she got married and she knew what she was getting herself into. That feeling of being tolerated was what I always carried with me. Until last summer: For some odd reason, I remembered the day Mom told me I needed to go away to school for myself or else she would tie me to her. That was without a doubt the most unselfish act a parent can do—to let a child go. It is hard to accept that I wasn't protected from my brother's abuse, but at least I can now believe I was loved.

I Felt Safe With My Father—Before the Heart Attack

My father was a little bit better. This is something I just remembered this winter in group, and I just about fell apart. Monique, our group therapist, asked, "Was there a time in our lives when we ever felt safe? And if so, where was the place that you felt safe? And where do we feel safe as adults?" Those simple questions really brought the entire group to a tremendous trauma. Everyone said no, there absolutely never was a time anyone felt safe, and the only time we feel safe as adults is when we are alone. For each of us it was a little different, but most of us like being in a car by ourselves, or in a room completely by ourselves.

Anyhow, I was saying, like everyone else, "No, I never felt safe. I can never remember a time when I was safe," when, for whatever the reason, I don't know, I made the connection. I remembered I felt safe before my father had his heart attack. My father had his heart attack, the first one, when I was in fourth grade, so I just turned ten. Up until his heart attack, my father had always gone to six o'clock mass every single day of the week, or at least Monday through Friday, before he went to work, and that year I went with him. All on my own, I decided to go with him, and what came back was this memory of a time that was very special to me, being alone with him.

I liked my dad, but I always would tell people I didn't know him as a person. When we came back that night at group, I was remembering what he was like before I was ten, before he got sick, and before I was abused. He was a really nice, gentle man. I can remember two times in my entire life when he ever raised his voice. All of us remember that he hardly ever got angry; my mother acted out all the anger for both of them. He didn't get angry, so it was very easy to remember that he was the good guy.

I remember he used to play with my younger brother and sister before he had that heart attack. He would take us to the movies, and that was fun. We were always dropped off at the movies on a Saturday afternoon, and afterwards he would take us out for a sundae or something like that. He was accessible, but then he had the heart attack in April, and I remember that the abuse started sometime around then.

Father Ill—Brother Abusive

He was in the hospital for six weeks, and my mother didn't drive, so my older sister drove her to the hospital every day when she got home from school. My sister was 18 then, and the two older kids were already in college, so that left Kevin and Jim—Jim who was 15 and Kevin who was 14—in charge of my two sisters and me. So you can imagine that essentially I played in the house with other children unsupervised. My brother, Kevin, had always exhibited a disturbed personality. I'm still not too sure why he did it, but I think it was a combination of, partly he was horny, and being in a Catholic home and a Catholic school, he couldn't jump in with his classmates. So part of it was curiosity.

He was 13, going on 14, when he started it. It lasted 13 months, and went from fondling me to raping me. He started it with me with the excuse that he was going to teach me about menstruation, and the way he would teach me was if I took off all of my clothes, he could show me the path of how the egg left the ovary and left the body.

When I remembered what happened, that was one of the first things that came back, that memory of the first time. I was standing in his room, and it was late in the day. It was just starting to get dark outside and there were no lights on in the room. I remember him explaining to me what was going on and at first being very curious about menstruation, because no one else would talk to me about anything related to that, and then realizing it wasn't right that he would have to show me this by me not having my clothes on. Actually, maybe he only took my shirt off, maybe not all my clothes, but I just knew it wasn't right. I remember him telling me it was okay; this is something I would need to know.

I have thought a lot about what motivated him. I think it may have been curiosity, and I was available. There was no adult supervision, and I was such an enabling child, anything to please people so they wouldn't get angry with me or reject me. I think the reason it went beyond that was that Kevin is a classic narcissistic personality.

My Brother the Abuser

Kevin has never taken any responsibility for anything in his entire life. He is 39, and he is one of the three people in the family who did not finish college. The other two who did not, which I think is significant, are the two younger ones, who lost their parents when they were in high school. One of the reasons we were motivated to go to college was for our parents. I think that had a lot to do with it, the two of them just went through such trauma losing our parents at the age they did.

Kevin, from the time he was very little, was a poor student—never did his homework, always was in trouble with the nuns, and then, like I said, he didn't even finish high school. He couldn't graduate from his class, so he joined the navy and was in the navy to avoid being drafted into the Vietnam War. Then he just started working as a waiter. Twenty years later, he is still working as a waiter. He has held more jobs in 20 years—he's probably held 40 jobs. I would bet he goes through two a year.

He was married once, and his wife left him after about three years of marriage, when their son was about a year old. She went back to Florida to visit her family, not telling Kevin she never intended to return to California. That was the only way she knew how to get out of the marriage. She just stayed there and stayed there, and it finally became apparent she was never coming back.

A Narcissistic Person

For Kevin, it is always everyone else's fault, never his. All these jobs he has gone through, they're never his fault. The reason his marriage broke up was not his fault; it was his wife's fault. He made a small attempt to move to Florida to be near his son because he wanted to be the proper father. But he claimed that when he got there his wife wouldn't let him near his son, so of course there was no point in staying there, so he moved back to California. The truth was when his wife did leave Kevin with his son, the boy was upset, started to cry, and Kevin didn't know what to do with him so he took him back to his mother. Then he would tell us, "My wife won't let me be near my son. She would take him away from me." He just doesn't take any responsibility, and it's always immediate gratification that he needs for everything. If you can't help him out right then and there, you are a rotten person. If you can't do what he wants, you're a terrible person.

When he moved to Florida to be near his son, at that time he had an apartment, a small studio apartment in California. I switched jobs right at the same time he was going to Florida and I needed a place. I was moving to the same city where he was. So he said I could take over his place. "When it's time to move out, you can move in and I won't lose my security deposit," and all that kind of stuff, so it was very convenient.

Once I got up there he hadn't yet moved all his stuff out and I had people there ready to move my stuff in, which is typical, just not responsible. So my friends had to end up moving his stuff out to get my stuff in. Then he said he didn't have a place to stay; could he just stay there with me? And I was paying the rent.

It was a studio apartment, and, by this time, not only had I remembered the incest, I had already confronted him on it. I said, "Absolutely not, you're not staying here with me," and then he started screaming I was a rotten sister. So I said, "So I'm a rotten sister, but you're not staying here with me. You will have to find another place to live." That's the way he handles his entire life—it's always someone else's fault. It's never his.

Why Did He Do It?

Anyway, recognizing now that he is a narcissistic personality, I guess part of what drove him to abuse me was he needed immediate gratification. Sex is one of the first things he would do. He soon taught me how to jerk him off. I can remember getting hysterical the first time he ejaculated. I didn't know what it was; it was all over me. I just started crying and screaming, and he kept telling me to shut up, threatening that if I didn't shut up, he was going to hit me, and telling me it wasn't going to hurt me.

Another thing, one of the reasons we lived in the suburbs and we went to Catholic schools is that my parents wanted to protect us. My sisters and I, from high school on, went to women's schools. They built the house so there were only two children in each bedroom and we each had our own bed and desk and dresser. My father, being an engineer, had designed it all to be a place where children could feel comfortable and they didn't have to worry about us ruining anything. Our family room had wood paneling that was done in chestnut because it had holes in it, and it didn't make any difference if we put holes into it. So all these efforts were made to protect us and take care of us. And the most horrible thing that ever happened to me in my entire life took place in the bedroom next to theirs in the house where we lived. That was sad.

I think part of it was because my brother did everything and anything to break the rules. That was why he was a lousy student; that's why he didn't finish high school. Wherever there was a rule, he broke it. That's why he wouldn't go to Mass on Sundays. He just would live for breaking rules; that is how he got his attention. We didn't get a lot of individual attention, so that's why Kevin, from the time I can remember, soaked up all of my parents' energy. He was the fifth one, third boy, so a real middle child. His way of getting attention—and he did a very good job of it—completely drained all their energy by being a bad boy.

I've often wondered if there is a part of him that was really pissed off that my dad had a heart attack and that my mother was at the hospital and there wasn't really anybody to get attention from, so he broke the ultimate taboo, which was to touch a girl in the nude. Maybe he was hoping to get caught and that's why he did it in the bedroom next to theirs. I just, I've often thought that; maybe he really did want to get caught.

Shame and Terror—I Couldn't Tell My Mother

I remember the first time my therapist asked me why I didn't tell my mother, I burst out laughing, "You've got to be kidding." In our family, which didn't discuss sex, to go and say, "Excuse me, but Kevin is molesting me," there is no way. They were people I'd run away from when I was little and when I needed help because they couldn't deal with emotional things. They were people who didn't talk about or acknowledge sex. Also, my father was sick and in the hospital and my mother was away a lot. It was not possible for me to tell her. I was afraid to tell her, afraid she would blame me.

I can see now how Kevin helped instill that belief in me, that it was my fault. He was doing this because I wanted it, that's what he always told me. He was doing this to teach me about it, he was doing this because I would need to know this when I had a husband; he was actually helping me. He also told me he was doing it because I liked it. Often, in sexual abuse, there is a stimulation that does elicit a sexual response—there is part of it that feels good. What stayed with me was the part that felt good, because Kevin would always say to me that I liked it. He would say, "You want it," and when he finally stopped it with me, he told me he couldn't do it anymore just because I wanted it. That was the feeling that stayed with me, this feeling of having enjoyed it, because Kevin told me he couldn't do it just because I wanted it.

What I didn't know, but what came back later, was this feeling of complete and utter terror. It was so different from the feeling I had carried for 20 years that it's taken a long time to reconcile them. I'm still not even sure I know how to put those two feelings together because they seem so separate.

It's so hard to reconcile the feelings of the sexual stimulation with the feelings of terror because you think they can't coexist. But they do, and that's what makes you crazy, and, I think, that's why I shut down the sexual part of me. I couldn't deal with the terror, so therefore I'd rather not have the sexual stimulation.

I think that's another reason why it was easy for Kevin to intimidate me into not telling, because I had this feeling of shame for having felt the sexual stimulation and I was afraid I would be blamed. And after he raped me, I was too terrified.

I Blocked It Out of My Mind

I was ten and it lasted for 13 months. I never completely blocked the experience like some other people do. I blocked almost all of it out, but there were two things I remembered when I started therapy. They were like snapshots. I didn't remember the rape. If someone had asked me to describe it, I would have said I was molested by my brother. But, I always told myself it hadn't really affected me because I was only ten when it happened and it hadn't been any big deal.

When I started therapy, I was suffering from depression, I also told my therapist I was afraid of men, but I never made any connection between remembering that Kevin had molested me and my fear of men. I didn't even tell my therapist about the incest at first.

By the time I went into therapy at age 26, I'd had years of believing nothing was wrong. I was terrified of men and afraid of sex, but going to all-girls Catholic schools for high school and college made it easy for me to avoid any recognition of my fears. I had a lot of friends; everything seemed okay to all appearances. But I had severe depressions. The period between the incest and starting therapy was not what it appeared to be or even what I thought it was. I thought I was coping with everything when I was really blocking it.

Today—Progress Through Therapy

Therapy helped me confront the abuse and see the ways it was affecting my life. I had been very successful with my work, and I had thrown myself into it. But I was not able to open up to people and depend on them. After eight years of therapy, I can see I am now more able to open myself up to people, and to lean on my friends when I need help. I am also starting to develop more interest in men, but I have to work on that because I still find myself looking for "safe" men—men who are friends that I work with, married, or somehow unavailable. But at least I now feel sexual attraction and I am available for a relationship. I've made progress.

Didi
Professional homemaker and mother
Age 24
Married; two children.
Paternal incest.
Two years of therapy.
Alcoholic mother.

Her mother died and her father abused her sexually. These two experiences occurred in tandem in Didi's life at the age of 11. As she tells her story, the two are so inextricably intertwined that it is hard to see where one loss ends and the other begins.

Didi's experience especially emphasizes the fact that incest is not an isolated phenomenon; that it is all mixed up in the victim's experience of the context in which it occurred. For Didi, the context was one of loss and abandonment, and the incest itself was another loss and abandonment. To recover, she not only has to grieve over the incest but also grieve for her mother.

Didi has an unusual experience to share with us, too. She was able to go to therapy with her father, who then entered therapy for himself (Chapter 7). Her experience with confronting her abuser turned out well for her and shows how it can have therapeutic value. The lesson for us all is that we should only attempt such a confrontation if we can be certain that it will help us in our recovery. Her father tried to accept some responsibility. Ask yourself how your abuser would respond, and how you would feel if he did not accept responsibility. Confrontation should not be undertaken without careful deliberation and professional support.

Another important part of Didi's story is the problem of being a mother coping with incest while trying at the same time to be a parent. Survivors with children will take note of how children introduce an added complication and how Didi responds to it (Chapters 5 and 7).

Incest does severe damage to our self-esteem. We all respond to that in our own way. Some of us give up, despairing that we will ever be good enough to achieve our dreams, and we suffer the worst loss of all—a loss of hope, of ideals, of dreams. Megan thought she could never marry or have children; Didi thought she couldn't go to college or have a career (Chapter 4).

Another response is to become a super-achiever, to adopt the "If I do this or that, then I will be somebody" approach. Many of us pile up our accolades hoping it will change us, only to find that it is never enough.

For all of us, the way to self-esteem is through confrontation of our victimization and our powerlessness. Didi has gone far in doing that, having confronted her father and having placed responsibility for the incest on him. She gives us all something to think about.

Abused After My Mother Died

I am 24 years old and a mother, a stay-at-home mother with two young girls, ages three and one-and-one-half. I come from a middle-class family of three children. I'm the youngest, with an older brother and sister. I was abused by my father for two years after my mother died. I was about 11 when it started. I was the only one at home then, basically. My brother was there, but he wasn't emotionally there. He never, never took care of me. My sister had gone to college, and obviously she wasn't able to help me. She never did anyway, but she pretended to.

My Mother Was Sick as Long as I Can Remember

My father had a job that required him to live overseas, and my mother was always very unhappy when she had to leave the U.S. and her family. Before I was born, she had breast cancer and had to have a mastectomy. Then I was born, and when I was a baby they had to go live overseas again. She was not happy overseas and became very ill. She was sick as long as I can remember, but she got seriously ill when we were overseas. She went repeatedly to an American doctor and told him over and over something was really wrong. Even knowing that she had undergone surgery for cancer, and without even checking her, he told her she was just under a lot of stress and to go home and take an aspirin.

By the time we were due to come back to the U.S., she was acutely ill. We couldn't even make it back. I was only four years old then, and I don't remember much of this, but my dad has told me about it. From what I remember and what I've been told, we had to stop on the way back to the U.S. so she could go into the hospital. Then we got to the U.S. and as soon as we got off the ship, she was taken to a hospital where the cancer was diagnosed. This was in New York. There were no family or friends there, and my dad had to spend a lot of time in the hospital with my mom. I was left for long periods of time in a motel room with my older brother and sister. My sister was only 11. It must have been frightening for me. And then my mother left that hospital and went to her home town, where she was hospitalized again. There I was left in the care of relatives. I don't know what her treatment was, but she seemed to get better and we finally went to our new home on the West Coast.

They Said She Might Die

For the next five to six years she was not well. I know she was ill all the time because she was so limited in what she could do. She underwent chemotherapy and, I guess, some radiation treatments. There were no family vacations, very few family activities. During this time I didn't know what was going on; I was not specifically informed that she had cancer or that she was dying. She just got sicker and sicker. Finally, she went in the hospital about four or five days before she died. I guess she knew she was dying, but my father never told me. My older sister sat me down one or two days before she died and said she "might die," but that was it. You have to understand that my older sister was not a warm person.

I Never Got to Say Goodbye

I guess one thing I think of that hurts a lot was that I never got to see her before she died. I remember we went to the hospital that morning with a bunch of relatives, and they all went to see her while my brother and I sat in the lobby and waited alone. Then, after a while, they all came back down and somehow I learned that she was dead. But I don't remember who told me, there was no crying or hugging me or anything. Then there was a service for her, but I did not get to go so I had no awareness of it. There was no funeral either, or I guess it was a cremation, and they have some sort of ceremony but I did not get to go. I had no involvement.

It was all unreal. We left the hospital, went home, and she was just not there anymore; it was like she might come back any time. I was almost 11 when she died, and up until I was 22, when I started therapy, I would see someone in the supermarket or on the street who looked like her and think it was her, that she wasn't really dead and had come back. I would get a surge of excitement and want to run up to see if it was her. It was very hard.

My dad never spoke to me about her death. After we came home from the hospital, there was no discussion of it. He started to sexually abuse me almost immediately, and it lasted two years. So I never got to grieve for her. I still haven't. The abuse started right away, so right away I had that to deal with and I never dealt with my mother's death.

Unresolved Issues—Death and Incest

Sometimes I get upset because I'm afraid I'll lose my memory of her. I have more pictures of her than anyone else, all of them from before she had the chemo. She would not let anyone photograph her after the chemo started. So all the pictures are of her when she was younger. I want to go back to her home town to see a cousin of hers who was close to her. I want to do that so I can get in touch with my mother and grieve for her. I have worked on the incest in therapy and I think I have to work on my mother's death, too, because they all happened so close together.

Two things in particular still bother me. My older sister once said something like, "Mom never should have had you," meaning that somehow her pregnancy brought back the cancer she had before I was born. My dad has since then told me that it is not true, that my birth had nothing to do with her cancer. But still I had grown up with this feeling that I was somehow responsible for her death.

The other thing is not getting to talk to her before she died. I found out that she had a long 40-minute talk with my brother, who was then about 14 or 15, while she was in the hospital, that last four or five days before she died. But she never did that for me. I think it would have meant a lot to me if she could have done that for me.

After Incest—Hard Years to Deal With

The years since then have been hard—in high school, the partying and drinking, taking risks, not caring about what happened to me. Luckily I met my husband when I was 14, and he was older and always there for me. We got married right after high school and I had my two girls. Trying to be a mother, trying to deal with the incest and all the related issues, has been very painful. But Danny, my husband, has been there in support of me.

I went into therapy a few years ago because of my sexual dysfunction and it turned into much more than just that. I've had to deal with the incest and the pain it caused me for most of my life. My dad has gone into therapy. He started therapy with me and now goes on his own, to deal with his problems of being abused himself as a child, abandoned by his mother. It has been very painful, very hard, especially being a mother, having to deal with young children while at the same time having all this pain. But it is better to do that than to do nothing. I reached a point where doing anything was better than doing nothing. I had to deal with it, and I am.

Ann-Marie
Vice-president of data management firm
Age 34
Married twice; no children.
Paternal incest.
Two continual years of therapy; previous intermittent therapy.
Alcoholic father.

Ann-Marie was sexually abused by her father between the ages of 7 and 13. Her response to it is tightly controlled and intellectual. She does not remember having any emotions while her father was abusing her (dissociation), and in telling her story her emotions are often distant or evoked by other events. Ann-Marie's emotions are channelled elsewhere for their expression—books, movies, and her family history with all its secrets. "I feel like I'm tapping into centuries of pain . . . and I feel like it is all focused on me now," she says.

We all have different ways of managing our pain, deflecting it from ourselves so it can be felt in a more removed, controlled, and less threatening way. Control is important. But eventually we all come to accept our pain for what it is and place it with the original trauma where it belongs. It will take a long time to do that, and rightly so. We only let ourselves feel what we can cope with at the time. If the slow, self-protective pace is not respected, we could be traumatically overwhelmed.

As we read through the stories of Ann-Marie and others, we will see how denial feels when the victim remembers the incest, but isn't able to connect the event to its effect in spite of a conscious desire to do so (Chapter 4). It shows how denial is an unconscious, protective process that resists even our best efforts to break through. We need other people who are outside our tangled emotional web to help us get through it—in particular, a good therapist and an incest support group.

A Closely Kept Secret

In my family, there are two family secrets. One of those falls in the category of "open secret," my father's alcoholism. We more or less pretended to the outside world that it wasn't there, although, of course, we lived in a small town and everyone knew it. The other secret that was much more closely kept was the incest between my father and me.

I remember from the very beginning the whole thing felt very strange and very weird, and being very confused and not understanding what was going on. But I don't ever really recall asking my dad, "Why are we doing this?" I mean, I don't think as a child I had that concept. I guess I didn't even know what was happening to me, much less why it happened.

To the best of my recollection, the earliest it started was when I was around seven. The only reason I've been able to fix that in my mind is that we moved between my first years of school, between second and third grades. I have a very clear remembrance of the very first incident because it took place in my parent's bedroom in the new house. It seems to me that it happened very early on, because I went into third grade that year and I had a best girlfriend named Amy at the time. I remember coming very close to telling her one day. You know how little girls get with secrets. Her grandmother lived on my street—that's how I knew her, besides the fact that we went to school together. I remember one time her grandmother had a male boarder in her home, an elderly gentleman who required some care. I remember one day Amy was saying something like, "Y'know, you tell me your secrets and I'll tell you mine" type of thing. Well, it was probably the first, the only time in my life I reneged; I made her go first and she said something about the boarder didn't take a bath or something. I remember being outside my house—my father was asleep upstairs in the house—just kind of looking back at the house. I don't know what made me do it, but I said no to myself, "No, I can't tell this, that Daddy does these things to me." When she told me her secret, I thought, "Big deal." I knew I had her beat!

I Didn't Want to Be Me

I do remember telling her at one time, around the same period, that I hated my name, I did not like being Ann-Marie. I didn't want to be Ann-Marie. I remember standing outside of school one day, and, all of a sudden, Amy just shouted it out that "Ann-Marie doesn't want to be part of the family," or however it was. I was mortified, I felt betrayed—all those kinds of feelings. I was absolutely mortified.

No one said anything to me; I'm sure they just thought it was an odd remark. In this day and age, probably a teacher or someone would maybe get me aside later or take me to the nurse and explain and see if they could find out what was going on. Because there is a lot more awareness that things like these usually signal something is wrong. But at that time, no one, not a single soul, I recall, ever came out and said anything to me.

We Were Never Caught

My father was careful and made sure we were never caught. He seemed to do it when no one else was in the house. My mother was a waitress for many years, until recently, so she was gone during the day a great deal. My father had sporadic work. I think he worked a fair amount, but he was a bartender. He was partially trained as an engineer but he didn't have a professional job. So, he was home during the day a lot when Mom was working, and often he worked in the evenings. So there was a lot of time when one was home and the other wasn't. Or when he was home for a short period of time, I remember a number of times him sending my brother out to play, telling my brother to leave the house. I do remember thinking, "Bobby's got to figure out." (He was young; my brother is 19 months younger than I am.) "He's a pretty smart kid. He's got to figure out something weird is going on."

Jealousy From My Mother

I grew up in my family with everybody saying I was the apple of my father's eye, and I always felt, "If they only knew." If this is what being the apple of my father's eye means, I don't want any part of it. So, I grew up getting that label on me and hating it every minute.

I could feel jealousy from my mother. I don't think she ever knew consciously what he was doing, or allowed herself to know consciously, but I felt what now, when I look back, feels like adult jealousy. There were a couple of specific incidences when my mother was very sarcastic to me, as if I were an adult. I was totally bewildered. I felt totally alienated from her and very bereft, because what little protection I had was from her. If she left, that was it.

I Don't Remember Much

After my father would abuse me and my mother would come home, I would go back to normal. Usually what would happen is that Daddy would fall asleep. In fact, I just had a flashback about this recently. Usually he fell asleep with his arm over my midsection, just loosely. I would go to great lengths to slip away without waking him. I got to be very expert at this, although I didn't realize he was probably sleeping soundly. I got to be very adept at getting out without waking him up, just placing that arm back slowly, literally inch by inch, or half-inch by half-inch, taking five, ten minutes, or whatever to do it. I don't remember what I would do after that; I don't remember.

I cannot remember anything specific after any particular incident. When I talk about dissociation, this is what I'm dealing with. That's why I say I've got chunks of time that I've lost. All that I remember is more a sense of feeling that, "Gee, I've got to go let Bobby in now." And I remembered the sense of having to pretend nothing weird went on. And nobody ever questioned this. If my brother ever said anything to my mother, she never came and asked me about it.

He Made Me Afraid

I did love my dad. I was also tremendously afraid of him. I think that has been a revelation in the last few years, that I had a tremendous amount of fear for him, too. I think that's one of the ways he got this all started. My brother and I both feared him. When he'd come home at night, from either drinking or work, whatever, Mom and I and my brother would be in the living room watching TV or something. My brother and I would literally scatter to our rooms and close the door and stay in there. I loved it when Mom was home because then she would have to cook him his meal and deal with him. If she was not home, I would have to cook his meal, whatever.

I was amazed that through all that fear, what finally stopped the incest was me saying no. It was before my period started. I was about thirteen years old. Most of the memories I have are of it taking place in his bed. My parents had two separate double beds in their room. The very first incident took place in my mother's bed, which was just masturbation-type things. The very last incident, we were in the living room. He was lying on the living room couch. I think he was beckoning to me and wanted me to come lie down next to him. I don't know where the courage came from, but I finally said, "Daddy, I just don't think that's right anymore."

For years, I felt guilty about the word "anymore" because I *never* thought it was right, but that's just the way it popped out. I was about 13 and this was the last incident. Remembering, I think he looked a little hurt or something, or maybe rejected. I don't know, it's kind of hard to classify now. But that was it; that's all it took to stop it. I remember being absolutely amazed that it was so easy. In a way, I thought, "Well, why didn't I think of that before?" If only I had known, I could have stopped it.

It Happened Drunk or Sober

The secret was fairly easily concealed because Dad slept a lot because of the alcoholism. That would knock him out. It wasn't unusual to find him sleeping a lot. My mom was gone enough that she wasn't around, and Bobby was almost always out playing anyway, or if he happened to be in that day, Dad would send him out.

This would happen when my dad was stone cold sober or when he was drunk; it really made no difference. I remember one of the instances (I was probably about ten, I guess, at the time), him sitting up in bed and having just woken up, and he had some pornography-type magazines around that he kept—he had a bottom drawer full of them. My brother and I would like to go in and peek at them when my parents weren't home. Calling me in then, and I remember thinking at the time—y'know, starting to get some consciousness about what was happening to me—and saying, "Now he's stone-cold sober and he's doing this to me."

I Think I Just Kind of Shut Down

I think dissociation may have been a regular occurrence. I don't ever remember him actually raping me in the strictest sense of the term. I do remember him trying intercourse once, very gently. I don't know where the knowledge came from, I directed his penis towards my anus instead of my vagina. He sensed the resistance, obviously, because he had asked me to help him. He got off me after that. I was probably maybe not more than ten, I would think. I really don't remember the age. If I had any emotions about it at all, I don't think I ever really felt them while it was going on. I think I just kind of shut down. Because it just . . . it's, I don't remember anything in particular.

Sometimes, when he was done, I would get a sense of feeling a little happy because Daddy loved me, that I was special. I always grew up feeling that I was special, that I was really meant for something. I always thought that, so when I did fantastically well in high school, straight A's, the whole bit—I was salutatorian—I thought something special was supposed to happen. In college though, I dropped a grade level, I did B's. I had some A's, but I did mostly B-level work. And I was bewildered by that. I thought, "Well, wait a minute, something really special is supposed to happen here." I kept waiting for it.

But aside from this feeling that I was special, I don't remember much about my life that I enjoyed as a child. I was looking for an escape. I read voraciously when I was a child. I was always in a corner with a book.

Escape Through Reading

My dad was a bartender, so he always had to look nice. He was always a nice dresser anyway. I remember him being in monogram shirts, nice and white and pressed. One of the things he would do is give me some money and I'd walk over to town, a very short distance, and pick up his pants at the dry cleaners. It was always the same amount every time, so I always knew how much money I had left over, and I always got to keep the change. So, often what I would do is, I would stop at the department store and buy a book.

In the children's toy department, in those days, they had these sort of hard, heavy-duty cardboard, plastic-covered books. They were like golden books, but much thicker. They had all sorts of good titles, like *Black Beauty* and all those. We had the fire in my home and they got wet, but I saved a few. They were great. They were only 59 cents when I used to buy them. Every time, I went out to the cleaners, which was once a week, I would buy a book with his money, and I always knew how much money I had to do this with. So, my parents were very proud of this.

We'd go to my grandparents' house, my dad's parents, occasionally, and I would get books there. He was a big collector of Reader's Digest condensed books. No one ever considered it rude or anything, but after a little while, I would just go off and sit in the corner of the couch and just read until we left. I remember doing a lot of wishing, as I read, that I could live a different life.

My mother used to tease me, because when I read a book, I had no physical awareness of turning the pages. When I read a book, what I remember is the internal landscape that I set up in response to the description by the author. I'm in the book, not outside it. I still, to this day, do this. Usually I cannot remember if I saw a movie or read the book, because the internal vision is so vivid. For those few hours it's pure escapism. Coming back out of it is literally feeling like waking up, I have to shake myself, and it will stay with me. That was how I escaped as a child, and I still do it.

It Was Over, But Not Over

My dad finally died of his alcoholism when I was 15, about two years after the incest stopped. I went numb at the funeral, and I don't think I've ever properly grieved. The feeling I had was, "It's over," and I was glad it was over. Toward the end, in the last few years of his life, I had talked to him about the dangers of alcohol and tried to get him to stop. I had this naive belief that if he knew how bad it was for him, he would stop using alcohol. Of course, it didn't work.

I finished high school, went to college, and I got married after college. Although my business career has skyrocketed, my personal life has had problems. My first marriage didn't work out. I knew something was wrong here, but I didn't know what. I went to counseling because of my problems with my first marriage. For one thing, our sex life was ridiculous. I told the counselor about the incest, but she didn't respond, so I thought nothing of it. The marriage fell apart, and I got out. I had several relationships after that, one lasting four-and-one-half years. When I married my current husband, I had been in therapy off and on, but not making much progress. I didn't really confront the incest because there was nobody to show me how it had affected me. I was searching, but I needed someone to show me the way.

Making Progress

I met my husband during this time, on a business trip, and we ended up getting married a year later. I stumbled on to a good therapist and finally got someone competent who responded when I told them about the incest. I got into a group, and things have really progressed. I feel that a group is an indispensable part of the process of working this out.

The marriage has gone through some very rough times, and I'm not sure what we'll do. I need support and help, and sometimes I feel that I'm not getting it from the marriage. I'm feeling my needs now and I'm not turning back, even if it means losing the marriage. I have lost my sex drive; I want no part of sex anymore, which is very strange for me. I suppose at some point we'll need a sex therapist, but it makes no sense now when I have no interest.

I see myself progressing with this, and it is hard. My life is in turmoil but it has to be better than it was. I can't go back.

Still Protecting My Family

Sometimes, when I look back at my mother's behavior, I wonder if she wasn't sexually abused too, and I'm almost afraid to even ask. In a way I think even beyond my own fears of rejection and stuff, I'm afraid if I bring that up now for her, she's going to start relying on me for help. Again, I'm in the position of protecting the whole family.

I wonder a great deal about my mother. She was a waitress and had to always be personable, take care of others' needs. She was well-liked by a lot of people. It was a situation where she had regular customers who thought a lot of her. She was very good in terms of service, and smiling all the time. I remember my father calling her in one of his nastier moods, "Miss Goody Two-Shoes," and not liking her.

I don't remember my father ever having any friends of his own. He had his drinking buddies that I knew, but nobody that was close to him. My mother had a high school friend that she stayed in touch with, and they were good friends. Her friend eventually moved to our town and remarried and as a foursome they would do things together. But I don't remember my dad ever having anybody come over to the house. I know my father resented my mother's popularity because he was not that well-liked.

About a year-and-a-half after my dad died, my mom turned around and married another man, a man who turned out to be another alcoholic. Now he is in recovery with AA, but we can't talk about it, it's a big secret. When I go home to see my folks, he gets dressed, cleaned up, disappears for a couple of hours. It's just done without any goodbye, hello, nothing—no discussion. Mom has asked us, when she has talked about it on the phone, not to say anything to him because he has to be the one to come to tell us all sorts of things. It's the same duplicity. She's asking me to pretend that I don't know something that I know. More secrets.

My Stepfather

In a way, my stepfather is a very immature man, even more immature than my father was, I think. My personal guess as to why he doesn't want it known is because, I think, he has accepted my brother and me as his own. He does have children of his own that he doesn't see very often. But there is a lot of love there; I've always felt that from him. He has never tried to become a father to me or anything like that, although he does offer advice.

So, my feeling is that, for whatever reasons, he's going to be afraid that if I do know, that he's going to lose whatever love and respect I have for him. I would like to have the opportunity to say that's not so. In fact, I'm very proud of him for going to AA. My dad tried it for a while, but it wasn't enough and it was too close to when he actually became ill, he was too far gone. Here is somebody who is really coming out of it.

Who Can I Tell?

What's happened now is my mother, in the early days of her marriage to my stepfather, confided to him a lot of the hurts and pains of that first marriage. Unfortunately, what he's done, he's turned around and used them on her in their own life, because he's very similar. He perceives himself not to be very popular, although he has a business and it's doing fantastically well.

Because he has been so warm toward me, I have thought of telling him about the incest. But I'm afraid, if I tell him, he's going to turn and say, "What kind of a mother were you to let that happen to your daughter?" I mean, I could just see it, it would just knife her right through the heart. So, that's one reservation that I have about telling him, because I think he would use it against her and that's not the intent.

But recently I've decided I don't have to tell him. If I tell anyone, I can just tell my mom and let her decide if he should know. I'm still struggling with this alone. I'm still the keeper of the family secrets.

Generations of Pain

The family secret issue goes even further than the incest. I started doing genealogy research on my father's side of the family a few years ago. I had information from my grandfather before he died. I found there were a number of secrets on my father's side. Then recently, in the last couple of years, I talked to my mom a little bit about her side, and there are a lot of secrets there also. There is alcoholism on both sides. My mom and her brother and sister are not, and neither of her parents were, but beyond that there was a lot in her family.

Worse than that, there was a case where my mother's grandfather killed a man because he thought it was the man his wife was having an affair with. I found another family secret there, that there was a child born shortly thereafter to my great-grandmother who was having the affair. He is a great-uncle, "great" in terms of ancestor, although he is a great man, too. I really enjoy him. He is crippled. I was always told he was a "change-of-life baby" and all this other stuff. One of the family secrets was that we heard he was punishment to my great-grandmother, the one who was having the affair. It was thought that he was the child from that affair.

This blows me away when I hear all this stuff. I feel very upset about all this. Any time I start thinking about getting back into the genealogy, what stopped me was, I kept feeling like I was running into walls of pain, like I was connecting with a lot more pain than just what I had. The farther I go back and find all these secrets and all that pain, I feel like I'm tapping into centuries of pain that has never been resolved, and I feel like it is all focused in on me now.

I'm Facing the Truth

I feel like I am the recipient, not just because of the incest, but the recipient of a tremendous amount of hereditary pain caused by these secrets. I don't know how else to describe it. Now, I understand that from a sociological point of view, back in those days, people couldn't face these things, didn't have the tools to do it, much less the therapists and everything else. But that doesn't make me any more forgiving. I'm angry about that. I'm dealing with these things up front. I'm facing it, as you say. It's a very, very painful decision. It has brought my marriage to its knees, I think we're recovering, I don't know for how long. I've only been married two years. I don't know how to make it any better, I can't make it better more quickly.

The other thing is I've always asked the question to myself all these years: How many of my problems derive specifically from incest, or specifically from the alcoholism, and how much of it is plain old me and is not that big a deal? Carrying what I feel to be the burden of these secrets all these years, I've been trying to sort out which things are mine and which things I should throw off. The issue of family secrets is still a hot issue in my therapy in terms of trying to decide what I should do with it. But I am finally dealing with it.

Brenda
Vice-president of a successful company
Age 39
Married twice; two adult children.
Foster-father incest; abuse from infancy through teen years.
Five years of therapy; previous incompetent therapy.
Alcoholic mother.

Brenda's experience represents the more extreme end of the spectrum of abuse. Her story is painful, so painful that you may wonder how she survived. However, you will find her successfully dealing with the same problems experienced by other survivors: difficulty identifying needs, inability to get needs met in a relationship (relational imbalances), difficulty in parenting, low self-esteem, depression, dissociation, hallucinations, fears, guilt, sexual dysfunction.

Brenda also gives us examples of the historical failure of the mental health profession to recognize and treat child sexual abuse. When she was abused as a foster child, the social workers refused to believe her. Later, her new foster parents (both psychologists) would not listen to her when she tried to tell them about the abuse she had suffered in her past. As an adult, her initial attempts at treatment made her feel exploited as a freak and left her with raw, exposed emotions without any resolution. Her experiences with the mental health profession constitute yet another layer of trauma in her life. Fortunately, she persisted and eventually found competent therapists with whom her recovery has progressed rapidly (Chapters 4, 7).

Brenda has never cried for herself. Like many of us, she is protected from overwhelming pain and grief by keeping those feelings at a distance. Her grief pours out for her brother, because that is safe (Chapter 5). You may recognize this mechanism in yourself and in others whose stories are told in this book. As we recover, we become more able to accept our pain and grief. Someday when Brenda feels strong and secure enough, she will be able to embrace the child, accept that she was powerless, release herself from all responsibility, and cry for herself.

Brenda's story, her strength, personal courage, and progress in therapy are inspiring at the times when we feel overwhelmed by the magnitude of our problems.

Abused at Age Three

I'm 39 years old. I was born and raised on the East Coast. My mother was an alcoholic and a prostitute. I never knew my father, he left when I was very young. I come from three or four generations of alcoholics, child abusers, sexual offenders, manic depressives, suicides, probably anything negative you can think of has been in the family.

I guess the first incident that I remember goes back to the time when I was approximately three years old. At that point my mother sold me to one of her gentlemen friends, and that was my first real exposure to sexual abuse. I guess if I could think back further I was probably exposed to it through my mother, but I don't recall any personal confrontations with it.

Caretaker of the Family

I am one of eight children, six of whom were adopted or sold on the black market. My brother and I are from the same father. However, by the time my brother was born, my father was gone. I was the caretaker of the family, the mother to everybody, even my mother. I was the one who scrounged for food. I was the one that made sure that we had some sort of safety, whatever was available, whether it was under a table, behind the door, under the bed, whatever. There was constant fighting, beer bottles being thrown, knives being thrown, screaming, yelling. In any kind of confrontation between my mother and any of her johns, my brother and I were totally unprotected. We lived in extreme poverty in a large city, in many, many slum apartments, which were generally one-room-type efficiencies.

Children came and children went. My brother and I clung to each other and probably feared that we would disappear as many of our sisters and brothers had. By the time I was five or six, the welfare agency came and took us, and we were placed in an institution here known as Children's Shelter, which was better than where I was, although not much better. At least we had food and shelter. My brother and I stayed together through numerous foster homes and institutions.

Sexual Abuse by Foster Father

We went to live with a family who had one child at the time we arrived, and we lived there with them for approximately six years. I arrived when I was approximately nine years old, and, never having gone to school, everyone's primary concern was that I be put in school and get caught up, if possible. I began school in the third grade. They felt through testing that I was intelligent enough that I could pick up things I needed, which only brought me one year behind.

The sexual abuse in the foster home began when I was about 11 years old; it coincided with the time that my foster mother was pregnant with their second child. However, the sexual abuse continued for two years. Part of that was a threat that if I ever said anything, both my brother and I would lose our homes. Knowing what the options were, the institutions where we had been, I opted not to say anything.

I Tried to Get Out

My mother had a sister who lived in Maryland when I was growing up, and she had what appeared to be somewhat of a normal family. Only now I know that it's filled with drug abuse and alcohol, depression and suicide, and a number of other things. But at the time, they appeared to be so normal, just the fact that they were a family living under the same roof with mom and dad and kids was more than I had ever known.

I remember turning to her, in one of my telephone conversations when I was in the foster home, when the sexual abuse occurred, and asking her for help—would she let my brother and I come and live with her? I remember distinctly her answering that she neither had room in her house, nor did she want to have the responsibility of her sister's children. We were her sister's responsibility, meaning my mother, and if she couldn't take care of us, that wasn't her problem.

This came from a woman, who, here again, was a very religious person, respected by the community, always involved in helping people who were poor or homeless or whatever, and here was her own family reaching out and she could have no sympathy for us. Even to this day, she doesn't understand why I'm so bitter, why I have no forgiveness in my heart for my mother, what happened to me, nothing. Here again, this is someone I thought was a good person. She was so heavily involved, she and her husband, in the church and always came across as such a Christian.

Rejection once again sank in that I just wasn't worthy, not even my family wanted me. How could anyone in the world want me for anything, other than to be abused?

I Was Blamed for the Abuse

The sexual abuse usually took place in a car or some sort of vehicle when he picked me up after church, where I was involved in the choir, and generally took place in construction sites or dead-end streets. I guess, as he felt braver, he decided that in the house would be another alternative, and he used to corner me in the kitchen when I was doing dishes or chores. The last straw was in the basement one night when I was doing laundry for them, and his wife walked in.

I was so humiliated and had taken full responsibility for his behavior and I couldn't face her, so I ran away and went to friends' houses. My social worker came to get me the next day and when I explained to her what had been going on, she was horrified that I would lie about such a wonderful family that had taken me in and given a person like me, whom she considered to be less than the scum of the earth, a home and opportunity. "Why are you lying?" she said, and she would make sure that I had every opportunity to rectify this.

Dissociation—What Happened When I Was Pregnant

Even after I was diagnosed pregnant in the institution where I was returned, she denied it. It was all hushed up, there are no medical records, I've searched and searched. There was a brief honorable mention in the welfare records that, at some point, it appeared as if I was pregnant.

At this point, I can't exactly remember what happened to me; it's all somewhat of a haze. I know I was pregnant. I assume that, at some point, I lost the child, that it was born stillborn, because I believe that I was too far along for them to actually perform an abortion. I remember growing larger, and I've confirmed this with several friends who came to see me during that time. They didn't say anything to me at the time, because they didn't want to make me feel embarrassed. But, they distinctly remember my being pregnant and seem to feel I was unaware that I was pregnant. Maybe I was just blocking out the fact that I was pregnant. But I remember one of the housekeepers at the institution, always trying to find larger clothes for me to wear. She was one of the few people who understood, or took time to try and understand what happened to me. Although the denial was still there and very strong, at least I remember her with some caring.

Another Foster Home

After the pregnancy was over and they considered me placeable again, I was placed in the home of two psychologists. They were a little backward in their thinking, because every time I tried to talk to them about what had happened to me, they didn't believe me; they didn't want to hear about it. I'm sure my attempts at that time were feeble at best.

I had a terrible fear of being alone with a man. I didn't want to be alone in the house or the car with the father, the foster father. I constantly tried to make them understand that I had these fears. I refused to go anywhere alone in the car with him. On a few occasions that I did, I always sat near the door with my hand on the handle, wondering when I would need to escape or what he was going to do with me.

Although I had many, many fears during that time, they also gave me many opportunities to better myself. They were an upper-level-income family, and exposed me to many things I probably would have never had a chance to see, feel, or experience. Having an opportunity to see how other people lived gave me additional new goals in life.

I Never Cried

I was a very hate-filled child, bitter, never trusting, very aggressive behavior, would not let anyone, any other child or adult, hurt me after that. I don't remember crying very much as a child. I remember thinking there's nothing anyone can do to me that's going to hurt me. After all, I had already been beaten to a pulp, beaten till I bled, cut with bottles, thrown out into the street, cold, hungry. There really was little left that anyone could do. And all through this I never remember crying, just being afraid. My brother has few memories of all this, which is, I guess, good. But it's hard sometimes for him to relate back. He deals with things in his own way, but they're not mine.

All through childhood I remember wanting to die. I even prayed at times for God to kill me, but also living with the fear that if I died, what would happen to my brother?

The Church

I had turned to the church many times as a child. As a young child living on the streets and when my mother would throw me out, the church was a refuge, and I could get food from the nuns and shelter for a while. As I got older, into my teens, when I turned to the church, no one was there for me. I guess I began to associate the sexual abuse coming home from church, that this was God's way of punishing me, and for whatever reasons he would never be there for me again. So eventually I stopped praying and I stopped going to church and I decided that I was alone and I would have to take care of myself, and whatever happened I would be responsible for it.

Fantasy and Determination—Survival Tools

As a child in elementary school, I remember living in a fantasy world, not wanting people to know who I was, where I came from, the fact that I was a foster child. It was thrown into my face periodically, because when parents found out, I wasn't allowed to associate with their children. But overall, I saw myself very differently in my fantasy. In my fantasy, I was a normal person, I had nice clothes, went to nice schools, could bring my friends home, could have parties, do all the things that my friends did that I couldn't do. I carried that fantasy into adulthood until I got into therapy, or I spent a couple of years in therapy.

I was a very determined child, very determined that I would get through this. My magic age was 18, when the government would release me on my own, and I could do whatever I wanted to do. I could be my own person and not have to always be afraid that I would lose my home if I spoke out or did the wrong thing. In those days, welfare children were basically in-house servants, to do what you are told to do; you didn't ask questions. No one cared how you felt, no one wanted to know what had happened to you in the past or present, just do what you were told and be quiet.

School—A Good Student

In school I seemed to go in and out of periods where I was extremely aggressive and wanted to hurt, particularly boys. Boys that got out of line, made innuendos to me or sexual advances—I wouldn't hesitate to fight them, physically fight them, stand up for myself. I was very intimidating. I wasn't a huge person in those days. I'm not a big person now, but I could easily intimidate. I think that the anger would come to the surface and they were afraid. I would go into periods of quiet, almost seclusion, and not want to deal with people, go into my fantasy world. I was always a very good student, although I must say that I wasn't always the nicest student to teachers, but I always had good grades and did what I was told.

Marriage—My Only Escape

As I became an adult or approached my eighteenth birthday, one incident led to another, and I ended up without any place to live. One of my mother's sisters took me in, and I was so excited to finally be with a relative, a blood relative, only to find out that she was half crazy. She threw me out in the streets after a few months, with absolutely nowhere to go. When I contacted my social worker again, I was told that my only alternative was to be returned to a girls' reformatory.

At that point, I made the decision to marry a man that I had known for a while, seven years my senior. We got married; it was my only escape. My drunken mother signed the papers for me, and I proceeded into married life with absolutely no skills. I had two children during the first three years of the marriage.

I was totally unprepared for motherhood. All I knew is I would never do to my children what was done to me. Unfortunately, that does not make a good mother. I gave the children everything I could. However, I didn't know how to love, I didn't know what it meant to be a child, I didn't know what was normal for a child. I guess I expected them, the children, to have the adult behaviors that I had always had. But, God knows, I tried.

Divorce and Another Marriage

That marriage ended in divorce. Then I spent many years raising the children as a single parent, working extremely hard, going to school at night, working two, three jobs sometimes to keep food on the table, a roof over our heads. Then I entered a second marriage that was doomed from the start because the man I chose was also needy. I thought I could take care of anybody and everybody in the world. That marriage ended and I went into a relationship with another needy man. The last husband, my second husband, and the man that I am dissolving a relationship with now are really good people. They are just very needy. My second husband thought that he should be my psychiatrist, that he should take care of me, that he felt sorrow and pity for me, and I couldn't deal with that.

Now as I'm progressing in therapy and I'm looking at why I choose the men I choose—that's another reason why I'm getting out of this relationship—it was an unhealthy choice. I hope as I progress into my therapy I'll be able to see more of the flags that come up, and recognize and try to be a little more analytical as to why I feel certain things, what it means, and to look at choosing healthy people to have relationships with.

Sexual Difficulties

I still am sexless; it's extremely difficult for me to have sex with a man. I'm okay in the first part of the relationship. Then, when something looks like it's going to be permanent, I start feeling controlled, like I have no choices. When I feel that I can't say no, I lose all sexual emotion, desire, and it pains me just to be touched, to be hugged, any-thing—a sign that someone's trying to be controlling.

I'm not terribly affectionate with the children, I never have been. That is something I'm working on now, even though my children are 19 and 21. It's never too late to show people you love them.

My Mother—Terrifying Even in Death

My mother died a couple years ago. And, when I went to the funeral, it was a very traumatic thing for me to do. I went to the funeral and I remember seeing my mother lying in the casket. I wouldn't go close to the casket, because I feared she would sit up and hurt me. Men-tally, I knew that she was dead, but inside, there was a fear of this woman. I kept visualizing, when I looked at her in the coffin, the wicked witch from the *Wizard of Oz,* the one who rode the bicycle. That's exactly what she looked like to me. I was afraid, so afraid. There was a power in that casket, a power over me that had been there all my life, that this woman could still hurt me.

I remember sitting through the funeral with the priest talking and trying to figure out who he was talking about. He was saying all of these wonderful things about this woman, how she suffered, how she was trying to turn her life around, and finally I had to get up and leave because I was so confused. I didn't know who we were talking about. It was making it harder for me to realize that she was in the coffin. Because when I looked in there, first off, I couldn't really see her, I saw the wicked witch. I was afraid to go too close, and here this priest was talking about someone I didn't know.

Denial—My Aunt

I went out and stood in the lobby with my husband (my second hus-band) and I remember my aunt, the one who rejected me, coming out and being appalled that I would leave the funeral. I remember look-ing at her and thinking and saying to her, "Who are you? Why do you pretend that things are so normal? There is nothing normal in this whole room. It's not normal that she is lying there looking like some-thing I've never seen before. It's not normal for a priest to talk about a woman who has been so cruel and dishonest and harmful to people, to talk about her as if she led a beautiful life and did wonderful things for people around her. It's not normal that you don't see things that are wrong. It's not normal that you sit here and talk about your daughter, who's a drug addict, and pretend that she's taking medica-tion. This whole room is crazy." I felt like I was crazy.

Denial—The Priest

When the priest came out, I remember asking, "Could I have a few words with you," and as we stepped aside, I expressed my concern about his sermon, about this woman who didn't exist. He apologized by saying, "I didn't know any other woman than this one, and she was good and she was Christian." I said to him, "Let me tell you about this woman that you think is so holy and so good." I proceeded to let him hear some of the things that I had been through. The sexual abuse, the beatings, the humiliation, the terror that I lived in. He looked at me and he said, "You know, you have to forgive at some point. You need to settle this, because, you know, God wants you to do this."

He proceeded with another small sermon about how I needed to cleanse my heart, and I remember looking at him and saying, "I'm not the one who needs to forgive; I'm not the one who needs to cleanse my heart. If this is the way the church deals with people like this, the church needs to clean up its act, not me."

I was so angry at this man. He was so placating, so really unconcerned about what had happened. He believed only what he saw, he didn't want to see anything else or hear anything else. He didn't want to be with someone who was so filled with anger and hate and hurt and humiliation. He didn't know how to deal with me, he didn't have the answers. I remember saying to him, "If she doesn't go to hell, then the church has more problems than God can ever contend with." He was just totally appalled with me.

"Why Are You So Bitter?"

I remember later, my cousin coming over to me and saying, "I don't know why you're so bitter, I don't know why you can't forgive people for mistakes." This came from a woman who had not been abused, who had lived with her family, who had a normal life, who was living a normal life now with children and a husband and not a fear of sex and men and poverty and humiliation and shame. I left the funeral home with so much hatred for these people and feeling almost crazy, like things were happening around me that didn't make sense. These people didn't acknowledge anything.

I remember at the grave site, my aunt insisting that I take these flowers, and I was afraid to touch them. I remember asking the funeral director, "Please remove those, don't touch me with them. Give them to anybody, but don't give them to me." And, my aunt being appalled that I was making a scene at the grave site of my mother and her sister, and how this woman needed peace in her life. I left the grave site, never to return again, knowing that I would never return. However, I did wait to make sure they put the dirt on top of her, because, here again, I still feared that she would find a way to come up and out of there, I had to at least know that they were going to put dirt on top of it.

It Is Their Problem, Not Mine

The whole craziness, avoidance, the not-acknowledging-what-really-is, pretending, hiding, secrets, all over again was just too much for me. I was just furious for weeks, and here again I felt the victim. Was something wrong with me? Was I the only one seeing these bad things? Had I really experienced what I thought I had experienced? Was that another fantasy? Had I read it in a book? Had I been asleep and had a bad dream? What was wrong with me?

Now I know that families do keep secrets and they don't want to deal with them, they're not ready. I feel sadness for them. I feel sadness because they can't even acknowledge their own problems in their own homes. They play these constant secret games. This constant masquerade that everything is fine, so they don't have to deal with any emotions. I began to feel that maybe it was good that I had never been allowed to come and live at my aunt's home, because maybe I would have been even more confused or more suicidal, or perhaps I would have turned to drugs like her youngest daughter did. It was a very painful experience.

I've Achieved What I Set Out to Achieve

Way back, as far as I can remember, my objectives were fairly clear for me—to be everything opposite what my mother was. If she drank, I'd never drink; if she beat her children, I would never beat my children. I was hungry, I'd never be hungry; I wore rags, I would dress appropriately. I'd never live in a slum area, I'd never go to bed with men, I'd never let a man abuse me the way she did. I'd be educated. And, I've lived up to those standards pretty much, as best as I could under the conditions when I was a young woman, without having had therapy at that point.

I've achieved what I set out to achieve, even though I have difficulty giving myself credit. I am the vice-president of a successful company. I am able to provide a very respectable standard of living for myself and my sons. I've worked hard in my therapy and I am able to see my progress in that area. I have yet to deal fully with my feelings for the child that I was. I will be able to do that in time.

Ellen
Internationally recognized scientist
Age 54
Married three times; two adult children.
Grandparent was abuser; sexual assault by unrelated juvenile
at age 8.
Intermittent treatment/counseling for 25 years; incest undiag-
nosed for 22 years.
Alcoholic father, grandfather.

Twenty-eight years ago, drugs, shock treatments, and hospitalization were common treatment for women like Ellen, whose chronic traumatic neuroses were mistaken for psychoses. The warning by Denise Gelinas that the intense emotional recurrences of incest trauma can easily be mistaken for psychotic decompensation takes on a heightened significance as we read of Ellen's traumas at the hands of mental health professionals in the late 1950s and early 1960s (Chapter IV). We are all fortunate today to have available to us trained practitioners who are familiar with the high incidence of incest and know how to treat the long-term effects. Twenty or thirty years ago, we might have had Ellen's experience.

Ellen has little memory of her grandfather's abuse, remembering nothing but what she initially dismissed as "fondling." She also was sexually assaulted by a neighbor boy when she was 8. She grew up with extensive denial of the significance of both traumas. Even today, at age 54, there is an element of disbelief as she tells her story. The denial from her family has been integrated into her thoughts and pervades her words with a sense of unreality that troubles Ellen herself.

Ellen has still not had successful therapy. We can feel it as we follow her story from chapter to chapter. Keep this in mind, and you will see how different she is from the others in the way she feels about herself and her experience. She is still uncertain, still trying to convince herself (Chapter 7). This is a stage most survivors who don't remember the incest must go through when they start to remember. It can last a long time because denial is a powerful protective force. A good therapist is needed to help the survivor confront the reality of the incest and break the denial without further traumatizing the survivor in the process.

Ellen's story is a lesson in the importance of demanding and persisting in our search for competent, experienced therapists. Misdiagnosis of an incest victim as being psychotic or borderline is less likely today than it once was. But a person could spend years with an unskilled therapist without achieving therapeutic results. Ellen's story is good motivation to demand and seek the quality of care we deserve.

What Really Did Happen?

I was born in a midwestern city in 1934. My mother had an advanced degree, and my father was working on his. My grandfather was a highly placed official and an active alcoholic. My grandfather did sexual things to me. For the last million years, I've had an inferiority complex.

Sometimes I question myself—what *did* happen? Did he really do it? Did he really have intercourse with me—a child? Suddenly I can't look at children, suddenly I'm afraid. I guess it's time to back off for a while. Actually things are going pretty well—I mean, I'm *acting* like a responsible adult now. It's just that I'm all jelly inside.

Until I was about eight—until my grandmother Nana died—I would spend weekends with my grandparents. I think this was when my grandfather abused me. My grandmother was diagnosed as having cancer sometime before I was five. And I recall an incident from back then that was probably bad—Grandfather wanted sex, Grandmother locked herself in the bedroom, and he tried to chop the door down with an ax. My grandmother wouldn't let him into her vagina—so he entered mine, her beloved little granddaughter's. He needed me—doesn't everybody?

Grandmother's Illness

Between the ages of 5 and 10, my grandmother's cancer got worse and so did Grandpa's drinking. He turned to prostitutes for sex, went to bars quite a lot. But he still kept his position at work. He hunted bear and moose in the winter. I remember the carcasses hanging.

My mother and dad had many physical fights during this time. I remember once when they fought in the front seat of the car over the car keys while my brother and I sat in the back, feeling trapped. I felt very protective of my brother.

My grandmother was pronounced terminal, so we went to stay at their house. Recently I remembered my mother fighting with my grandfather because he wanted me. My mother fought him to the floor. She told me to stay away but not leave, and the way she said it—I was so ashamed and so trapped, like it was all my fault.

Another Sexual Assault

Also at around this time I was invited by a neighbor boy to have chocolate cake—what else?—at his house. I went readily. He performed sodomy and ejaculated in my mouth. I was seven when it happened. I felt so dirty and ashamed.

Then I was running across the dirt banks with semen and dirt on my chin and on my dress front, and I was running up the back steps and into the house, and my mother was *angry*. She grabbed my hand and pulled me upstairs to wash me off. She took me up to the bathroom upstairs, I think. Anyway, I remember washing my face off and having clean clothes on. I remember the waiting—glad it was over (like a terrible scare), but afraid of what would happen next. I waited in the shadows of the kitchen and tried to be invisible and not there.

And then my father was coming in the front door, and Mom and he were talking, and then he was not talking and he was questioning and thinking and squinting his eyes. Then *he* was *angry*. He came at me and grabbed me, and I knew the world was ending. And I was so frightened because it was all turning black and gray and unreal. Then I was lifted and set on the toilet seat and it hurt my bottom and the handle on the tank hurt my back. He was on his feet hunched down, sitting on his feet with his tie hanging down in front of him. And he was crying. And then he was touching me and he was pulling at me, and I think I wet all over the toilet seat. And I cried, and I was so frightened and so ashamed, and so hurt, so deeply hurt.

I was never allowed to cry and be held. He tied me out in the backyard like the "bitch-dog" I was and told me I couldn't come into the house until I admitted how ashamed I was. And my mother was not available to help—she was not even there for me. So I lost both of them that day. Actually there wasn't much to lose because they hadn't been very caring parents—we kids (my brother and I) were a bother to them and they didn't try to change. Soon after the rape Nana died and I lost *everything*. And I sent myself into exile—an exile which has lasted 45 years!

Afterward—Death and Disruption

When, a few months later, my beloved Nana died, I was not allowed to attend her funeral. We moved about a year later. The next few years were hard for me. I do remember much time spent sailing on my dad's boat. I remember some storms where I was scared but felt like my dad was a god.

Then we moved again to a farm and I went to a new school. I felt painfully embarrassed much of the time. I even changed my name because I hated the name I had carried from my childhood. In high school, I felt dumb, dirty, naive. I was near the top of my class, but it didn't matter.

My grandfather moved in with us, living in a separate little house near the main house. He got drunk on binges periodically. I considered him a disgusting old man, and laughed when our dogs chased him when he was drunk. I couldn't invite friends to our house. My dad started drinking then, too.

College and Marriage

I went to a good college; was surprised when I got accepted. I nearly flunked out freshman year, but loved my science courses. I spent a great deal of time at a horse barn where the old couple caring for the animals offered me friendship and love. They were pure country. I loved to be with them. But I needed to study.

The next year I made the dean's list and transferred to another school with better science departments. In spite of everything, I graduated with a degree in science and a promising job in my specialty.

I met my future husband on a field trip for a science course. We were married a week after graduation. I didn't really love him but felt he was socially right—the first of many distorted relationships.

We had two children. My daughter was born 12 months after we were married. I didn't want to stay married, but my parents talked me into staying. I was unhappy but got busy with graduate school. My son was born three years after my daughter.

Things Come Apart

The marriage seemed to allow feelings to come out that were a problem for me. When with him, I felt so very inferior, and those feelings intensified. But an opposite feeling also intensified—that of superiority. And I began to feel disgust for him. I didn't enjoy sex at all, and it seemed to me I didn't really matter to him. I felt trapped and wanted to get away to establish myself as a person.

When my husband was working on his Ph.D., I decided to do some of my own research in my field. I decided this was a good time to leave my husband and told him I thought the marriage was over. I went off to do my research and got mono. While I was gone, for about one month, he met someone else, fell in love with her.

I was 26 years old and had never loved the guy, but I went off the deep end. I went into a horrible depression, lost touch with reality, had amnesia, threatened suicide. I knew I had an emotional problem. I couldn't control the feelings of rejection. The result of all this was that I was hospitalized and given shock treatments.

After that, I was angry, depressed, confused. I felt the shock treatments were a punishment. I went to my parents for support and they told me to stop feeling sorry for myself. Three years after I left my husband and went off the deep end, I finally got mad enough to get myself together and start over in a new place with a new job. It took three years because there was yet another completely useless stint in a mental hospital and a very messy divorce.

Struggling With Depression

From about ages 30 to 40, I fought off depression every day. I tried Freudian psychiatry and group therapy. I did work my way up professionally. I had an affair with a nice guy I didn't love, and I tried to be a perfect single parent. I felt guilty that I could not fall in love. My son had dyslexia and was in therapy quite a bit.

I met, and after two years, married an abusive guy—an uneducated, ex-Marine alcoholic. He tried to molest my daughter. The marriage lasted two months. It seemed like marriage was the only way to end the relationship. Somehow my kids survived this—I think I was good at protecting them. But the depression was always there—a heavy weight. I felt dirty, inferior, insecure.

Changes

When I was 40, the kids left home—daughter to college, son to special school. I was lost, yet relieved. I took in college students as renters. They were my "kids." My career really took off at 40—I began to travel a lot, got international recognition for my work, published, was active in the community. I feel like at 40 my body chemistry somehow changed or something. The depression lifted and I actually started feeling happy. I felt more worthy and I went back to grad school.

Then in my mid-40s, I met Brett, a younger guy, and I fell in love with him like a ton of bricks. He turned out to be needy, selfish, and ultimately abusive. But even now, after a separation of three years, I am still tortured by the pain of rejection.

At about the time I met him I began to experience what I now know to be professional burnout. I had gained international recognition in my field; I was a successful scientist. The more successful I was, the more terrified I became that when "they" found out about how dumb I was, I would die. My successful public image seemed totally out of sync with what I felt about myself inside.

I had impulses of running away, of escaping by sailing around the world on my 53-foot sailboat, the *Spirit*. I wanted Brett to go with me. It took me five years to realize he wasn't going to let me use him in my escape plan. We split up. Then the depression came on like a lead weight, like it had twenty years before.

Just before this split he suggested I was acting like a victim, and he thought it was because I had never dealt with the childhood rape by a neighbor boy. For the sake of keeping peace, I called a rape crisis center and they referred me to a sexual abuse group. After the interview for the group, the therapist said, "You sound like an incest victim."

At about this time, my mother became disabled with rheumatoid arthritis and came to live with me, my son came home, and my daughter and her family came to live with me, so I had quite an uproar. Finally, my son got married and moved out, Mother went to live with my brother, and my daughter and her family settled in with me. I live in the basement.

My mother has turned out to be a real bitch—manipulating, playing victim. My brother couldn't keep her in his home for the same reason I couldn't—she was vicious and critical of everyone. After a year with a housekeeper in a house in a bad part of town, I brought her home with me again. She's on a waiting list for a good nursing home. I actually feel a great sadness about her.

A Growing Feeling of Self-ness

Recently I started having memories, real memories of my grandfather's sexual abuse. I still have not gotten over the first one, of my mother fighting off my grandfather who wanted to fondle me. I sense in myself a real terror that I have not felt before, and I'm running away from it. I'm forgetting therapy appointments and staying up very late so I won't sleep and therefore won't dream.

I'm in an incest survivors' group, and sometimes I'm afraid of it because of powerful feelings of being bad. Yet there is a growing feeling of "self-ness" in me, a self that is different—stronger, less euphoric, more stable than before. It is very slow, but at the same time I'm afraid to go faster, afraid of what I will feel next. The process of remembering the incest is like knowing that somewhere, sometime, someone will drop a bucket of the water on you and you may drown or die of a heart attack.

Today, this moment, I am pretty happy. I am alone a lot because I prefer it that way. I spend weekends on my sailboat. It scares me when people tell me they love me, but I am trying not to run. I feel like a survivor.

CHAPTER 3—FOOTNOTES

1. Gelinas, Denise J., "The Persisting Negative Effects of Incest," *Psychiatry* 4 (November 1983)313.

4

Between Incest and Therapy: Denial and Dysfunction Running Amok

"After the incest, there is denial. Total denial about the occurrence of the event is infrequent and associated with abuse in a very young (preschool) child . . . Most common is denial of the significance of the event. Victims will report that they know something is wrong with their lives, and they are aware that some sexual activity occurred, but they do not connect the two . . . It is also common to repress elements associated with the experience such as the time period, the emotional content, or the place[1] . . . Some victims try to find validation that the incest was damaging, unable to make the connection themselves. Others may have no memory of it, or no awareness that their destructive behavior is a consequence . . . The incest, denial, and family dysfunction produce depression, anxiety, fear, alcohol and substance abuse, low self-esteem, exploitative relationships, sexual dysfunction, suicidal behavior, and dissociation."

The awful thing about untreated incest trauma is that it is not over when it's over. The abuse may stop, but the destruction continues. And usually we don't even know it. In fact, in the time period between incest and therapy, most of us either forgot the incest (like Noelle and Ellen) or put it away in response to the denial around us. We were hurt children, trying to get on with our lives as children do. But we were ill-equipped to do it.

This is the middle part of our story, the part where we got bogged down. Deprived of any effective response to incest and family dysfunction, the behaviors we developed to deal with them became dysfunctions in themselves. This secondary layer of dysfunction absorbed our youth and our energy. Instead of growing and becoming ourselves, we got lost in a bog of dysfunctional adaptive behaviors. Eventually most of us went into therapy to get out of the bog. Until then, we were stuck in dysfunctional behavior that we couldn't even recognize. How could we see it when it was all we knew?

Many incest survivors reading this book will be in this middle period, stuck in the bog. After reading the first three chapters of this book, a common response will be, "Those people really had problems — not me. Maybe you can call what happened to me 'incest,' but it didn't affect me that much. It was no big deal." As the stories in this section show, many of us went through a middle period when we felt just like that. We couldn't see what was happening to us. We got so used to feeling bad that it felt like normal to us, until a crisis made it unbearable.

This section will identify the whole range of dysfunction that emerges in this period — some subtle, some not so subtle. Some of it comes directly from incest; some comes from family dysfunction. Some of it comes from a combination of the two. It all has one thing in common: It feels like loss of self-possession when it is happening. It feels as if we don't quite own ourselves. But remember, we don't have to be stuck in these patterns. We can and do possess ourselves again, and the first step is to recognize the ways in which we are dispossessed. This section will help by showing us the many ways in which our loss of self-possession is experienced.

The stories in this section start with childhood as it was experienced after the incest stopped. In the period between incest and therapy most of us went from childhood to adulthood. The transition from child to adult is a precarious time even for children from functional families. For the children of incest, it is the period when our self-impairment begins to emerge. Our behaviors may be aimless or destructive or pervaded by an urgent need to achieve. The violation of self that we experienced as children is manifested in a whole range of behaviors that have one thing in common: our impaired sense of self. In this period, the impairment of our self-identity is experienced as a loss of self-possession. It feels as if something outside of us is always too much in control of our identity and self-worth. Relationships of any kind are difficult.

How did this happen to us? Part of it was our family dysfunction. We all come from families that to some degree had a problem with us as people. Our parents typically didn't have secure identities themselves, and they felt threatened when we as children began to become people in our own right. Their responses to us ranged from extreme withdrawal to extreme control over us.

Self-image is literally just that. We actually acquire an idea of ourselves through "mirroring," by seeing ourselves "reflected" in our parents' responses to us in our early childhood.[2] Our parents tended to be too withdrawn or too controlling, so our self-identity was not very clear or consistent. We couldn't get a constant, steady reflection of ourselves to carry around. We weren't sure of ourselves.

When our parents are uncomfortable with us as people, so are we. Because we don't learn to be ourselves comfortably, we are either too close or too far away from others, just like our parents were with us. Much like them, we don't have a comfortable spot to stand on and be ourselves as we grow up. Our boundaries aren't clear. Unsure of ourselves, in adulthood we are too vulnerable to being defined by another person's expectations, which can feel overwhelming and produce anxiety. Or, to avoid being overwhelmed, we become estranged and distant from others, leaving us needy and feeling that we are nothing.

Incest further damages our sense of self. To be sexually violated by the very people we rely on for our developing self-identity is to be told in a very tangible way that we have no self-rights. Incest is thus an ultimate expression of our families' inability to respect and nurture our sense of self adequately. More important, we experienced the use of our bodies by someone else at a too-early age. When children are used sexually, it feels to them as though their bodies are literally taken away. And when it is over, the body that is returned feels alien, dirty, and damaged. Thus incest actually impairs our sense of our own bodies. It doesn't feel like it's all ours. Our boundaries and the body part of our identity are seriously damaged. We are pervaded by a sense of shame for the dirty thing our body has become, and this shame gets incorporated into our self-image.

Denial is also a part of the family dysfunction that damaged our self-identity, described in detail in Chapter 1. *Denial* is the word used to describe the way our thoughts and feelings were discredited. Denial made it impossible for us to connect the incest with its effects, thereby turning "something bad was done to me" into "I am bad." Much of our dysfunctional behavior in the period between incest and therapy was a response to "I am bad," as we either acted it out or tried to disprove it.

Denial also contributed to our incest trauma by depriving us of a resolution to our pain, anger, and grief, forcing us to carry those feelings unresolved into adulthood. Denial severed the connection between our feelings and the incest trauma that caused them. These unresolved feelings surfaced destructively in our lives in ways we couldn't understand, because we couldn't recognize what they were.

In this section we will see how our impaired sense of self and the unresolved incest trauma emerged as broad patterns of behavior as we moved from childhood to adulthood. As we grow older, society presents us with an increasing array of options. We go out into the world and find new ideas, new values, new ways of being. Children with a healthy, developing sense of self go through a process of "trying on" new behaviors, new values, new ideas, new people. With a healthy idea of who they are to start with, their selection has some coherence. And even if they get a little wild in some of their choices, they'll feel free to discard something that hurts or doesn't fit. They'll try on something else and keep what feels good. In this way, they acquire an elaborate self-identity "wardrobe" that can accompany them through life, give joy and satisfaction, and enrich the lives of their own children.

For the children of incest, this process doesn't work so well, because we are responding to "I am bad." Without a clear, positive sense of self to start with, our anxiety escalates when faced with choices. What are we supposed to do? What are we allowed to have? We feel inadequate, and have an urgent need just to have *something* on—to acquire an outfit, anything to give us form and definition. With our feelings of shame and guilt, many of us are afraid to try anything too "good," while others rigidly conform to the "good" choices to disprove their sense of shame. And we also don't feel free to cast away anything—even things that hurt—because what if we don't find anything else? We would have nothing. Like bag-ladies, we tend to take what we can get.

Some of us are less destructive than others in the acquisition of our identities, giving ourselves to more socially approved sources of self-identity—schoolwork, careers, children. But it is still a manifestation of the same problem—as adults we have to rely too much on outside sources for our identity and self-worth. We never developed beyond the childhood need for validation. How many of us went with the first needy man that came along, stayed with him even when it hurt, and felt shattered when he left? How many of us became too closely identified with our work, unable to take risks or assert ourselves for fear of rejection? How many of us gave too much of ourselves to boyfriends, husbands, children, religion, or peer group for self-definition and self-worth? Or we go overboard with fads and trends, from the latest in pop-psychology to the newest health concern.

By giving ourselves to others for identity and validation, we get stuck, unable to make choices, unable to assert ourselves, merely adjusting to whatever comes our way until we break. Or, we experience the only alternative we know—protective isolation, withdrawal. Sometimes we became involved in substance abuse when we couldn't deal with the anxiety of having any identity at all—the ultimate annihilation of self.

Remember, too, that our choices in this period are also distorted by unresolved emotions from the incest trauma. Feeling abandoned and hurt, we might cling to intimate relationships, seeking but unable to get the nurturing we missed. Our confusion about sex and love often made these relationships sexual at too early an age. Or, fearful of intimacy and sex, we might bring our expectations of nurturing to our work, making far too much of an emotional investment in our jobs or our schoolwork. And within the context of all these relationships, intimate or not, we might play out our unresolved feelings of shame, anger, betrayal, grief, and pain, miserably confusing past and present.

The confusion of past and present happens when we bring our feelings from the past to some event in the present, such as getting inordinately hurt and angry over some little thing said or done by a friend, maybe even severing the relationship because of it. These incidents can be recognized by two characteristics. First, the feelings we experience are always excessive or inappropriate to the occasion, and second, we are unable to resolve them. They keep occurring. These incidents, compounded over time, destroy our relationships and disrupt our lives. Until we identify those feelings, reconnect them to the incest trauma and deal with them appropriately, we will continue to play out our victimization in every relationship. Our lives will not belong to us, but to the past.

You will see this reenactment of victimization in many stories in this section, as in the way Noelle isolates herself from "nice" kids because she feels "dirty and jaded," or in the way Megan always finds something wrong with a man when she starts to feel too close. And note that at the time, neither Noelle nor Megan realized they were responding to the past, not the present.

These are the ways in which we lose ourselves to the past, missing the real possibilities of the present.

As you read the stories in this section, look for all these patterns of incest and loss of self-possession. Try to find them in your own life. Remember that the way to regain our self-possession is to recognize all the ways in which we give ourselves away. We can and do possess ourselves again. And we always have a chance to go out and "try on" the world again.

NOELLE

How does it feel to not remember the incest? How does the incest trauma manifest itself later when there is total denial? Noelle's experi-ence in the years between incest and therapy is especially helpful to those who are struggling with an "invisible" monster. It isn't so "invis-ible" when we can see its destructive path through our lives. Only when we see its damage can we take the steps needed to stop it.

This section is especially important to survivors who don't remember the incest. Those who don't remember, or who are starting to remem-ber, have a difficult time accepting the reality of it because their mental construct of themselves and their experience doesn't include incest. Be-cause they have no prior consciousness of it, the emerging memories threaten to shatter their sense of reality. It feels like trying to force in a piece of a puzzle that doesn't fit, and in the process breaking apart the whole puzzle. The mind protectively resists this, by denying the reality of the incest. An effective and less traumatic way to overcome the de-nial is to examine the past behavior and identify the dysfunction cre-ated by the incest, gradually adjusting the picture so that incest, rather than appearing as something alien and new, is seen as something that was there all the time. The reality of the incest doesn't shatter the pic-ture—instead, it begins to fit. This was an important process for No-elle, and in this section we will see that she was able to identify a his-tory of dysfunction that was indicative of abuse.

Denial shows itself most destructively in Noelle's family. Denial so thoroughly repressed any response to her father's abuse (both sexual and non-sexual) that Noelle was only able to express her feelings about the abuse in "crazy" or destructive ways: depression, dissociation, sui-cide attempts, destructive sexual behavior, hallucinations, and night-mares.

Responding to unidentified feelings of victimization, Noelle acted out those feelings, as seen in her childhood isolation, her premature sexual relationships, her suicide attempt, and in her inappropriate sexual re-lationships as an adult. She did this with no awareness that her be-havior was dictated by her past, or that she actually had other options. For example, in college Noelle experienced a need to isolate herself and attributed it to the way the other students treated her. Only later, after therapy, is she able to look back and see that it was her old feeling of shame that she was responding to, rather than any real rejection by the other students. Similarly, as an adult, she "found herself" in exploitative sexual relationships and experienced men as abusive. Therapy enabled her to realize that she was responding to her own programming of sexual victimization, and that there are "nice guys" but she could only respond to them in a victimized way. These are some of the ways in which we lose our self-possession to the past, until we confront the past and recognize what happened to us. Until then, we don't own ourselves and we have no choices.

Noelle could not be herself—she was too busy dealing with things that just "happened" to her. The damage done to her self-identity is evident in frequent dissociation, isolation, compulsion to achieve, and unbalanced relationships. The pain Noelle feels is the pain of looking back at a life lost to an invisible monster, against which she was defenseless. But having recognized it, she can now free herself from it. From the pain of recognition comes the freedom to choose.

After Incest—Fear and Abuse

After the incest, I either blocked it out or forgot it. I had no memory of it until it came back when I was 36 years old. But the years between the incest and therapy show the devastation. My father, who quit drinking but remained an alcoholic and also remained out of control, continued to abuse me. It was not sexual, not beatings, but something horrible. I can't describe it; it's hard to describe what life in my family was like because the type of abuse he practiced is so unlike what people typically think of when they hear the word "abuse." It was a combination of terrorism, psychological terrorism, and abuse and neglect. Instead of helping me recover from incest, he just compounded the effects.

As far back as I can remember, I found it best to hide. I was like a little mouse living in his house, trying to hide, but I had to come out for dinner. Dinner was involuntary. We had no choice; we had to come and sit at the table. And if we happened to sit at the table the wrong way, if we happened to answer one of his questions in a not-quite-perfect way, then spewing out would come his hatred and rage and invective on a child.

He would treat us as if we were grown people, as if we were convicted felons and it was his job to destroy us, and that's what he would do. He would viciously tear apart anything we said. He would use twists of logic and hurl accusations at us, cursing and screaming, and I would sit there in the chair just feeling my body go numb. I would dissociate. I would try not to hear him, and I'd blank out. I wouldn't be able to eat. It was a reign of terror until I could leave the table and crawl off by myself to hide.

There was no protection in my room either. He would come in the room and corner me on the bed, spewing forth his rage and violence. His rage would intensify if I cried, because crying meant, to him, that I was indicating he had done something wrong, and of course, I couldn't do that. If I cried, he would hit me for crying.

This whole thing would escalate until I would be screaming with hysteria and begging him to go away and leave me alone, and then he'd go out of the room and say "I didn't do anything to you! Shut up!" Then I'd be restricted to my room for hours or days at a time. This happened on a regular basis until I left home to go to college.

Dissociation—A Survival Mechanism

Maybe this would not have hurt me so much if there had ever been any happy times at home. But there were none. There were no occasions of joy or play or laughter with my father. It was unrelenting fear and abuse. I look back and have no good times to offset the bad. No birthday parties, no family outings, no moments of just sitting around together talking or enjoying ourselves. It was like growing up in a concentration camp.

I learned to dissociate very early. I probably dissociated while he was sexually abusing me, and then the daily abuse I got fostered this habit of dissociation, which is one of my biggest problems right now. When it happens, my mind stops working and I either freeze or get confused. I can't think or say what I know, or do anything. I just become whatever I'm supposed to be at the time. I go away, mentally, and don't come back until the conversation or action is over. It happens at the slightest little hint of stress or power imbalance. That comes from a childhood of abuse, having my physical and mental boundaries violated again and again.

Intelligent Enough to Escape

I attribute my survival to the fact that I was extremely intelligent. When I was 10, my mental age was measured at 17, which gave me an IQ of about 155. I used my mind to escape. I was an avid reader. When I was 5 or 6, my favorite book had a refrain in it: "A person's a person no matter how small." I remember reading that book over and over again. When I had a child of my own, I read it to my daughter and cried.

In grade school, I would go to the public library and stay at the library all day on weekends and read everything I could get my hands on, sitting on the floor in the stacks in the adult section or children's section. I developed this ability to live a fictitious life. For several years, I read books about horses and I became a horse. I saw myself as a powerful horse, and I played this all the time. Then I became a deer—a large, wise old stag from another book I read. I remember sitting on my bed crying one day when I realized I wasn't really able to be a deer. I read many other books, but I really loved animal books. I felt safest with animal books. Now I can see that's how bad I felt about my life. I wanted to be an animal.

"Noelle Was Always Smiling"

I look back and realize the horrible feelings I had about myself came from shame. Although I could not have identified these feelings at the time, I felt disgusting and repulsive, I wanted to cringe when people looked at me. My parents tell me everyone says I was such a happy child, always smiling. I still had that smile when I went into therapy at age 30—and it was a smile of embarrassment, of apology.

I was painfully self-conscious, especially about my body. I dealt with it by dissociating frequently. I remember wearing ballet costumes as a preschooler and feeling ashamed of my genitals, feeling everyone could see them. Later, at age seven or eight, I felt ashamed in a swimsuit, wrapping a towel around my waist. I think throughout most of my childhood, I was trying to be nonexistent. But mostly I remember feeling ashamed, that I was disgusting and repulsive. I wanted to disappear when anyone looked at me, so I dissociated. I felt I was always being looked at, examined. When I walked home from school, I felt the houses looking at me, as if the windows were eyes. I was afraid to stop or do anything, feeling I was being watched and would be punished.

That was my childhood: depression and a need to escape. My teachers would send home report cards saying, "Noelle dreams a lot. She'd do much better in school if she didn't daydream so much." Yes, I was "daydreaming," I was off somewhere else, because I had to dissociate, because I just could not deal with myself, my life.

From Tomboy to Femme Fatale

Then I became a tomboy. I didn't want to be a girl, I wanted to be a boy, I guess because in some way I knew boys had more power and I wanted to have some power. So I wanted to be a boy and I dressed like a boy. It was very hard for me to become a girl.

Later, when my family spent two weeks on a ship, there was a little girl there who was very feminine. I noticed she had total control over the boys. They would do anything for her. She would be sitting in the lounge and say, "Could somebody go get me a box of Cheezits?" and ten little boys would jump up and run to buy her a box of Cheezits. And bingo, I went back to my cabin, put on a dress, put on some of my mother's jewelry, put my hair on top of my head, got a handbag, left all my jeans in the suitcase, and from that day on I became a girl.

I suppose subconsciously I decided there was some way that girls could have power too, and I was going to do it. And that was the day I realized that somehow sex had some power to it, and that's when I entered into the realm of sexual behavior, when I was 11 years old. My adolescence, I think I can safely say, was a series of inappropriate sexual relationships.

Some Hints of the Hidden Trauma

Prior to age 12, I had no memory of any sexual experiences and yet I had sexual awareness. A few things stand out in my memory that I believe were indications of the sexual abuse.

One was when I was 10, and I became very sick. I had to go to the hospital for an EEG and skull X-rays. As I lay on the table and the male technician began moving my head around, moving his hands through my hair to make marks on my scalp, he said, "You have beautiful hair." I recall becoming terrified and freezing up, feeling he was going to do something to me, although I didn't know what. I was intensely aware of his maleness. Looking back, I can recognize it as sexual fear.

I remember my mother buying me a bra when I was about 11, and I was afraid to wear it. I lay in bed one night and heard her tell my father I was going to be "very well-developed." I lay there in fear, angry and scared that she would say that to him, afraid he would do something to me. I cried because I did not want to be that way. But somehow in becoming an adolescent, I made a transition into sexual behavior that was too much, too early.

Looking back, I can see how odd I was. I was mature too early. I didn't fit in with other children. I was too smart in some ways, reading literature and science on an adult level, taking over the household chores, assuming responsibility for my parents' relationship. In other ways, I was backward and inept—I was a social outcast. I did not know how to be, how to act. I knew how to do one thing, and that was to have a secret sexual relationship. That is what I felt comfortable with, so that is what I did starting at age 12 with a boy I knew was "bad" and much older than me.

Groping and Stumbling Through Life — A Non-Person

During my adolescence and my teen years, I continued to be lonely and isolated, and felt unable to cope with the rest of the world. I was totally withdrawn, in a fog all the time. I honestly did not have much idea of what was going on around me, at school or anything. I was very, very bright, but nobody believed me, because I ran around with bad kids. The only kids I felt comfortable with were bad kids, because at least I wasn't as bad as they were, and I guess I could feel some sense of power and security when I was with them. And I couldn't hang out with the nice kids, I was too ashamed.

At the time, I could not identify my feelings, but I had what I now realize was a sense of shame. I couldn't bring nice kids home. Nobody could come to our house, my father made that impossible. And I couldn't go to their houses because I just didn't know how to act around normal people. I felt incredible anxiety around nice people, I just didn't know what to do. I didn't know what they did. I hung out with the bad kids because that just felt right.

Being Whatever I Had to Be

So, my boyfriends were always bad kids who were much older than me. I didn't have a lot of them. I went steady with one boy from age 13 to 16. When I was 13, my boyfriend was 18. He had been in jail and I was trying to "save" him, and I did. I worked with his probation officer, I got him back in school. He was earning B's, he was doing really well until he was hauled away in handcuffs from the school cafeteria for a robbery he didn't commit.

He sexually abused me. I was a little girl, and he used me sexually and I didn't derive any joy or satisfaction from sex. I went through it with a feeling of numbness and grief. But I felt I had to do it. Looking back on it now, it hurts to think of myself as this. I was such a lovely, smart, wonderful child. I love the child I was, and yet I let her be so badly hurt and mistreated, it kills me now. And I feel so sorry for kids who are going through that now, just throwing their bodies away, throwing their lives away to people who can't possibly treat them well because it's what feels right. That's what I was doing; I didn't know how to be in an unabusive relationship.

School—Another Trauma

I was really sick a lot, and when I was home sick, some of my teachers would talk about me in class to the other kids as an example of a kid gone bad. I remember once, in eighth grade, my teacher took the opportunity at one of my absences to lecture the whole class on all my faults and what was wrong with me. Other kids said she told them I was far too mature for my age, far too grown up, and I didn't have any business being that way. She was one of the principal people who harassed me. She was responsible for the school authorities opening up my locker in my absence looking for alcohol, evidence of delinquency, which they found pretty easily. They found notes and things in my locker that indicated I was drinking and having sex, and they wanted to make me a ward of the court.

I felt hounded, persecuted, with nowhere to go. At home, life was hell. At school, I could find no peace. I just wanted to be left alone. I withdrew more and more, into a fog. But there was nowhere for me to go to be left alone.

I Was Not in Control

Looking back on it, it's amazing to me that even though I was so evidently such a "problem child" it never occurred to anyone that something really bad was going on in my family. No counselor, nobody, offered to help. Nobody ever asked me what was wrong. It's almost as if they assumed that a child who's behaving that way is in complete control and knows exactly what she is doing. I would not have known what was wrong even if they asked.

I was not in control, I didn't know what I was doing. I was so confused and dissociated most of the time, I didn't have any idea what I was doing. It would have been a relief for someone to take me aside and say, "There is something wrong in your life. What's it like at home?" Just to have someone offer to help, to have an idea that something was wrong. I had no awareness of my behavior. I had no connection to the abuse I had suffered. It was automatic behavior. I needed someone to point out to me that there was a cause for my behavior, and that there was an alternative.

Crises—School, Abusive Psychologist, and Suicide

When the school authorities tried to make me a ward of court, they said I was out of control. My father said, "I'm only fighting this because it's a dishonor to *me* to have my child made a ward of court," and he successfully combatted the school's attempt. So of course, I didn't get any help.

Later on, when I was a freshman in high school, I became sick and despondent and missed so much school that they required me to go to a psychologist. I was 15, the psychologist was only in his twenties. He was very young and very nice. He was really great. He listened to me, he became my friend. I really liked him. Then later, after only a few months, I started to cry one day in the therapist's office and he sat down next to me, put his arm around me, and I think he started kissing me. It gets kind of foggy here, because I got terrified and I dissociated. I remember the fear that he was going to have sex with me. I left and never returned. Now I wonder if it was just harmless affection, or if I was right. I don't know. I still did not remember the incest, though.

Also when I was 15, I tried to kill myself by eating a combination of aspirin, Darvon, and other things I found in the medicine cabinet. I was so depressed I felt I could not go on living. I lay down on the living room couch and passed out. I was there 16 hours and regained consciousness. Nobody noticed. I had trouble hearing and was dizzy for weeks, but I was alive. Since nobody seemed to notice or care, suicide seemed as meaningless as the rest of my life.

A Glimmer of Awareness

When I was 16, we moved overseas, and I thought, "Okay, I'm not going to throw my life away anymore. I'm going to pull myself together, I'm going to become totally self-sufficient, I'm going to be a successful person."

The psychologist I saw for a short time had been able to open up one little glimmer of awareness in me. He gave me just enough insight for me to start to change my life a little. He did a whole battery of tests, and after he saw the results, he sat down with me and held my hand and said, "There is nothing wrong with you, but I'd sure like to get my hands on your father." He asked my father to come in, but my father had nothing but contempt for psychologists.

But that comment stayed with me. I felt a wave of relief when he said it. It helped me believe I was right in thinking my father's treatment of me was wrong. No matter how much he justified himself to me and heaped criticism and abuse on me, *he* was wrong, not me. I began to have some faith in myself and somehow I began to stand up for myself.

Starting Over at Sixteen—Almost

I went to a very small private school overseas that was academically very rigorous. I was very alone, terribly self-conscious, no friends, in a very friendly school. The other kids were so nice, so clean-cut. I felt dirty and jaded around them.

True to form, I found older men to go out with. This time they were educated members of the upper class in the country where I was living. They were sophisticated, witty, and intelligent. I was usually silent, and functioned mainly as a decorative object. I was a novelty as a foreigner, and somehow they took my silence and knowing looks for intelligence. I passed myself off as sophisticated and mature when I actually felt old and tired. I developed a secret sexual relationship with one man for whom I pretended to have no feelings. Actually, I felt I was in love with him and would have married him at the drop of a hat. I didn't know how to deal with those feelings, so I completely blocked them when he was around. He thought I was very cool, very controlled. What a joke.

This relationship was the main thing in my life throughout the rest of high school. It kept me apart from the other kids. They went to games and dances, I went to black-tie cocktail parties and country weekends.

My parents at this time were completely out of my life. One thing did happen in my senior year. My mother tried to commit suicide on Christmas Eve. I went out to a party, came home, and found my brother sitting alone in the living room while my father was carrying on upstairs with my mom. He told me she had overdosed, and my dad found her and called the doctor. I remember having no reaction. It was like just another routine event. I always felt very sorry for my mother.

College—Compulsions for Success and Secret Sex

In school I worked compulsively hard. I wanted to be the best. I became a top student and earned honors. I got advanced placement when I started college. I needed these achievements to bolster my almost nonexistent self-worth. It became vitally important to me to be a scholastic star. I could find nothing good in myself except my intellect. I could not relate to the nice kids on any other level. I felt that they would reject me if they knew me.

I started college in Europe. Again, I worked hard to excel and won academic awards. I loved Saturday nights because that was when I had the library all to myself. I didn't party, had only one friend, and did not date. I tried going to parties, but would have to leave, not knowing how to act or what to say. I wandered the streets alone, spent lots of time in the museums and galleries alone.

Any relationships I had with boys were secret and sexual. I did not know how not to do that. I didn't know how to act around nice boys, or what to say. The tension I felt with them was unbearable. The only thing that felt comfortable was a secret sexual relationship with one boy, which would be very intense but not acknowledged socially by the boy. I would spend the night with him, but the next day we would totally ignore each other in the student lounge. I needed to do that. I didn't know why, even though it hurt. I just did it.

I educated myself through undergraduate, graduate, and postgraduate degrees on a series of grants and loans because my father would not pay for my education. At one point, because of lack of money, I had to go live with my parents in the U.S. and go to school there.

Living at Home Again—Breakdown

I hated to go back to the U.S., and especially did not want to live at home, but I could see no way out. I was not able to see there was an alternative. When I came back the first thing I did was start a sexual relationship with someone who was completely inappropriate. I was very unhappy, fighting with my dad and hating him. I got more and more depressed as the school year progressed. I met the man who would be my first husband and attached myself to him. Again, I had to have one sexual relationship.

My depression became overwhelming. My boyfriend (my first husband) was a very helpless, childlike, "pure" boy who I felt safe with because I could be his mother. He was too afraid to go into the student union alone for a cup of coffee. I thought he was a beautiful, pristine child. I took care of him. I loved him deeply. I was his mother, he was my child. But my own sense of helplessness, of being overwhelmed escalated. I could not keep up with my studies. I could not stand my father at home, my mother became dangerously ill. I hated the brutality and violence I felt in America. I began to fall apart. I cried all the time. My grades fell and I panicked, thinking I would lose my grant money. Also, during this time I went to the school clinic to see a doctor for a urinary tract infection, and he molested me on the examination table. I dissociated and couldn't respond. I never told anyone. This made my depression worse.

Finally, I found it impossible to dress myself, to get out of bed, or to stop crying. This is all sort of a fog. I wanted to kill myself.

Somehow, my father found a psychiatrist he thought was suitable. Now, I think it highly significant that the shrink was a foreign male who hardly spoke English. I recall going before this man in his office, crying uncontrollably. He looked at me very coldly, and never spoke to me. He told my father in broken English that I should be in the hospital.

I went to the hospital, and they put me on the mental ward, took away my mirror, comb, shoelaces, belts, and so on. They kept me drugged out of my mind. I remember little. The shrink came around once a day and said brokenly, "How-you-do-feel?" and of course, being drugged, I felt nothing. I read a whole book and never remembered it. After a week I went home. The following week I got engaged. Two months later I was married and left home.

First Marriage—Me Against the World

In my first marriage, I was angry, so very angry about everything in the world. I had opened up some needs in myself that could never be met in my adult life, but I did not know that. All I knew was that the world was an overwhelming, disappointing place.

For the first few years, I did everything I could to insulate myself and my husband. We were two against the world. I took great care of him. I picked out his clothes, got him up, fed him, arranged his social life, handled the money, advised him on his work. This was fine until I became aware that I wanted someone to take care of me, to guarantee that the scary, uncomfortable world would not get to me. Then I began to hate him, because he could not do that. I felt he couldn't even take care of himself. He could not find and keep a job, he could not even put food on the table. He could not grow up and reciprocate my nurturing, and he especially couldn't be the superman I wanted to meet my enormous, overwhelming needs.

Children—First I Didn't Want Any

Eventually, we broke up because I wanted children and he didn't. The whole issue of having children evolved in a strange way. When I first got married, I did not want any. I grew up without knowing parents could like their children. I grew up thinking children were horrible, awful things, to be avoided. In fact, I hated children, and when I was 22, I tried to get a tubal ligation because I didn't want any children. I remember my first husband, who was very passive, said, "Oh, all right, anything you want." So I went to the doctor to get a tubal ligation and the doctor refused. I was outraged. That shows how I had internalized my family's rejection of children.

Children—A New Awareness

Well, when I was about 24 years old and out of graduate school, I separated from my husband and I started making films on crime for a special film project some friends and I put together. It was funded by a federal grant. I had been teaching at a university, but at this time I was trying to change, to be loose and adventurous, to open up to life. I knew I could not continue the way I was, which was like my father—rigid, angry, and controlling. I had to change or die.

So I threw myself into this project. One of the films was on child abuse. My technique was to go in and literally live with the people I was filming. So I hung around with a bunch of families in Parents Anonymous. I also went to the police and spent a lot of time interviewing and looking at files on child abuse. I worked with doctors and teachers. I interviewed Raymond Helfer, who wrote the first definitive book on child abuse, called *The Battered Child,* and I got really immersed in the subject.

Light bulbs started going off in my head. I didn't remember the incest, but I knew I had been abused! And I realized there were people in the world who loved children, and it was actually normal for adults to like their children, and that people who didn't love their children had something wrong with them. I started noticing. I'd go to the swimming pool at my apartment building and sit on my lounge chair, and all of sudden I noticed fathers in the swimming pool playing with their children and having fun, and it wasn't a chore. They were actually enjoying their children. This was a huge revelation to me. My father never showed the slightest enjoyment of his children. He was most interested in getting us out of his way.

Falling in Love With a Father

At that time, my husband and I were separated and thinking of getting a divorce. He was living overseas. I met a man who had taught at my grad school and I became involved with him. There was nothing sensational about him, but I was completely infatuated with him because he had two children and he loved them. He was divorced. He and his wife lived within a block of each other, and he kept two bedrooms in his house for his children. They could come over any time they wanted, and they did.

He loved his kids. He had fun with them, he enjoyed them, and talked about them all the time. He would talk about how great babies were. I remember how he would say, "If I ever get married aga n, I'd like to have a few more children, because I just think babies are so neat. I just love the infant stage." He would talk about holding them and how cute they were and how much fun it was to play with them and to take care of them.

I had never been around a man who was nurturing, who loved children. It was almost like a window opened up on a whole beautiful world or state of being I didn't even know existed. I think now he opened up my feelings from back before the incest, when I felt love from my father.

This infatuation lasted for years, and it was almost entirely because he loved his children. I found that irresistibly attractive. He got me in touch with feelings about being a woman and having children that I didn't even know I had. Those two things, finding out about child abuse and finding out fathers could like their children, really changed my life. My eyes opened to another way to live. It made my marriage intolerable, because I wanted to have a child and my husband wanted to be my child. After ten years our marriage broke up.

Breakup of a Friendly Marriage

Now, during that ten years I was pretty much estranged from my family. We traveled a lot, my husband and I. I engaged in all the fantasies I always wanted. I gave myself a childhood. It was wonderful. I had a sailboat, I joined a great racquet and health club, with swimming pools. I had a workout coach, and I went backpacking and hiking. I did everything I'd always wanted to do. I loved camping and hiking. My family never did any of that. Growing up, my family was totally isolated. We had no recreational activities, we had no family vacations, no activities at home. Life was just a day-to-day struggle to avoid my father, to be nonexistent. So when I got away from home, I gave myself a childhood, and I had a lovely time. My first husband and I had fun, we really had fun. I did love my husband. The marriage just fell apart because I learned I had needs for the first time, and I didn't know how to deal with them in the marriage. I thought he couldn't meet them.

I Ran Away From the Men Who Had Something to Give

The breakup of that marriage and my realization that somehow I could not get my needs met in a relationship put me into therapy. I was still in bad shape. On the surface, everything looked right. I had a successful career, a house, a sailboat. I had a racquet club member-ship. I had two advanced degrees and a promising future. I was very attractive. I could have any man I wanted, but I honestly didn't know how to have a relationship with a healthy, normal, giving man. I didn't know how. I couldn't understand why getting what I wanted was not possible for me.

I now realize, after years of therapy, that my inability to accept care or love from anyone came from the abuse I experienced as a child. First, I learned the price I paid for needing my parents was to be abused, that having needs made me vulnerable and helpless. Sec-ond, I learned love is abusive, that loving others gives them the right to take over my mind and body, that it is a form of self-annihilation. I learned to be loved is to be abused, to have no rights of my own. Love was a license to violate me. Having experienced that kind of "love" all my life, I had a distorted and impossible model of love and need-fulfillment as an adult.

The Typical Self-Defeating Pattern

I had trouble at work because I always ended up having a secret sex-ual liaison with someone in an authority position. The typical pattern was that I would be very anxious and have no confidence in my work at the start. I would feel nothing was good enough, and I would knock myself out to excel. Since I was a professional, I had a lot of responsi-bility, so I could justify the hours I worked, having no life outside of work. But the anxiety and sense of being out of place would be over-whelming until I fell into a sexual liaison. Then, suddenly, my confi-dence would blossom, my anxiety would disappear, everything would feel right—until the other people in the firm caught on. Then I would lose their respect, and no matter how hard I worked or how good I was, my work would be discredited. This happened repeatedly. I was tortured by this behavior, but I couldn't stop it and had no idea how it was happening.

I can look back and see that I was behaving seductively and dress-ing in a way that attracted a lot of sexual attention, without knowing I was. I blocked out all awareness of my sexuality, and I also blocked out all awareness of the responses I got. Then I would "find" myself being pursued sexually and it would "happen." It seemed to be just done to me, and when it happened it felt right. It was a relief.

The relationships I had were tortures in themselves. I felt rejected and hurt, but highly desired. I would want to kill myself and get de-pressed for weeks, but I could not stop.

A Compulsion at Work

The entanglement that got me into therapy was with a partner in my firm. Before the affair started, I could not function well at that job. I was not able to tell how much initiative to take or how far I should assert myself. I felt lost. I got confused easily. In conversations with the partners, I couldn't understand simple things because I couldn't focus my mind when I had to discuss something with a man in authority. I would lose grasp of things I knew quite well. I know now my confusion and mental chaos was dissociation, but at the time I thought I was just no good. I would perspire buckets when I had to review a job with a partner. I felt as if I may as well be a creature from another planet, I felt so unable to connect on any level.

Then, when one of the partners seemed to pay personal attention to me, I began to feel different—here was something I knew I could do. As soon as that sexual connection was made, I felt comfortable. This was the base I needed to stand on, I guess. My management skills would improve dramatically—I would feel it was okay for me to make decisions, step into responsibility, assume authority, because I felt accepted.

Things That Just "Happened" to Me

I attempted to go out with other men who were available and attentive. I couldn't because I couldn't stand them. I didn't know why, but I always found some reason to reject them.

Another feature of this behavior was that I would have strong sexual desires for unattainable men, but if I actually had sex with them I would dissociate. I would not be able to keep my mind on it, my mind would wander off somewhere—to work, shopping, the beach, anywhere—until it was over. On rare occasions when I could respond sexually, I would cry uncontrollably with grief after orgasm. I would feel depressed for hours. I thought everyone did that, although it always upset my partners.

I saw myself as a sexual magnet, and I created a fantasy that I liked sex. I did not realize it at the time, but my sexual victimization was the central part of my identity. The way I saw myself and presented myself to my therapist was as an innocent child with an irresistible sexual attraction, helplessly attracting men and bewildered by all the attention I got. I had no awareness that I was doing it to myself, or that it could be different. I just felt I was powerless over things that "happened" to me.

Starting Therapy

When I entered therapy at age 30, my anxiety and depression were serious. I felt worthless, and I had serious fantasies of running away to the desert in Utah to live. I was impulsively running away from work, crying in the bathroom at work for hours, waking up at 3 a.m. afraid. I felt worthless, and in a futile attempt at being someone else I changed my name.

Other things got bad at that time. I had hallucinated spiders for years, but while I was living alone they got worse. They developed red front legs and dropped on me from the walls and ceilings. My recurring dreams bothered me, although I'd had them for years, too. I would wake up from them and be unable to sleep.

The biggest problem was that I didn't seem to be able to fit into any human relationship in my life—not at work, not with friends, not with men. Every relationship was unworkable, I never got what I wanted. I could not connect in any way that didn't result in damage to me. Thank God I found a good therapist, or I don't know if I would be alive today.

MEGAN

In the period between incest and therapy, Megan kept up a good appearance. For those of us who felt everything was "just fine" after the incest, it helps to read Megan and see the subtle signs of incest through the denial. For Megan, fear of men and fear of sex were there but didn't surface because she didn't let them become an issue—she simply avoided intimate relationships.

She did that by avoiding her own feelings, as in the way she repressed her grief over her parents' death. In Megan's story we have an example of the way avoidance of our own feelings works to isolate us even within relationships. Many of us might have an active social life and a circle of friends who freely share their thoughts and feelings with us. But we are still effectively avoiding intimacy by avoiding our own emotions. We can know others intimately while remaining strangers even to ourselves.

But depression and suicidal intentions could not be avoided so easily, and they compelled Megan to seek therapy and to become aware of the effects of incest and family dysfunction.

After Incest—Fear of Intimacy

The best way I know to describe how the incest invaded my life is this: It's as if you are walking along just fine and then you trip, and you don't know who tripped you, why they tripped you, where it came from. All you know is that you tripped and now you are flat on your face. I blocked out most of my brother's sexual abuse and all of the rape. But it came out in other ways, like severe depression, suicidal periods, fear of sex, and fear of men. I could not have intimate relationships with anyone. I took care of other people emotionally, but I did not let them do it for me.

High School—Easy to Avoid Boys

While in an all-girls Catholic high school, I could avoid facing my fear of men because they were not there on a daily basis. Only the real "cool" girls, those more mature and sophisticated, dated regularly and had boyfriends from the boys' Catholic high schools. There were a lot of us, though, who did not date and only went out with a boy to a high school dance. And since we were an all-girls school, if there was a dance, we invited the boy.

I made friends with a group of girls like myself—nice girls interested in going to college—so we did what we had to do to get the grades but we didn't kill ourselves over it. We were not too ugly, so we always had dates for the dances. We were right in the middle in our peer group. No Einsteins, no Candice Bergens, just average. And no one blinked twice in our culture that we didn't date. It was comfortable for me. If I did go out, it was with my girlfriend's brother, Kevin, (that is really his name and that becomes important later). My mother did not encourage me to date—my parents were strict and did not promote getting serious until after we finished college. Education was everything to my parents, and my mother especially exhibited this fear that if you got involved too young, you'd marry too young, which was absolute disaster in her eyes. First you went to college, then within a year after you graduated, you were to meet someone, then get married. If not married by 25, you were written off as a confirmed single person; obviously there was a tight time frame here, and the first three in the family followed it precisely—all finished college and were married within a year after graduation.

Since I was the sixth in line, there were plenty of role models in front of me and I was prepared to follow in their footsteps. All the men in our family went to a Catholic men's college, the women to a Catholic women's college right across the street from the men's college. It was destined before we were even born. There is this picture of the first six of us lined up when I was about two, all wearing college t-shirts with the year on it that we were expected to graduate.

All of us fulfilled the prophecy except Kevin, my abuser. An interesting footnote.

Dad Died, But Life Went On

My world appeared to be fairly safe, and then six weeks before I graduated from high school, my father died of a heart attack. Although he had been sick since I was ten with heart disease, it was still a shock. It changed our lives irreparably. My mother had always been a full-time mom and had devoted her life to my father. She was lost without him and I was afraid.

Among the fears was what to do about money. I was already scheduled to go to the women's college, but I told Mom that if there wasn't money, I could go to a state school and put myself through or go to a college in the city and commute. She said no, if the others got their chance, so would I. She also said she was afraid that if she let me stay home she would become dependent on me and then when I wanted to leave home, she would make it difficult for me. She said it was important for me to leave home then and to go away to college as planned. So I followed the family's blueprint to go to the Catholic women's college.

College—Still Avoiding

My problems with men were not at all apparent at first because the odds were four to one in favor of the girls. The men's college was not yet coed, and there were 8,000 guys there and less than 2,000 women at my college. Only the truly shy never went out. I was immediately thrown into meeting guys because I took a lot of classes at the men's college—there was an exchange of classes and you could take a lot of courses on either campus.

I was overwhelmed by the attention and went out all the time. For the most part it was very safe, sexually, because it was a Catholic school. The boys made all the regular advances, but because we were Catholic girls they were surprised if you said yes. Many of the boys were from all-boys high schools and were as uninformed about girls, sex, and relationships as we girls were. Again, I was in an atmosphere that protected me from facing my fears. I never knew they existed.

A Close Call

In the middle of my freshman year, I started dating one of the guys I met in class—we had known each other since September. And here I continued the pattern I started in high school by only going out with men I knew as friends first. Bobby and I were as hot and heavy as the average campus couple—a lot of heavy breathing and petting, fully clothed. He was as afraid of sex as I was, so we were ideally suited. Bobby lived on the East Coast and I was in the Midwest, and he went to study in Europe our sophomore year. We kept up the romance through letters and phone calls and I was content. I had a boyfriend and did not have to worry about advances from anyone else.

Bobby came back second semester of sophomore year at a time when my life was literally falling apart. My mother was dying of cancer and I was terrified. It seemed to me that the people I depended on all died (which was literally true—first my father, and then, 20 months later, my mother was dead. The two most influential people in my life were gone by the time I was 20 years old).

Bobby and I had known each other long enough to have gotten intimate emotionally, and it frightened me terribly. He had cut short his European program to come back to be with me. But I refused to accept that anyone would do that for me, so I told everyone else, and convinced myself in the bargain, that he had come back to straighten out his major courses. The day after he got back I broke up with him. I told myself if I didn't break up with him, I would become dependent on him and that would be terrible. Becoming dependent on anyone or anything became my biggest acknowledged fear.

Valid Reasons to Say Goodbye

For the rest of college I went out sometimes, but most often I hid in the protection of a group—I always had big groups of friends, both male and female. If a guy took interest in me, okay, but as soon as there were sexual advances I got frightened and got out with some excuse. Now these excuses were valid reasons to me. I never looked upon my retreats as running away. There was always something wrong with the guy to justify my flight. The feeling really was that there must be something wrong with the guy if he was interested in me. Nobody normal could find me attractive.

A Well-Controlled Relationship

After college, I returned to my hometown and resumed my friendships with high school friends and again was in a group of males and females. A couple of guys I worked with took an interest in me—I had enough confidence then to know that all I had to do was to show interest and we'd start dating. I unconsciously chose the guy who was the least stable and the one who was going to move down to the state capital to work for the governor in a few months. He was therefore the one I felt the safest with. And he is the guy I slept with. The whole relationship fell apart six months after it started; partly, it was the distance, partly, it was his reluctance to make a commitment, and partly, it was mine—I wanted all or nothing, and if he wouldn't make a commitment, well, then I was out.

Looking back, I know I wanted out—it was all too frightening, so I put pressure on him and he pushed back, and, lo and behold, I was out. I was always able to manipulate things so that I could get out without facing my real problem with the relationship.

Suicide

Three months later I moved to California. And now I lived near my older sister who was in therapy and finding it extremely helpful. As I talked about my depressions that had become a part of my life since my father's death, she encouraged and pushed me into therapy. And she became the second in a line of a half a dozen people who have saved me in the last 15 years from committing suicide. The first was my friend Rachel. The summer after my mother died I decided to kill myself. But before I did, I called Rachel and asked her to talk to me. I didn't tell her what I was going to do, just told her I needed someone to talk to me and she did. She saved me and did not even know.

Denial

Now, through all this time, I rarely remembered the incest—I blocked it so thoroughly that it wasn't a part of my life, at least as far as I knew. But I did do an odd thing. I moved to California in September 1977. The following summer Kevin, my friend Rachel's brother, moved to California after his marriage dissolved. Kevin and I started dating again, and this time, unlike high school, sex reared its ugly head. Kevin wanted us to sleep together. I told him I couldn't, that it felt like incest since he was Rachel's brother. Incest is exactly what I called it. Kevin was flabbergasted, and, of course, the whole thing between us fell apart. Surprise, surprise. We were 26 that summer.

Depression Leads to Therapy

And I thought my brother's molestation of me at ten had not affected me. I was crazy. After that, I started therapy because I was suffering from depression. I had suffered from being depressed for years, and I had gone through a really severe depression the year my mother had died. Since then, for six or seven constant years, every three months I would go into a depression that would last about two weeks. Then I would come out of it again, and I would kind of stumble along. Right before I started therapy, I had gone into another depression, only this one lasted three or four weeks, and I was afraid it was going to be a permanent one, or a long one like when my mother died. That one lasted a year.

Dealing With Death

When I went to the therapist, I went in talking about being depressed and connecting the beginning of the depression with my mother's death. That's the area where my therapist spent a lot of time with me. We started on my relationship with my parents and how I dealt with their deaths. It came out that my father had been dead almost ten years, and for ten years, I had never talked about him, not even to my supposedly close friends. If anybody asked me anything, I would just say, "He's dead."

I had never really dealt with his death because I really wasn't given the chance. Before I had the chance to really absorb his death, my mother was ill. Eight months after his death, she was diagnosed with breast cancer and had a radical mastectomy, and then she died almost a year to the day after that. So I really never had a chance to deal with his death. Then trying to deal with my mother's death, with the two things, I just blocked it. I thought I had dealt with it really well. If anybody asked me, I would tell them I had dealt with it without any problem because I had kept going. I finished school and I got my job and I didn't have a nervous breakdown. So I thought I had done great.

In therapy I learned that I hadn't dealt with it. We worked on that at first. I mentioned my brother's "molesting" me but we didn't pursue that. I wasn't ready. That came next.

Incest Was Still Invading My Life

During this time, I was still avoiding men, still not able to let myself depend on anybody. I started a relationship with a man who had been a friend of mine for years. I'd call him up to go do things, and he would call me, and he never pushed me sexually, which was fine. Then finally I reached a point where I thought I wanted more than this buddy-buddy-type thing. I started to wonder why he never actively pursued me.

I had always thought that he never approached me sexually

because of something wrong with me—I wasn't attractive enough or something. I had lived with that feeling ever since the abuse —that there was something wrong with me—what man would want me? Finally I began to wonder if it wasn't because of something else.

So I pushed him on it, and pushed and pushed, and finally he told me that the reason he never approached me sexually was because he was gay! I was in love with him, and he was gay! Here I had finally reached a point in a relationship where I thought I could really get serious and take a commitment from someone, and he was gay.

I guess that all along it was the distance and ambivalence from him that I had sensed and that had made it possible for me to feel "safe" with him emotionally and sexually. It shows how the incest was still invading my life. I still couldn't have gone that far with a really available man.

DIDI

Destruction took over very quickly for Didi when she suffered the death of her mother and sexual abuse by her father in rapid succession. The feeling we have with Didi is that of abandonment—an abandoned child overwhelmed by abuse. The impaired sense of self and damaged self-worth are evident in her drinking, drugs, partying, premature sexual relationship, depression, and suicidal feelings.

Like Noelle, Didi was responding to her feelings from her past victimization by bringing them to the present, without any awareness of doing so and no awareness of having any other choice. This is the effect of denial, the major feature of our "middle period." We get bogged down by our dysfunctional behavior, behavior that is a response to our unidentified and unresolved feelings from the past. Without any awareness on our part, "Something bad was done to me" becomes "I am bad." Most of our dysfunctional, destructive behavior is a response to "I am bad." Didi, for example, felt she was "not good enough to meet up with other people's standards" so her drinking, drug use, and bad grades followed naturally. In "trying on" the world, her choices reflected her negative self-image. She was, like Noelle and other survivors, robbed of her choices and her self.

The part that hurts the most is seeing how, at one point, she tried to get some positive reinforcement from her studies. But the moment passed, ignored by her family. Her negative self-identity was established. Didi's recovery was precipitated by a crisis in her marriage, pushing her into therapy and into an awareness of what had happened to her.

A Terrible Time in My Life

After incest, before therapy: this was a terrible time in my life, a very, very painful time, and a time where I was very self-abusive. I was 22 before I went into therapy, so there were ten years of damage. I did drugs and drank a lot, a lot of alcohol, did a lot of running around, trying to see how much I could get away with, trying to find out if anybody really cared enough about me to stop me, to say I was in a self-destructive mode and ask what was wrong. But of course no one did.

Trying to Be Good

I did go through a very short time when I was probably 12 or 13, when I was a straight-A student. I think it must have happened right after or right toward the end of the abuse. It was really the only point in my life where I did that. I remember feeling as though that would be the only way I would get recognition and respect as a person. I worked and worked and worked and I got straight A's. I was studious, and everything I was supposed to be. But that didn't work, and I didn't try it for very long. I worked hard for six months or a year, one year, I guess, in school, but it didn't do anything, nothing changed at my house. No one recognized me more because of that.

Easy to Be "Bad"

So, then, at 14, 13, entering junior high, eighth and ninth grades, I guess, is when I really fell into a group of people who were rebellious, liked to drink, liked to party, liked to do everything, run around. We were just normal, I suppose, but if there isn't anybody there who requires you to stay in line, if there aren't parents there who love you and want to show they care about you by stopping you from doing whatever you want to do, then it gets out of control. I was staying out as late as I wanted, going here, going there, going to people's houses and parties, and, I don't know, my parents never stopped me and they never asked enough questions.

A Stepmother

Then there was my stepmother who, I suppose, was afraid that it would be too much of trying to be a parent if she showed some love and caring for me, I think. That is very painful now. She stepped into the family after the abuse ended. She stepped into the family, and she fit right in with the denial, the attitude that if anything is painful, ignore it. My relationship with her was strained at best.

Naturally it would be like that anyway, regardless of the incest. She moved into my mother's house, with all my mother's belongings still there. She used my mother's things, my mother's dishes, my mother's utensils in the kitchen, my parents' dishes they had collected, and their silver, and my mother's furniture. That was very painful in itself. But some people have no idea of boundaries and where you stop, where you end as a person, and where they begin. So moving into my mother's house and picking up my mother's things and using my mother's things — she had no idea that this was an intrusion on what my family was and what my mother was to us, and it left all of us extremely bitter toward her.

It Never Was Terrific

My family from the beginning has never been terrific, and that was the painful realization. To me, I always thought everything was fine up until the incest began, but it wasn't. We were always extremely closed, and no one ever even talked about my mother dying of cancer. At one point, when I was very young, about three or four, my mother was in the hospital for several months and my brother and sister and I were left in a hotel room while my father went to the hospital to be with my mother. It was right for him to be with my mother, but he did not provide anyone to take care of the three of us. The emotional neglect of his coming home from the hospital and not even discussing with the children what was going on is real apparent to me now. Parents are like that. They try to shelter children, but it's worse because you need to feel the pain in order to feel and to heal. You have to feel the pain. I guess he wanted to protect us from that, and I guess that's why it was never something that was brought up in our family.

You Just Don't Care What Happens to You

But, after the abuse, besides the drinking and drugs, skipping school, and bad grades, I had feelings that I suppose were suicidal. They were feelings that it would be the ultimate way to get back at my parents — to kill myself and leave a wonderful note making them feel so guilty that they would have to live with that pain for the rest of their lives.

At the time I never realized what it was that had actually caused my pain. A lot of times I thought I was just a normal teenager hating her parents, but it was never that. It was an extremely intense hate for them and an intense self-hate. I couldn't regain any good feelings about myself. I think I must have had good feelings at one time when my mother was alive. But after the abuse, I lived constantly hating myself and wanting to kill myself, but not consciously wanting to, and letting it come out in the self-destructive behavior of the drinking and the drugs, partying.

You just don't care what happens to you. I was terribly risky in things I did, hitchhiking with my girlfriends and walking around in the middle of the night. We just had no problems with getting a six-pack of beer and sitting in the park at midnight or one a.m. and getting drunk. It was crazy. But then, I didn't care if anything happened to me, I was sure my parents didn't care. It was a very painful time.

Danny—My Husband

I did have Danny, and a lot of people don't have a Danny. He was 18 when I was 14, and, of course, I was madly in love with him, because in some respects he was an enabler, helping me to get drunk and do drugs later, when I was around 15, 16. But he was also a very good person who believed in me and loved me incredibly, and it just grew. I don't know, I think I was a good factor in his life, too, although I never saw it. I think I was, because we both have come so far from that point, from the way that we were then. We have kids now, but we are different. We've grown a lot and grown together instead of apart and that is just very important.

But Danny was, too, a way of getting back at my father, because he was older than I was. He was a Marine, and my father told me I could not see him. So I did secretly, but letting them know that's what I was doing. I didn't care what they thought, and I was going to see him if I wanted to. They didn't care. They would say that they did, and they'd get angry, but I would go ahead and do whatever I wanted, and that was that. That was the way a lot of things went. I would do whatever I wanted and they had no recourse. They never said they loved me, or, "Please don't hurt yourself because we love you." They didn't have it in them. I don't think my father has even said it to this day. He might have, I don't know. I guess I don't hear that.

Marriage for Love

It was a terribly destructive time. It was also around the time when my sister got married. I guess I was about 19 or so when she had a baby. My dad and my stepmother just loved them, I mean just doted on my sister and her kids. Her children were just exquisite and she was just perfect, you know, stay-at-home mother and all this. I thought, well, that's what I'm going to do. I'm going to get married and I'm going to have babies, and then my dad will love me as much as he loves my sister. I don't know when the realization came that no matter what I did, he couldn't love me as much as he loved my sister, period. He just couldn't, because of what happened between us. I can see it clearly now, but, of course, I couldn't at the time.

I Never Felt Good Enough

I think the sexual abuse distorted my life in terms of my self-worth and what I could have become and what I could have achieved. My life was just thrown out the window. I feel like a lot of me was wasted. I could have done a lot more than I ever did. I could have gone to college, but I felt I wasn't good enough. I felt I wasn't worthy of anything good, so I guess I didn't try to make anything of myself, because I didn't think that I was worth it.

I also think, when I look back, that in many respects I felt so different from other people, not good enough to meet up with other people's standards. I wasn't smart enough, I wasn't pretty enough, I was never enough. That kept me from building relationships that I might have been able to build with other people, friends and lovers. I could have met more people and done more things, but I felt different from everyone and that separated me. I felt like I was bad.

I remember being in different groups of people, at a party or a class, or whatever, and knowing that I was not like them, I was different, and never realizing at all what the incest meant to me. That never, ever, became a factor until I was 22 years old. Up until that point the incest was never ever a factor. My problems were always my own fault. I blamed myself and I was a horrible person to myself. A lot of times I did think I was going crazy. I thought I was going nuts, but it was me, unable to see what had happened to myself. It was like that until I got into therapy.

ANN-MARIE

Many times incest victims respond to the damage done to their identity and their self-esteem by finding positive ways to try to restore what they have lost. Ann-Marie was able to direct her intelligence and her strength into her studies and her career, deriving a positive self-image from her many activities and achievements. But if you pay attention to her story, you will see in it signs of vulnerability, pain, and damaged self-identity, particularly in her relationships. All of the relationships she describes are a problem—somehow a satisfying give-and-take is never established. Her story is useful in helping us to see through our protective armor of success to the pain and damage it may mask.

Her need to achieve at school and at work is in part an expression of her fragile self-esteem, because, as she says, being just Ann-Marie was never good enough, she never had that luxury. Ann-Marie, like Noelle and Ellen, achieved a lot, but with the sense of urgency that comes from feelings of inadequacy and a need to acquire a positive image from the outside because it isn't there on the inside.

Ann-Marie's story is also helpful in showing how denial works as a powerful unconscious process, preventing us from recognizing the nature of our problems even when we make a conscious effort. A good therapist is essential to the process of breaking through the denial.

I Never Really Grieved for My Father

My dad died about two years after the incest stopped, or rather after I stopped it. I don't have much of a feel for those years, except for maybe my drive to be academically at the top of my school. The feeling was there that I was special, that something special was supposed to happen to me.

Then my dad died of illness related to his alcoholism. At the funeral, I cried very little. I remember, in fact, that the moment we were told (we were in the hospital) my father had died, feeling relief—the nightmare's over. The alcoholism had really become an issue in the last couple of years. I remember this feeling of numbness. I think when I look back at high school, college, that numbness lasted the whole time.

On trying to look back at this period, after the incest and up until I got into therapy, real therapy that is, I am beginning to realize that I wasn't there. Or at least I can see that I haven't spent much time on it, particularly college and my first marriage.

I never really grieved for my father. Less than six months after my father died, we had a fire in my home. We got our personal belongings out, but mostly everything was either destroyed by fire, smoke, or water. So, all the memories were gone. Since we didn't live in that place, in a way, it was a real fresh start all the way around—as fresh as you could get.

Guilt, Numbness and Relief

Anyway, in high school I had to write a descriptive essay, and I chose my father's funeral. I remember writing about it, describing feeling very numb the whole time when he was dead, the funeral, that I had a mask on. I think I was really confused. I didn't know what to feel.

I felt very guilty about my feelings of relief that the nightmare was over, and I felt sad that he was gone, because I did love him. I do remember feeling that feeling. You know, I loved everybody in my family. I often felt that in alcoholic families you have all the roles, and I was probably the hero, that was the role I played. I remember feeling very resentful of being in that position, because I felt that if I told this secret, especially the incest, the whole family was going to fall apart.

I always had that feeling that I was the one who had to be responsible and that my needs always had to be deferred because they required too high a price to be met. This never changed.

The years after high school, as I said, are a grey area. I went to college, did well, although I was shocked when I went from being a straight "A" student in high school to getting some "B's" in college.

Graduation Was Great

When I graduated from high school, I was number two (out of 122) in a small town school. I only missed being number one by a few hundredths of a grade point. I wasn't terribly disappointed because I knew I had taken a more demanding course load senior year than the valedictorian, who also happened to be a close friend. She was from a family with a much higher income than mine, and we didn't mix socially much, but we talked on the phone a lot and shared activities at school.

Anyway, graduation was great. Despite (or maybe because of) my father's death the previous summer (1970) and a very damaging fire in our home just before Christmas of 1970, it was a great time. The fire had elicited sympathy and support from my classmates such as I hadn't had.

A Very Busy Life

The spring of my senior year I was able to travel to Europe for ten days with a group of high school kids, and my family—Mom and my four grandparents—kicked in the money so I could go. I had been active in a variety of extracurricular things all through high school—

chorus, library club, school newspaper—and senior year I hit the big time. I was editor of the paper, president of two or three of the clubs I was part of and active in a few more. I also had a solid part-time job that was full-time in summers, a good money job that basically paid for my books in college.

At the graduation ceremonies, it was embarrassing. I had won several awards and ended up staying on stage so I wouldn't have to keep walking up and down. I was a National Honor Society student, and I had won three scholarships that, together with a student loan, enabled me to go to an expensive school that my mother would never have been able to afford.

Dismissed to College

Shortly after I turned 18, I remember my mother had what was to me a very bewildering and hurtful conversation with me. The basic gist was that now that I was 18 I was responsible for my own decisions, but my memory is tinged with feelings of being "dismissed," sent off on my own, and so on. On the other hand, Mom did most of the preparations for college—bought me some extra blankets, things for the dorm room, and so on. And she did drive me up every fall and back home late spring each year, except for my senior year, when I had stayed in town the previous summer.

Anyway, I went to a college about a five-and-one-half to six-and-one-half hour drive from home. I had a very nice roommate and we shared our room easily enough with few arguments, but we were not friends, really. I remember sitting in my room after the first month on campus feeling lonelier than I ever had in my life up to that point. I had sort of made a couple of friends, mostly boys, but I felt pretty isolated. Freshman year I went home for the weekend every month.

He Needed Me

My relationships in college were dominated almost entirely by one man, someone I met freshman year and proceeded to take care of for the duration in a roller-coaster relationship. He always said he would never have made it if it weren't for me. He was younger—he had skipped some grades, so he was only 16 when he started. He needed me, so I did what he needed, which mostly was to study since he had a tough pre-med course load.

I met him purely by chance at a "Welcome Freshman" concert. Jeff just happened to sit down next to me and we struck up a conversation. He was good looking and "normally" dressed—no outlandish style, et cetera. All-in-all, I subsequently went after him pretty aggressively. He was a little shy, but mostly very focused on his studies. He was Jewish and thoroughly imbued with dedication to making his parents proud, becoming a doctor, and earning enough to support them in their old age.

I Supported the Relationship

The religion issue (I'm Catholic) pervaded our relationship all three years. Mostly Jeff (with prodding from his family) was concerned about it. I really didn't care one way or another. He and I had a really different relationship than any I'd had to that point. We appreciated each other's "brain power." I was very supportive of him—emotionally, especially. I'd sit and comfort him with his worries before exams. I'd type his papers. Almost all our "dates" were study dates. He and I probably went to less than a handful of social events while we were together.

But he had a lot of respect from our classmates, and I felt a lot of that reflect on me as a result. People would see one of us and ask where the other was. We ate our meals together. We began sleeping together midway through freshman year. It was truly just sleeping. Our "sex" was really mutual masturbation at that point, and we were both virgins. He was also deathly afraid of getting me pregnant, although I had every intention of also seeing to it that that didn't happen.

When I think about it, it seems I was the major aggressor when it came to sex. I very often would tease him unmercifully when he was trying to study—seduce him. He always gave in sooner or later. I was head over heels in love with him and I was very attracted to him.

A Roller-Coaster Romance

We had numerous ups and downs. I remember Jeff and I would have major fights, me ending up crying my eyes out and going back to my room. (We almost always stayed in his room, not mine.) I remember once accusing him of being a "rock" as portrayed in the Simon and Garfunkel song, "I Am a Rock," because of the walls I felt he put up between us. We were intimate in some ways and like strangers in others. I remember one really bad fight sophomore year where I was hurt so badly that I took the next bus home immediately, at 2 a.m. And I cried most of the trip home.

Summers in between we rarely saw each other—maybe I'd get a

few letters. Once I was home and settled in, I'd usually start seeing the boyfriend I'd had on and off during the last couple years of high school. He was also the first boyfriend I had. Good ol' Stanley. Unlike Jeff, I definitely had the upper hand with Stan. I always knew he wanted to marry me, but I knew it wouldn't work. He seemed to be a dedicated hometown boy, and I was *not* staying in a small town for the rest of my life. Shortly after I turned 19, I "lost" my virginity to him—it seemed sort of inevitable. But then each fall, I'd go back to school and to Jeff, and he and I would begin again and Stan would fade away.

Goodbye Jeff, Hello Dave

Then, in the middle of my junior year, I began to work part-time at the campus computing center. I was the only female on staff except the boss, and I got lots of attention from the staff and most of the users (mostly male) as well. After the "yo-yoing" with Jeff, my ego really got a boost. I remember Jeff actually getting jealous, but by this time I was starting to get fed up with our on-again, off-again cycle. Many times, *he* was the one to convince me to be with him again.

Also, he and I knew that he wasn't coming back for senior year—he was going to med school one year early. We stayed with each other until the end of the school year. I still cared for him a great deal, and when he finally left, I really hurt. In fact, I remember Carly Simon's song, "Haven't Got Time for the Pain," had just come out, and I sorely wished it were true. I knew he and I would not marry—the religious difference—but I still was ambivalent myself.

I stayed near school the summer before senior year, sharing an apartment with another girl from the computing center. Sometime in late spring of 1974 is when I met the guy who would be my first husband, Dave. He was a full-time staff computer operator over at the main facility about a mile away. We first "met" trading wisecracks via our respective system consoles; "computer dating" was our joke. We began dating that summer. He was about three to four years older than me, had been on his own for quite a while, but never did finish his bachelor's degree.

He was nice looking and fun to be with. Late in the summer of 1974 he took me home to meet his family, and I really think it was them I fell in love with more than him. Basically this big loving family just took me straight to their hearts. To this day I far more regret hurting them with the divorce than I do him. By Thanksgiving my senior year we were engaged, and by two weeks after graduation we were married. Two weeks after that I started work at a major corporation.

College Retrospective—Feeling Lost in Poor Relationships

A few things about my college years that are important: I remember very little emotional support from home. There weren't many letters or phone calls from them. Sometimes a month or two would go by if I let it. I remember coming home for a Christmas holiday, and my mother and stepfather (Mom remarried in January 1974) getting my brother something expensive, like a small color TV set, and me something minor, like a sweater. That same Christmas Mom griped about the long-distance phone bill when I was there, because I called Jeff and other people while home. I hit the ceiling and exploded. I was furious because I was already fully and completely paying my own entire way to college, and she was begrudging me a few bucks on the phone bill. I don't remember her reaction, but it seems she apologized.

The other major incident freshman year was Jeff's and my involvement with his roommate, who turned out to be a basket case with an attempted suicide at the end of the school year. During one early "hiatus" in Jeff's and my relationship, Jay and I went out, and he really emotionally grabbed onto me.

The main thing about college was that I was mostly focused on other people, particularly men. I have no sense that I did any thinking about what *I* wanted. I did mostly reacting to others. It's a weird sensation to describe—maybe feeling lost, or numb.

Also, senior year was a bad year. I was sharing a campus suite with five other girls, one of whom had been a very close friend up to that point. However, the previous summer, Sally's boyfriend graduated and dumped her. I think it was a combination of jealousy at my engagement and hurt at my preoccupation elsewhere, but she basically tried to rally our suitemates together to kick me out. It never came to pass, but I was extremely hurt, and a friendship I had really enjoyed and valued died.

On top of that, I had a real SOB for a sponsoring teacher at the high school where I was student teaching. I still don't know what went wrong. For a reason never revealed to me she seemed to decide early on that I was not cut out for teaching and was quite discouraging to work with. Instead of applying for teaching positions, I applied and got a job as a programmer at a major corporation.

First Marriage—Running Away

My first marriage was a case of running toward a fantasy family and running from the woes of senior year. Basically, I feel my marriage decayed as I grew. I went through substantial changes my first three years at the corporation where I worked. It was almost as if I had finally awakened from the sleepwalk I did throughout college in terms of exploring what I wanted. I became career-oriented, and enjoyed my independence. My husband grew more threatened with each advance I took. Toward the end we had numerous fights over whether I could have savings and checking accounts in my own name. By the way, I did change my name in my first marriage, but got it back in the divorce decree. I was uncomfortable with the name change the entire time I was married.

I guess the first couple of years were okay. We took a trip to Florida. We saw his family often. We had a social life pretty much bounded by his friends because I had none of my own nearby. We became the godparents for his best friend's first baby.

The Illusions Fade—Divorce

Late spring and summer of '77, things began to come apart. We had one awful fight that summer about the marriage, him wanting to know when I was going to be a "real" wife, and me shouting back that my job gave me more satisfaction than the marriage. At one point he wanted me literally home, barefoot and pregnant, selling off our second car, and wanted me to quit my job even though (or maybe especially because) it paid 50 percent more than his and we were in debt.

The night before our third anniversary, I couldn't take it any more, and I couldn't bear the thought of going through the anniversary motions—cards and flowers and sentiments that weren't meant. That morning at work I told my boss, who knew what I was going through, that I had decided to get away for a while and asked if she knew of an inexpensive place I could stay for a couple of weeks. She ended up offering her house. So I went home in the afternoon, packed some clothes and left, writing a note that I needed a "time-out" to think through all this.

I was scared to death. I had never done such a substantial, rebellious act before in my life. I was also a little afraid of my ex's temper. His male ego was about to take a beating, and I was afraid of his reaction. I wouldn't have put it past him to report my car stolen. He didn't. I would not let him know where I was staying, and I went through all kinds of efforts to steer clear of him.

After only a few days I knew I was doing the right thing. I agreed to meet him in a public place to talk, but it was over and I wouldn't be budged. It took eight months for the divorce to become final, but it was worth it.

Of course, he had his own perceptions of the marriage's failure: people at work had filled my brainless head with a lot of "women's lib nonsense"; that I was given an ultimatum at work of my job or my marriage. I was in "marriage" counseling by myself for eight months—he refused to come. He also blamed the failure on the incest (I had told him about it), and he threatened to tell my mother about it.

Our sex life was down to nothing, except I would occasionally masturbate him. He actually claimed he didn't know how!

We really were worlds apart, and he could not accept the changes in me. I still don't think having one's own checking account is earth-shattering!

I Was Glad to Be Out

I haven't seen or heard from him since the divorce was final. Once in a while I would drive by the old neighborhood out of curiosity, but I wouldn't stop, of course. Eventually, his name disappeared from the phone book. Occasionally I wonder how he's doing, but never enough to track him down. I was just glad to put it all behind me—especially when I realized I could have come out better financially than I had. We had a house and furniture. I only came away with what I had brought into the marriage—some furniture my grandparents gave me—and my car, as well as its payments.

My lawyer was a bastard sometimes, especially after I told him about Dave's threats concerning the incest. The lawyer had no compunction about making passes at me, actually suggesting I sit on his lap and stroke his beard! Of course, I didn't, but I was furious—someone else who was supposed to protect me, betraying me. And he advised me to sign over the house, with no provisions for getting my share in it back. I was very glad to be out, but it seems he could have fought harder for me.

Starting to Take Control

After that breakup I tried to get counseling, but my attempts to address the incest were unsuccessful. The therapists and counselors didn't seem to know what to do, so they simply didn't respond. I had two significant relationships before I met my second husband. At the time I met my second husband, Jack, I had finally found a therapist who realized incest had had some impact on my life and I was starting to make progress in therapy.

After I married Jack, I got into the incest group and found a very skilled counselor and the process has really accelerated. I'm going so fast and the changes are coming so rapidly, I feel the stress on my marriage, but it has to be done, the therapy can't stop now. I have begun to be able to look back and see how my life was distorted, changed, or whatever by the incest. For me, this is the beginning of being able to take control. That is a big issue with me.

BRENDA

The mechanism by which denial of our trauma contributes to our loss of self-possession is clearly visible in Brenda's story.

Accepting responsibility for the incest she experienced as a child led to self-rejection and loss of self-esteem. Instead of feeling "something bad was done to me," she experienced herself as "I am bad," an experience compounded repeatedly by multiple abuses. When she began to feel "I am bad," the secondary level of dysfunction began, including a withdrawal into fantasy life from which she emerged to throw herself determinedly into school work and career to bolster her sense of worth with her outstanding achievements. In her personal life she experienced the isolation that comes from feeling we are not good enough to be seen as we are. Most relationships at this stage are exploitative, as we see in this and other survivors' stories. We did not learn to identify our needs and meet them, finding it much safer to take care of others rather than risk the dangers of exposing ourselves.

Also evident in her story is the distorting effect of incest on our sexual behavior and the way our impaired self-identity makes parenting a struggle. Brenda's sharp insights give her painful story an overtone of hope. She is no longer controlled by the past. Aware that she accepted responsibility when she actually never was responsible for the abuses she suffered, she has escaped the bondage of denial and is taking possession of her own life.

Accepting Full Responsibility

After the incest stopped, I accepted full responsibility. I assumed I did things to make men turn on to me. Maybe I did, maybe that was my only way of seeking acceptance, thinking it was love, although horrified that this was happening to me. But when it was happening, I wasn't there anyway. I could go off into my own world. When it was over, it was over.

I remember anytime someone would try to be nice to me, whether it was counselors or teachers, I would turn on them so angry, so hateful. I'm surprised that people kept trying when I look back now. I'm sorry that I never saw that they were sincere. I never knew sincerity, so I assumed that no one around me really cared. They just wanted something from me, and I wasn't going to give them the opportunity to get it.

As a teenager, I never participated in school dances or went on dates. I'd get involved in athletics or some scholastic project. Reading was an extremely important getaway for me. I could read and read and not be whoever I was. I could be somebody else, go other places, and just become other people, people I considered normal. I really just felt that everybody who looked at me, hated me. They could see who I was, this horrible person that let men abuse her, led men on. I could see my mother when I looked in the mirror. I hated myself.

I guess I hated myself pretty much through about three years ago. I'd look in the mirror and I'd see this hideous, ugly person who was stupid, couldn't do anything right, who could never be accepted by other people. I would have to lie if I wanted to be accepted.

Defending Myself

I remember quite clearly back in junior high school when one of the young men, who was constantly making jokes about me, sexual jokes in particular, came up one day and sat on my lap on the school bus and pretended that he was going to make love to me or something. I remembered how appalled and humiliated I was, and the sense of being out of control and his being able to do whatever he wanted at my cost and my own expense. The anger welled up, and I remember beating him almost to a pulp at some point.

Another incident was in an English class when one of the more colorful kids from school, a boy who was behind several years in your typical kind of juvenile delinquent mentality, walked by me in English class one day and grabbed me by the boob, I remember turning on him with an anger that was just powerful and decking him to the floor, and he was a kid who was a lot bigger than I was. How appalled the English teacher was that I had demonstrated this kind of behavior!

Accepting the Blame

Once again I accepted responsibility for something that wasn't my responsibility. When I look back now, it was a defensive behavior. I was protecting myself. It was one of the few times in my life that I stood up and decided not to let someone abuse me and get away with it. At the time I couldn't understand why the teacher didn't understand and didn't protect me—even when she found out what had happened. Perhaps it was that the behavior itself wasn't warranted to be so abusive. Obviously decking someone isn't considered a normal way to handle difficulties, but it was my only way of lashing out. I'm sure years of pent-up anger came rushing forward.

Normally I was somewhat of a withdrawn child who had taken the abuse and just welled up inside. But, in these particular incidents, I remember standing up and defending myself, then later suffering ramifications from both my foster parents, who at the time were the psychologists, and the wrath of the principal. How horrified I was that when they came to school I would have to face them. The shame that I felt and the humiliation in knowing that once again I had failed them and their expectation that young women just didn't behave that way. They expected me to be able to control myself and to present a certain kind of image. And at this point, of course, that wasn't the image I was projecting going around decking people. I felt shame in just knowing once again I was going to be rejected by them, because I just couldn't fit in.

Feeling Inadequate

All through my life, and particularly in my teenage years, I was always envious of other young girls in the class, feeling that they were prettier than I was, they were smarter or better than I was. Always the sense of inadequacies, always the sense of not measuring up. Only recently have I begun to feel that perhaps I'm not as ugly as I think I am and maybe I'm more of an average person, that I have abilities, that I have something to offer the world, that I wasn't put here just to be a doormat, to be abused by whomever. But, during school, that lingered over my head like a black cloud so heavy I didn't think I would ever get up and above it. It stayed with me day in and day out. Everything I experienced, I experienced through the eyes of a person who's totally unworthy of any kind of life, any kind of goodness, any kind of caring. I just couldn't visualize myself any other way.

Foster Home—Denial

I don't remember any Christmases, or celebrating birthdays, or any of the usual occasions. I don't remember getting presents, or, even later, I don't remember wanting a present because I knew I wouldn't get it. When I was older, for my sixteenth birthday my foster parents bought me a pearl ring. I guess I broke one of the rules and the birthday present was withheld for a while, which took a lot of the specialness away from it. Having it withheld was just another controlling device. It's sad that this happened with the two psychologists. I look back now and remember, at the time, thinking how wise these people were and how normal they were, and how I just couldn't fit in, I just didn't have it, I wasn't perfect.

It seemed no matter how hard I tried, my behavior was wrong, my background was wrong, everything was wrong. I again retreated into my fantasy world. I look back now and realize they probably weren't the best psychologists in the world. I guess at that particular time, incest and child sexual abuse weren't part of their professional awareness as it is now. They couldn't deal with it, and therefore they couldn't help me deal with it. They didn't recognize the depression was brought on probably from the incest and all the physical abuse I had suffered. They just labeled me moody and hard to get along with. It's too bad. I thought in some ways they would be my salvation. But it wasn't a total loss, as I said, I got a lot from them, I learned a lot about life from them, good life. Even though I have a lot of problems.

At Work—Superwoman

In my years between the incest stopping and going into therapy, I was terribly self-destructive, my self-esteem was probably nonexistent. I did very well at my jobs; I was probably one of those employees every employer dreams of having. I worked myself 'til I dropped for perfection, for acceptance, and no matter how hard I worked, it was never hard enough, it was never good enough. If I worked 10 hours that day, I'd have to work 12, and when I worked 12 I'd have to work 14. I had to do the work of three or four people to be accepted.

I was always very quick to acknowledge when a negative was stated about me, it's like it was presented to me carved in rock. Give me a compliment and I'd toss it aside because I wasn't good enough to receive it. Somebody was lying; they wanted something. So, the drive just continued to feed upon itself—work harder, do more, be more, and the more compliments I got, the harder I worked, because they weren't true, and I wanted them to be true. When someone said,

"You're a beautiful woman," or "You're a pretty woman," flags went flying—what did they want? I'm one of the uglier people in the world. How come they can't see that? Why are they lying to me?

When someone said, "You're smart," again I thought, "What do you want?" But give me a complaint, acknowledge some weakness, I'd be devastated, and I'd work harder and harder and harder, not realizing that every human being has weaknesses and makes mistakes. A mistake was totally unacceptable to me.

As a Parent—I Gave Everything I Could

I'm sure I carried this forth to my kids. "You can do better in school, participate in sports, be somebody," not allowing them to grow up and be whoever they were going to be, so afraid that people would look at them the way they had always looked at me, and that they wouldn't be accepted. I wanted so desperately for them to be accepted by their friends. I overcompensated for everything, except the things that were really needed, the expressions of love, the emotions, actions. I gave them everything I possibly could, but unfortunately, most of it was material things.

When I look at my own children I realize that my oldest son suffered the most. He's probably the most sensitive—he's withdrawn, extremely low self-esteem. He had a great deal of therapy when he was young in elementary school. I didn't know how to help him, so I took him to doctors to try and help him. He spent a year-and-a-half in a psychiatric hospital when he was in his teen years.

I guess I carried forth my ideas of perfection into my children, probably demanding far too much, far too much for a child, and probably maybe even far too much for an adult, for that matter. Being a single parent wasn't easy, and working all the hours, I wasn't there for them. Basically just not knowing how to be a parent. I regret that. Even now I wish there was something I could do to help my oldest son. He really doesn't know where he fits into society, although at least we do talk about things now. He tries to tell me things, and I try to listen. I've suggested therapy for him again, but he's not ready yet. The youngest one is different; I guess he had more protection from his brother, and maybe I wasn't quite so severe by the time he rolled around.

Traumatic Therapy

I had been in and out of psychiatry with a multitude of different kinds of therapists and came away feeling more helpless and more of a bad person. It seems that most of the doctors I went to got so caught up in the horrors of my childhood that they forgot I was there for help, not there for a freak sideshow. I'd come away with raw exposed feelings and not know what to do with them, which became more and more detrimental to me. I finally let go of therapy and shut the door again, thinking I could deal with it a lot better on my own.

Always at the Command of Authority

I've never acknowledged that I have needs, never wanted anyone to think that I couldn't take care of myself and 25 others at the same time. I'm drawn to people who need something. I think my only worth is when I can do something for someone else. To acknowledge a need is to acknowledge a weakness, and even now, after therapy, the healing process, it's still very hard for me to express a need that I have. Always feeling that I had no choices, that I was always at the beck and call and command of anyone who was an authority.

Male superiors were extremely intimidating. Working in a male-dominated world, I had an awful tough time. I was petrified constantly that one of the men would touch me, make advances to me, and I would be victimized again. And, here again, thinking I couldn't do anything about it because I would lose my job.

Indeed, I lost two jobs because of sexual harrassment. But at least I didn't let them get away with it. I made a choice to say no and was struck a tremendous blow by being fired. Trying to raise two young children by yourself and getting fired can almost make you crazy and want to die.

Thinking again, always the victim. Why me? What did I do to make these men react this way to me? Never thinking for a second that they had the problem, but just that when they looked at me, they saw my mother, the prostitute. No matter how I dressed, how high my collars were, how tight my buttons were buttoned, always I saw the prostitute in the mirror and blamed myself for these men coming on to me and then, ultimately, losing two jobs, being fired.

Sexual Manipulation

One of the things I learned about sex early on in my life is you can use it. If people were going to use me, I think subconsciously I knew that, "Okay, fine, you can use my body. Then I can use you." And I think that happened during my marriages when I wanted peace and quiet, when I wanted things to look normal. I guess I used it as a manipulative tool. Even though I hated it, I knew that it would bring me things. I never associated that that's how my mother functioned until years later. Thinking that I had conquered the alcohol and child abuse problems that were prevalent in her family and families before, I never realized what I was doing was a sexual thing. That disturbed me when it finally dawned on me what was going on.

I guess, even in my first marriage, sex was a matter of convenience. Things got so tense, I would give in, and things would be fine for a while. Then they would build up again and I would repeat the same behavior, hating the act of sex. Then my first husband cheated on me and gave me venereal diseases, and that even more impressed me that nobody cared. If they did, why would they do this to you? Sex was a vehicle to manipulate and control, to abuse people. I decided I wasn't going to do that anymore.

I Loved My Children But Couldn't Say It

I refused to let anyone get close to me, to know me, or to do anything harmful to me, and whenever I felt threatened or if my children were threatened, I would lash out with a vengeance. Whatever I had to do to protect my children, I would do it. So although I was probably one of the not-so-good mothers, I had their best interest at heart and wanted desperately for them to know that I loved them.

But it was hard for me even to say those words. It's still hard for me to say, "I love you." To me the word "love" means you have a license to abuse me. "If I say I love you, then I have the right to do whatever I want to you," is what I heard growing up. So, of course, in a marriage or a man-and-woman relationship of any kind, when I start hearing those words, it triggers old feelings that, "Oh, my God, I'm going to be abused again." So I've trained myself not to believe that love exists. I want someone to care about me as a person. I want someone to try and understand me, but I have no interest in hearing the words "I love you."

What Should I Become?

When I was a young woman, in my mid-to-late twenties, I remember people saying to me that my friendliness could be misinterpreted. I was trying to be friendly, so as not to carry forth all the hurt inside of me. I didn't want people to know, so I tried to be friendly. I tried to appear happy and laugh and be fun to be around. And to be told that people misconstrued this to mean that I was trying to seduce men with my flirtatious, friendly overtones—I was horrified. I was always horrified of men. I didn't want them; I just wanted someone to like me. I wanted to be friendly.

When my friends told me this, and when my first and second husbands both said, "Why do you always flirt? Why do you try to come on?" I had no idea that's what I was doing. Now I realize that was their interpretation. I'm a friendly person, generally. I try to be friendly; I try to be outgoing. It's been a long, hard challenge to do that, because when you are friendly and outgoing, you're taking a risk. And to be told this by my husbands and friends—that my behavior was once again unacceptable—was so confusing to me. It left me again wondering, "Well, who am I? What should I become?"

It was so easy for me to admire other people and take on their qualities to change myself, to be them. When I started therapy four years ago, I really didn't know who I was, I had taken on so many personalities.

I'm Turning Negatives into Positives

I look back now, I can see all the different moods, all the different stages that I went through and why they occurred, how I was a product of all the horror and all the abuse. I think back now, and yes, there was a lot of sadness, and many, many things I wish I could change, but in some way I take great pride now in having conquered so many obstacles with the only tools I had.

The more I go through therapy, the more I challenge myself, the more I look back and analyze. I'm feeling better and better about myself, and I'm turning negatives into positives. I'm taking pride in having the courage to face those things again that are so painful. I'm taking pride in overcoming things and overcoming the fears and overcoming the low self-esteem and recognizing some of my abilities and taking pride in those abilities. I'm not always so quick to put myself down.

I find myself becoming less fearful of men. I'm a long way from conquering the sexual problem. I still don't want to have sex. But right now that's really not one of the most important things in my life. I want to feel good about who I am, and I want the right road to do that.

I've built good support systems for myself. I've chosen my friends extremely carefully. They are there for me; I can talk to them. Several of them come from alcoholic families, but none of them come from incestuous families. There's a lot of support, a lot of empathy, a lot of caring. Not pity and not sorrow, some sadness, yes, of course, but a willingness to support each other and be there, and that means a lot to me. They're just like my family, as what I would have fantasized the family would do for one another.

ELLEN

Impaired self-identity and intense denial are particularly evident in Ellen's story of the period in her life between incest and therapy because it is such a long period—more than 40 years.

In Ellen's story we see what happens when we cannot connect our disruptive emotions and behavior to the sexual traumas of our childhoods. This is the working of denial, as we have seen in the other stories in this section. As long as the connection between our feelings and the original trauma remains severed, our lives are disrupted by emotions and behaviors we can't control because we don't really know what they are. We usually attribute them to other things, such as the break-up of a marriage or pressure at work, as Ellen did. And, like Ellen, we might proceed to obsess about the marriage or fantasize about leaving work to sail around the world. But all our responses, all the energy we expend trying to regain possession of ourselves from our disruptive feelings and behaviors will fail, because we will not be addressing them as what they are. We can't do that until we reconnect them with the original trauma and place them in the past. Ellen could not do that without professional help, nor can any of us.

Unfortunately for Ellen, 30 years ago there was little knowledge of incest or its long-term effects. Ellen's story gives us a historical perspective on the mental health profession and demonstrates how bad treatment can be a trauma in itself, hurting us even more than no treatment. We can all be grateful for the progress that has been made and the availability of good therapists today.

Ellen's loss of self-possession was severe. Her successful career as an internationally recognized scientist was her redeeming identity, but even there she was vulnerable to low self-esteem. Her relationships display the familiar lack of balance, each one an expression of low self-esteem. Other familiar signs of incest are her depressions, characterized by feelings of worthlessness and need, guilt, shame, and episodes of dissociation. In Ellen's story, we have a vivid example of the way denial creates dysfunction in this "middle period" after incest.

The Sound of Denial

My feelings about what happened to me as a child are a mixture of grief and fear, and then it feels like I'm not really here. I guess I've been able to rationalize not dealing with this by saying, "My problems aren't really that bad—these other people really have a lot of problems. I haven't." It's my mother's tape playing inside my head, "Forget it, there's nothing wrong with you." That is what denial sounds like. For too long I listened to it.

I know something about the events that happened to me, and I certainly know how I've felt all my life. But I've only just begun to connect them. What I'm sensing is that somewhere along the way, I'm going to have to really deal with it.

There are two parts to what I'm feeling now. One is there are things that are happening now that I can identify as a result of the incest. The other part is what has happened to me in the course of my life that I now realize is related to the incest, although I did not know that at the time.

Feelings of Inferiority

The thing that took me into treatment and forced me to start to deal with the incest was a feeling of inferiority. I can remember walking home from the first grade or kindergarten and being sure that everybody could see me; I assumed that because they could see me, what they saw was a rotten person. And this was at age five! I look at my grandchildren today, and how happy they are, and I'm constantly amazed that they don't feel that way. So that was the first thing.

My mother told me that an inferiority complex came with our family, that it was just part of our family. So I sort of accepted it as part of being who I was, but I really wondered about it.

The First Breakdown

My history is really punctuated by a couple of events—the worst and the first was after my husband and I separated. We were married five years and had two children. I was 27. I didn't love him. I knew when I married him I didn't love him, but he was wealthy and money had always been a big problem in my family, and he had a sense of humor and seemed to be relatively harmless. But there wasn't a lot of love there.

It would have been okay, I think, if he had been involved in science and the things that I thought were important. I thought we were going to have a team, a professional team. I'm a geologist, and so was he. But he didn't make decisions. I had to make all the decisions. And then I found, after a while, that when I made a decision, he withdrew, so I was just sort of dragging him along all the time. And I thought, "This is silly. I don't really love this man, and I don't really like being with him, so I may as well go off on my own."

I wanted to go to graduate school, so I said in a very straightforward way that this wasn't really working and we should go off on our own. Well, he sort of panicked and started being very passionate and pleading, "Don't do this. I love you so much, and so on and so forth," and I just felt cold. So about that point, I decided to start working on my own science. He was doing his Ph.D. research in the field, and I had a babysitter and I started doing my own field work. I got mononucleosis and went to my parents' to recuperate. When I left, I said, "This is probably a good time for a separation." I felt that I could just up and do my field work and carry on and he could do what he wanted.

Well, he met a girl within a couple of weeks after I left, and he fell madly in love with her. I thought it was because of the mono, though it turned out it was because of my problems arising from the incest— but, when I found out that he had found someone else, I went into a nervous breakdown.

Dissociation

I dissociated, almost completely, from everything. I knew there was something very wrong, because I shouldn't have been acting that way about this man I didn't really love. In fact, a part of me was really relieved that he had somebody else and now I could carry on with my own life. And yet, everything about me was falling apart. I didn't want to kill myself, because I really enjoyed life, but I couldn't live this way. I thought, "I've got to find someone who can tell me what is happening to me."

So, I went back to live with him, but the pain was so great being near to him, I walked out of the house one day and went into town. I was going to find a place to live where the students live. I was spaced-out completely and some people took me in—an old couple who kept me in their kitchen a few days, and then they said, "Well, you really should go home." I didn't even know where my home was! I went out of their house and wandered around until I found a street on the campus that looked familiar, and then somehow I managed to find my house. I walked in and announced that I was going to kill myself. At that point my husband called his father. That was the standard technique for him, "Call Father, he'll know what to do."

Hospitalization and Shock Treatments—Another Trauma

They put me in a hospital in the city where his parents lived. I was relieved because I thought someone was finally listening to me. I needed help. A psychiatrist came in and saw me, I think for an hour, for maybe three days. Then, on the third day, he came and said, "We know exactly what your problem is." Being a scientist I thought, "Great, they must know." And he said, "We've got a new technique to cure you."

Well, what he was talking about were shock treatments, but I didn't know what that was about—I was just happy thinking they had an answer. They sent a telegram to my husband, and he signed it—a release for my shock treatments. I had seven. The first one told me what this was all about. At that point, I should have done something. But I was in the hands of mental health "professionals" and they were giving me drugs and stuff—plus my self-protection mechanism wasn't working.

"I Deserved This"

At some level, an important level—as I now understand it—I was thinking, "I deserve this. I'm being punished. I deserve this."

Shock treatments are awful. I almost decided to switch fields and go into psychiatry, just to do some research on what shock treatments do to people's brains.

I came out of that fog. That was 1959. At that point, if I could have found someone who knew what was happening to me, I could have very easily trusted them and probably dealt with the incest successfully. But there was nobody there for me.

Instead, I went into this weird state of mind where I felt that I deserved the shock treatments. My inferiority and everything were still there. I had these two little children, and my husband was with this other woman. And I remember thinking that they were like gods, this woman and my husband, and that I was just a nothing.

Second Crisis—Another Hospitalization Trauma

The worst thing I did in that period—my daughter and I have talked about this. My daughter looks a lot like her father—and I transferred to her the feelings I had about him. It was like, "This child is looking at me and thinks I'm disgusting." So I withdrew from her and pushed her away and did all sorts of things.

One day, she was sitting up on the counter in the kitchen. And she didn't do anything bad—just some little thing—but I hauled off and hit her and knocked her off the counter. As she fell off the counter, I looked down at her and I thought, "She looks like a frog." It was the antithesis of motherhood.

At that moment, I knew something wasn't controlling my emotions, and I committed myself to five weeks in a mental health center. I thought, "I'm going to get some heavy-duty treatment here—I'm going to get out of this thing." And all that came out of that was a lot of drugs and a psychiatrist who talked to me every day—and his analysis was that I was a latent homosexual!

It was good in a way because I had exhausted this big hospital treatment of my in-laws, and I had exhausted the honest-to-god mental hospital, and I was still feeling awful. So I said to myself, "I've got to survive." And somehow or other, I just decided to grit my teeth and survive.

Dissociation Again

At that time, there were other people—my mother—saying, "Well, you're just feeling sorry for yourself." After I got out of the mental hospital I was over at their home one day, and she said, "You're just feeling sorry for yourself." And I could feel the anger just coming out of me, and the frustration. I felt she was right, and yet I knew she was wrong. I knew something was happening to me—I wasn't feeling sorry for myself. I had to fight to stay alive—to keep from killing myself!

Well, at that point, my father jumped on the bandwagon, and I remember him saying, "And when are you going to pay back all your long-distance phone bills?" Well, something went off in my head. I ran out the front door, across the street, and into the woods. I felt that I just wanted to get lost. That was something else—after the shock treatments, I felt that I wanted to be this little pinpoint of light, and just disappear. That seemed to be the only escape—to become a pinpoint of light and disappear. And running into the orange grove, I had those same feelings. I thought, "They can't ever find me here. I'm gone."

I Had to Survive and Do It Alone

Well, they got the police and the dogs, and they came after me, so finally I said, "This is ridiculous," and I got up and walked out. Then I knew I could not go to my parents for help. And there was no help from mental hospitals or psychiatrists. So whatever survival I did, I had to do it alone. So from then on, I tried to just *not* feel.

So I moved here, and it took me about nine years to feel any confidence in myself at all. It was an uphill battle—every day. And I almost gave up—if it hadn't been for the kids, my kids, I would have given up. Oh, so many times I wanted to die—with cancer or a heart attack—"Please, God, just let me die. But what will happen to the kids? No, Ellen, you can't die—you have to keep on facing your ugliness day after day."

Another Try at Therapy

It turns out, I've been really quite successful, professionally. But I've never dealt with the other stuff, my personal stuff. I had another marriage, to a guy who tried to molest my daughter. He was a sergeant in the Marines. I met him at a county mental health center, where I had been in therapy since moving here.

When I came here, I decided to get into therapy with a Freudian, thinking Freudians know about trauma. I had known that my grandmother died, and that she was the only one I had loved. I knew that my grandfather had "played around" with me, and I knew things like that can cause problems. I also knew that I had been raped when I was eight, and my father was alcoholic and abusive. I mean, I knew all those things. And I thought, well, the Freudians believe in all this trauma stuff, so maybe by working with a Freudian psychiatrist I can deal with this. So I was going, and it wasn't doing a thing. I told her all this, but it seemed to me that she didn't like me. I remember, I had an affair with a guy, and I couldn't enjoy him sexually. So she said to me, "You're just teasing him. You're lucky he didn't hit you."

Disastrous Second Marriage

So I switched therapists, started going to the mental health center, met the Marine, and went with him for two years. He drank and was violent. He said to me, "I want to put a gun up my wife's ass and blow it off," because she had gone off with somebody else, had five children. A friend of his called me and said, "Do you know he burned two houses down to support his wife, and that's why she had to go off and find a job and then met someone else?" I didn't believe them.

I finally married the guy, was married about six weeks, and I just couldn't stand it. I had my own house and my own finances, and it just seemed to me that I didn't want him in my space. And I knew this was not good, so I got divorced rather quickly.

After the divorce, my daughter told me he had tried to molest her. It happened one evening when I was out. I was very active in the community at that time, and I was out one evening at a meeting when he got drunk and tried to get into bed with her. She was in a bunk bed, fortunately, and she put her foot on his shoulder and pushed him off the bunk bed. She said, "You stay away from me," and he did, fortunately.

Feeling Guilty, Going Nowhere

When she told me about this, I felt nothing. It was like a blank. I felt a little anger at him, but not intense. Inside there were these things pulling in opposite directions, and all I could feel was just grey. I can understand now how mothers can just watch these things happen and not protect their daughters. I was relieved that I was separated from him, and I felt guilt, of course. It was like—"I'm so rotten that that's the kind of man I would pick." It seems like through the years so much of the things that have happened to me have led to this place where I feel, "Of course, you're rotten, so you just have to accept this and go on." It's sort of like something I just carry along with me.

Well, that led me to going to another psychiatrist, but it didn't really go anywhere. I was in a group, but I didn't seem to be getting anywhere. I felt very guilty, and then I got out of therapy completely and moved overseas to another country where I was doing some good things professionally. I was gone quite a while. I started doing work on my master's degree.

Another Involvement—Love and Disgust

I met Brett after about two years. He was eight years younger than I was, and I fell in love so totally—it was amazing—just ten months after I met him. I was in outer space. All three of the men I've married have been only children—and he was, too. He was very selfish, and yet I loved him. I would have done anything for him, but after about a year, I started feeling disgust for him. His sneakers—I'd see his sneakers on the floor and I was disgusted. Watching him walk, I didn't like the way he moved. And yet, I loved him. It was the same way with my first husband. I loved this man and yet the disgust was very strong.

Four years after we'd been together, he said, "You know, I don't think you've dealt with the rape." So I called the rape crisis number, and they referred me to a women's center. I started with an incest group although I felt I didn't belong there. I told myself I didn't have any problems, not like the women in the group who had "real" problems.

About a year after I was in the group, Brett and I broke up. It happened when my son got married. He came over for the wedding, and I wanted a commitment from him. After the wedding, we went to have breakfast, and I put my hand on his arm and asked, "What about our relationship? Do you think you could make a commitment?" He said, "I don't know." It was just the offhand way he said it—I felt, "What am I doing with this guy?" So I got angry, and he went to Annapolis and I went home.

Later on that evening he came back, and I confronted him and he said, "I will not make a commitment under fire." So I said, "Go find somebody else." And I felt very calm, like steel. He walked out and a month later, he did find somebody else.

History Repeating Itself—Almost

I didn't find out about it until six months later. A mutual friend told me he had met this woman, gone to Europe with her, and was now living with her. I could almost hear a click in my head. I went from feeling a little rocky about splitting with him—from thinking of him as this big kid that I didn't really need in my life—to thinking that all of a sudden he was this handsome, perfect being, and I was right back in the dirt where I had always been. I went into a horrendous depression. That was two years ago, and I'm just fighting my way out of it now.

Now I'm in this place inside where I'm trying to understand the incest and deal with that, and working my way through the depression. Things are kind of confusing right now. It's funny, talking about it makes me feel a lot of relief. That tape that says, "If you hadn't done this or that," and, "It's all your fault," is not playing.

CHAPTER 4—FOOTNOTES

1. Gelinas, Denise J., "The Persisting Negative Effects of Incest," *Psychiatry* 46 (November 1983):316.
2. For an excellent discussion of how a sense of self is developed in the first three years of life, read *Oneness and Separateness* by Louise Kaplan. She "translates" the definitive clinical work of Margaret Mahler into language that is understandable to the average reader.

5

Parentification: Or the "See What You Made Me Do!" Effect

Gelinas describes the pervasiveness of incest family dynamics as they extend into the next generation. For the victim, the long-term effects of incest and relational imbalance together do most of the damage . . . The parentified child learns to take care of everyone but herself. In adulthood, the parentified child will not know how to get her needs met and will not even be able to recognize her needs . . . She therefore adjusts readily to an exploitative job and may typically be underpaid and overworked . . . The man she will attract will be narcissistic, immature, insecure, and dependent . . . She never has a childhood, so she has an overdeveloped sense of responsibility for others and an underdeveloped sense of self . . . She will be markedly lacking in self-esteem, having grown up without the concept of self-rights . . . Guilt is an important feature in her psychological landscape . . . The degree of guilt is related to the degree of parentification whereby she was taught that she was responsible for everything . . . It is also magnified by the victim's awareness that she may have loved her abuser . . . and may have experienced sexual arousal . . . She will have serious trouble in all other relations . . . [she will] not know how to balance "obligation and entitlement . . . "Friendships will be difficult and in sexual relationships they will be exploited . . . because those will be what feels familiar to them . . . As parents they will feel depleted and overwhelmed . . . will not know how to establish boundaries, set limits, provide structure, administer meaningful discipline, or nurture beyond the biological level . . . They may withdraw even more from their children . . . As a result, her own children may also be at risk for emotional and physical abuse . . . Parentification of their own children will begin . . . leading directly to the third persistent negative effect of incest: the intergenerational risk of incest."[1]

In Chapter 4 we looked at ourselves in our bogged-down period, the time when many of us didn't recognize our dysfunction because it was just business as usual for us. After reading Chapter 4, many who initially may have said, "I don't have a problem with incest," may have started to question that belief and look a little more closely at their lives.

Now we're going to look closely at something that is even harder to recognize when we are in it. We will examine a process, the process of role-reversal with our parents. Gelinas calls this "parentification." We will look at how it contributes to a large part of our dysfunctional behavior—specifically to our problems with relationships.

When I think of "parentification," I hear someone yelling, "See what you made me do!" First it was my mother and father when I was little. Then later, it was me yelling at my daughter when she was little. That is what parentification is. It is always being responsible for everyone else until you are a parent, and then the converse is true and you expect your own child to be responsible for you because you are so wiped out from having never been cared for. Then your child carries it into her family when she becomes a parent, and then her child, and so on and so on. Until someone stops it, which we intend to do right here.

We will examine our childhood relationships with our parents and siblings and try to identify the ways we experienced parentification. Most of us find that our mothers were parentified as children. Then we will turn to our adult relationships with spouses, boyfriends, co-workers, employers, children, just about every adult interaction we have. We'll see how we carry forward our parentified behavior into these relationships in our adult lives.

The problem with our relationships is the way they end up devouring us. We always seem to lose ourselves to them. They own us, and we resent them. It doesn't start out that way. We usually start out masterfully taking care of someone, and we end up losing possession of ourselves. Without knowing it, we're experiencing the long-term effect of two forces in our lives—parentification and incest, each one reinforcing the other, as we will see in the examples given by each survivor in this section.

Denial of our incest trauma contributed to the process of parentification. It made us ripe for it. Denial taught us to discredit our own feelings and perceptions. We didn't learn to cope with them or resolve them, we simply learned to stuff them away. Denial also went a step further. Not only were we denied our own perceptions, we were forced to accept the perceptions of others as our own. Usually, those alien thoughts and feelings didn't feel right and made it hard for us to function. But we got used to that, as we saw in Chapter 4. We grew up continually adjusting ourselves to accommodate the thoughts and feelings of others, until there was not much left of us.

Children who are already primed by denial are especially suscepti- ble to the encroachment of parentification. Parentification does what denial does, only it does it specifically in the area of nurturing. De- nial teaches us that our own thoughts and feelings are wrong and someone else's are right. Parentification teaches us that our needs don't matter and someone else's needs do.

Put simply, we learn to build our sense of self-satisfaction not around the fulfillment of our own needs but around the fulfillment of others' needs. We are only allowed to feel okay if the people around us feel okay. In this way, we are made servile and dependent on the people around us for our self-worth and self-identity. If Mom and Dad are happy, we are good. If they aren't, we are worthless. In later years, if our boss, boyfriend, or child is pleased, we are elated. If not, we are devastated. Thus denial and parentification work together to place us continuously in peril as we enter the world of adult relation- ships, dispossessed of ourselves.

As parentified children, we developed a model of relationships based on dichotomous roles—the caretaker and the recipient. Later, as adult caretakers we unrealistically attribute to ourselves more power and responsibility than we can ever really have. Conversely, the only other role we can conceive of is that of recipient, in which we see ourselves as more helpless and more needy than is appropriate for an adult, and resentful that others always fail to fulfill our expecta- tions. We find ourselves unable to break out of these dichotomous roles. When we aren't being caretakers and assuming inappropriate responsibility for other people, we are being recipients and resenting our caretaker for failing to meet our overwhelming needs. Either way, we fail to achieve reciprocity, balance, give-and-take in our adult relationships. We can't understand why we never get what we need.

The big problem with parentification is that we grew up with it so it feels natural. Another reason why it feels natural is that the fe- male role model in our society is built upon parentified behavior in women. Women are depicted as selfless, suffering nurturers of our husbands and children. We are applauded for being helpless when it comes to taking care of ourselves; vulnerability and passivity are des- ignated as desirable attributes of femininity. But we are contradictorily expected to always be capable of caring for others. This sets us up for victimization in every facet of our lives. It is no accident that the greatest female sex symbol of the century, Marilyn Monroe, was an incest victim.

Aside from the obvious issue of how we overcome self-destructive behavior when it is accepted as the essence of femininity, there is the basic problem of recognizing this behavior when it is so ingrained in our identity.

Most of us found it hard to recognize parentified behavior until a crisis made it intolerable for us—like finding ourselves married for the second or third time to another baby in men's clothing. Until a crisis hits you in the face, you may still be able to recognize parentified behavior by its more subtle effects. For example, you may notice a nagging frustration or resentment in all your relationships. Sometimes you might find yourself blaming other people, feeling that you are not "allowed" to be yourself or ask for what you need. Or you'll find yourself saying resentfully, "See what you made me do!"

You assume that someone else always has to come first, and you might even glorify this generosity of yours, until you find yourself hating the other person. These are some of the feelings by which you will recognize the dispossession of parentification. Look for these feelings in the stories in this section and in your own life.

I have found that I am still trying to throw off the effects of parentification long after I have dealt with the more direct effects of incest. You will find that other types of dysfunctional families suffer from parentification and denial. This is particularly true of alcoholic families. In this area we find that we have much in common with Adult Children of Alcoholics (ACOA) even if there was no alcoholism in our families. Many of us refer to the ACOA literature to help identify our dysfunctional behavior.

There is a difference, however. Parentification compounds the damage done by incest, because it teaches us that we are always responsible for what happened to us. So, when our abusers told us it was our fault, we believed it, leaving us crippled with shame and guilt. Incest, in turn, intensifies the damage of parentification. Incest is a uniquely traumatic physical violation of the self. It damages the self-esteem and self-identity of the victim to a greater degree than would the family dysfunction (denial and parentification) alone. Incest leaves the victim especially vulnerable to the message of parentification which is: you have no rights. So even though we share many of the effects of family dysfunction with ACOA's, we have to be aware that for us there are additional elements of sexual trauma.

By identifying these effects of incest and parentification, we will take yet another step toward freeing ourselves from them. We will begin to have choices. As you read each story, try to be sensitive to the different expressions of parentification. In each story you will find two types of statements. One is the person's description of her experience and the other is her interpretation of it. You will notice that sometimes the interpretive part may sound inconsistent or misguided, indicating the limits of that person's understanding at that time. So, if you read, "My mother was devoted to me," in one part, and, "My mother told me she didn't want to hear about the incest," in another part, you are witnessing the disparity between fantasy and reality.

Another thing to look for is areas where the survivor herself is unaware of the significance of the behavior she describes. You can't always rely on the subject herself to identify parentified behavior because each person is still in the process of therapy and, to some degree, still parentified. Sometimes it is easier to see it in others than it is to see it in ourselves. Or you might find that the effects of the parentification are more evident in the subject's attitude toward herself or toward other people rather than what she says about them. For example, Noelle evaluates her marriage mostly in terms of a caretaking arrangement for children. The idea of self-gratification in the form of love rarely enters into her consideration. That tells us more about the effects of parentification on her than all the things she has to say about herself. Another example is the way Brenda is able to express pain and cry for her brother, but not for herself.

This section is to help you become aware of the many ways in which our own behavior may be controlled by the abuse of the past. We cannot break the chains until we see them. Don't be dismayed by how many there are—instead, be glad that we can finally be rid of them.

PARENTIFICATION

NOELLE

Noelle is very typical of incest victims in that she only began to recognize through therapy some of the more subtle forms of parentification. She easily recognized the overt forms of abuse she had experienced, but the general neglect and lack of nurturing were hard for her to see. Similarly, in her adult life, she is not yet fully aware of how her own needs were not met in her marriage. Notice that she identifies many of her husband's abuses, but she rarely addresses the subject of love.

Marriage was experienced primarily as a caretaking arrangement for children.

You will see the dynamics of parentified behavior in the way Noelle was continually frustrated in her attempts at fulfilling her needs. She was not able to pursue reciprocal relationships because she grew up with her self-worth dependent upon meeting the needs of others, not her own. And because she grew up experiencing her parent's negative responses to her legitimate needs, she herself experienced them as bad or wrong. As a result, she ended up in caretaking relationships feeling resentful and hurt. Any assertion of her own needs was usually short-circuited by her own expectation that she was going to be mistreated or punished for them. She would experience tension or anxiety when the opportunity for need fulfillment was presented to her, as when she "ran away from nice guys."

You will see that Noelle did not have a clear idea of what she could legitimately expect from an adult relationship in terms of need fulfillment, having had little experience in testing her needs. Which ones were appropriate? Which ones could she expect to be met? And which ones were unmet needs from childhood that could never be fulfilled in an adult relationship? She did not know, and as a result she either expected too little or too much, feeling dissatisfied in all relationships. When she became a mother, the consequences of misplaced needs could have been serious when, in her depleted state, she inappropriately began to bring her needs to her daughter and resented her for failing to respond.

I Was Responsible for My Father

My father acted as if nobody in the world had any function except to serve him in some way. People didn't exist except in terms of the way they served him. So, as a child, the parentification I experienced was not only in terms of physical tasks, housekeeping chores and so forth, it was also emotional. I learned very quickly that my job was to take care of my father's ego. He wasn't ever supposed to be hurt or angry. I learned I should do nothing to displease him, that my father's state of mind, his self-esteem, and his emotional state were my responsibility. I know that compounded the shame I felt about incest. Within this framework, I would have felt I made him do it.

I think that is the most grotesque form of parentification. The housekeeping chores and all that stuff—big deal. But this business that I was responsible for my father's feelings while my own feelings and needs were not recognized, that was the most devastating.

For example, when I was ten I became very ill. One morning my parents woke up and found me lying with my head out the back door, unable to move. My father tried to pick me up and stand me up. Every time he stood me up, I'd fall down. I kept crying and asking him to please not do that to me, because it made me feel horrible when he would stand me up. I just wanted to lie there and be left alone. So I began to cry and begged him to stop. He went into a rage, and he said, "I'm not doing anything to hurt you; you just don't trust me. You won't let me help you!" Now that is real typical of my father. I was not allowed to feel pain, I was not allowed to be hurt, I was not allowed to have any feelings that in any way might make him uncomfortable or reflect badly on him. That was the way I had to grow up.

I Saw How Pathetic My Mother Was

I was responsible for my mother, too. I became aware of how pathetic she was. She cried all the time. He bullied and abused her and humiliated her. For example, he'd walk around the house pointing to little spots on the walls and say, "Look at that! Look at that! Isn't that disgusting? It's filthy. Can't you keep this house clean?" and she'd follow him around like a humble servant with a little bottle of cleaning fluid and a sponge, wiping off these spots he would pick out. Or he'd find little pieces of lint on the rug, and he'd point to them and say, "Look at that. Look at that," and she'd run around on her hands and knees, picking up little pieces of lint from the rug. So I saw her being abused, and I saw how pathetic she was and how unable she was to help me, and I began to take care of her, too.

My mother was sick most of the time, sometimes seriously. She was overwhelmed. For years she had to go to work full-time, and she would come home totally exhausted, and yet my father wouldn't lift a finger to help her. He wouldn't boil water for his own cup of tea. As a result, my mom would be up until two or three in the morning doing all kinds of things. I remember coming home from a date once and finding her at two o'clock in the morning, in the basement, ironing his underwear and crying, she was so exhausted.

So, I took care of my mother. I began at the age of 11: cooking the meals, doing the vacuuming, the laundry. Whatever I could do to help her, I would do. The chores were not significant, what is significant is the fact that my parents could not take care of me, and I felt I had to take care of them.

What Else Could I Do?

That's the way it was when I was 14 or 15 and I was going around with criminals who were violent and carried guns. I would come home at two or three in the morning after having had my boyfriend use me as a sex object all night. I'd come crawling home, and the next day my father would sit at the table and cry and say, "How can you do this to me?" He couldn't care less that his child was being destroyed. All he cared about was, "How can you do this to me?"

It never occurred to him to ask, "How can you do this to yourself?" Most significantly, I never thought to ask myself that question either.

The parentification, as far as I can see, follows naturally. It is an extension of my father's selfishness, narcissism, immaturity, and my mother's helplessness. What could I do? If I didn't do what they needed me to do, what would have happened? The fear I had was of some undefined horror.

Sacrificing for Daddy: A Daily Ritual

I've realized recently that my mother did a lot to teach me that my job was to "do without" for my father's sake. One way she did it is my mother never made enough food. I didn't figure this out until just a couple years ago. Every time we sat down at the table, there was never enough food. Now this could not have been an accident. Maybe the first time we ran out of mashed potatoes, or the first time we didn't have enough gravy, or the first time we didn't have enough strawberries, maybe it was an accident. But, when, year after year, there was never enough food when we sat down at the table, you know my mother was doing something here.

The rule was my dad served himself first. My dad would take as much as he wanted of whatever we had regardless of whether there was enough. Since my mother never made enough, a couple of us sitting at the table never got enough food.

Not only that, if my dad ate all his share and then wanted more, he would say, "Where's the potatoes?" and my mother would say, "We don't have any more." So he would grunt and reach onto the plate of the child sitting nearest him and take the food he wanted and laugh about it. Then if we cried or said, "No, Daddy, I want my food," he'd go into a rage and scream at us and say, "You don't have to get so upset! You didn't need all that!" and he'd take it anyway.

Now that I have a home of my own, when I go out and buy strawberries or when I make potatoes, I make sure there is more than enough. Nobody ever sits down at my table and faces a food shortage.

I can't imagine why my mother did that. She seemed to enjoy the prospect of her and her children going without something so that my dad could have it.

Ignoring My Own Needs

For me, the parentification I experienced at home was a combination of having to care for my parents' needs and having my own needs completely ignored. When I was 17, I had endometriosis, only at that time, nobody knew what endometriosis was. I hemorrhaged real bad. I would leave bloody footprints in the morning when I walked to the bathroom.

This hemorrhaging went on a long time. I got severely anemic. I was so anemic that I would get up and go to work in the morning, come home at five o'clock, walk up the stairs, fall on my bed fully clothed, and lie there all night. I wouldn't move, eat, or anything. Then I'd get up in the morning and go to work. I was exhausted and lost weight. My parents never noticed, though it happened right in front of them.

Finally, one day at work, my hands and legs started going numb. I couldn't hold a pencil, and there were lines in front of my eyes like I was going to pass out anytime. I couldn't hear very well. One of the doctors I worked for said, "There's something really wrong with you." I told him how I felt, and he and the other doctors said, "We want you to go to the hospital."

I went to the hospital emergency room; they ran a blood test and admitted me right away. My hematocrit was something like 14. If it gets below 20, I think you're supposed to be dead. I could have gone into shock and died any time.

My parents showed up at the hospital and said, "Why didn't you tell us something was wrong?" Well I had, but they hadn't heard. I had to take care of myself, but I wasn't very good at it. I was very sensitive to their problems, to every little discomfort, but I was almost oblivious to myself. Looking back, I am aware of their inattention to me, but even more aware of how unable I was to attend to myself. They did a good job of keeping themselves at the center of the universe.

Adult Relationships—Friends

The parentification is reflected in the fact that in my relationships I didn't know how to be cared for. This is true of everything—friends, work, men, business transactions, even the way the teller at the bank treats me.

For a long time my few friends were people I took care of. I wasn't good at identifying my own needs, but I was sure as hell good at taking care of everyone else's. I had friends who would not call or come see me for months, then some problem would come up in their lives and they would come to me. And I was always there for them. Often I was crumbling inside, overwhelmed by my own problems, but I couldn't tell anyone or ask for a sympathetic shoulder. I liked it when people came to me with problems—it made me feel powerful and I played the wise old sage.

Sexual Relationships—Secret and Unsatisfying

I would have clandestine sexual relationships with men in which I was always there when they wanted me, but I could never call them when I needed them. If I was hurt or sick or lonely, I just had to tough it out. I had no right to ask for them to see me. I could only see them when it was convenient for them to sneak away. Everyone's needs were met but mine. The role I played was the all-patient, forgiving, understanding mother. I saw that as my power in the relationship, never seeing how abusive it was.

If someone who actually had something to give would enter my life, I would try him out for a while, but the anxiety would overwhelm me. I remember one guy, he was great, he was so crazy about me. He was loving and affectionate and very successful in his business. He showered me with gifts, he took me out to dinner, theatre, concerts. He was crazy about me. I was terrified of him. I couldn't stand to be around him.

When I was with him, my anxiety was so intense I found it hard to breathe. I couldn't wait to go so I could relax. The important thing is I did not have any awareness of this. I just knew I wanted to get away from him. I didn't know I was unable to accept anything from people. I would find some fault in the other person so I could somehow cut him down to size. Or I would reject him by simply withdrawing, finding excuses not to go out, not returning calls—just cutting him off. I rejected this man because he was too thin. Another man I rejected because I decided he would be a "burden."

Other Relationships—None of Which Worked

The parentification is reflected in my first marriage. I married an immature, dependent man who was not aggressively abusive to me like my father was. His abuse took the form of passive aggression. He had difficulty with work, had no confidence, and was unemployed for a period of time. I took care of him.

When that marriage broke up, I tried to have other relationships, none of which worked. The only relationships I seemed to stick to were ones in which my needs were ignored. I never again got into a relationship like my first marriage in which there was an obviously helpless, dependent man like my first husband. Somehow, though, men who were like that but who were hiding it real well would find me, or I found them.

Second Marriage—A Hidden Agenda

When I got married again, I married a man who had a problem with intimacy. I thought I was doing great because I finally got together with someone unattached—but he had his own way of being unavailable. We went through a rough time dealing with the fact that he was rejecting me and not communicating with me and hostile because he was afraid of his own feelings. And I had to realize how he was using me by not reciprocating any of the love and care I provided for him. I could not see that for a long time.

Essentially what I did is marry a man who seemed not to need me. He projected not needing me by his rejection and hostility. I even liked that because I consciously thought, "Here is a guy who is never going to depend on me and use me as his mother." I was not aware that it was just another form of using me. After I married and got pregnant, I became aware of real needs I had. I wanted to be loved and cared for and reassured, and he couldn't do that.

Fortunately, we stuck it out, and he wanted to change. He went into therapy, and we have worked very hard. I've worked at helping him get in touch with his feelings and be a loving person, and I've worked on myself to be receptive to that type of person. So we've both come a long way, but it's been a horribly long and difficult process. It is not over; we are still working on it.

Work—Underpaid and Overworked

Another area where parentification is reflected is in my work. Again, the relationship was always a one-way street—my giving everything, expecting and getting nothing until my resentment boiled over and I would leave. I was always underpaid and overworked, even though I was a professional. My work was never good enough; I could never do enough. Every little mistake was a catastrophe to me and would destroy my relationship with my partners.

I would lie awake all night agonizing over a mistake, sure that my partners would kick me out and hate me, and angry at them for not allowing me a mistake. I did not realize that I was the one for whom the mistake was intolerable, not them.

I also felt guilty about making as much money as I did. I would get checks from clients and feel I should return them because, to me, if I had not solved all their problems for them, my work was worthless. And since I never could solve all problems for everyone, I never felt comfortable with the money.

I didn't have the ability to recognize the resources I needed at work to do my job competently. I didn't know how to ask for help when a job was too much. I didn't know how to seek advice without appearing stupid and incompetent, so I rarely asked for information even when I couldn't do my job without it. As a result, I was frequently in over my head, spinning wheels. But somehow, in spite of this, I was successful, although it's only recently that I've been able to give myself credit for my achievements.

The Doormat and Superwoman Are the Same

I am beginning to see that every relationship I've had has been distorted by what I learned as a small child, which is, "I have no rights in a relationship." Instead of becoming a passive doormat, though, I assumed the role of being the "in-control, strong, supercompetent, I-don't-need-anybody" type.

The way I see it, there are two types that you can be when you are parentified. You can see yourself as the doormat, the person that's the real wimp and gets hurt and stepped on a lot. Or you can create the illusion for yourself that you are the tower of strength and you don't need anything and you can take care of everybody. That's what I did. Actually, they are the same thing. Everyone else gets what they want and you never get what you want, either because you deny your own needs or because you put yourself in relationships that can't satisfy them.

Intergenerational Effects of Parentification

This part of Noelle's story is particularly important. She explains the intergenerational effects of parentification. A parentified child grows up to suffer serious inadequacies as a parent, with destructive effects for her own children.

Parentified children don't really grow up, they just learn how to pretend they are. Inside them are deprived children with unmet needs and little experience of nurturing. Under the demands of adult life and parenting, they experience depletion as their superficial maturity proves to be inadequate and their inner pain and neediness is exposed. The normal demands of children conflict with the parents' own acute needs, and with little experience of nurturing, the parentified child who is now a parent herself may respond abusively to her own children.

Noelle discusses how her depletion almost leads her to abuse of her own child. She also discusses how her parentification and denial contributed to the sexual abuse of her child by a babysitter. Fortunately, through therapy, Noelle will be able to help her daughter recover, and the destructive process of parentification will end.

Repeating the Pattern of Abuse in My Marriage

Now, the big question in all this is not why my husband was so rejecting, but why I was dumb enough to put up with it! I believe this is the way I was treated in my family of origin. I was supposed to put up with neglect and abuse from my parents, to have no needs of my own while being understanding and sensitive to theirs. I grew up feeling this was the way things were. It was all I knew, so it felt right no matter how much it hurt.

I could not get out of the relationship. Shortly after our wedding, he moved out and I decided I would divorce him. Then I got pregnant the next time he came back and used that as a reason to stay. I ask myself over and over, why? In therapy, they call it "learned helplessness." To me, it was just an unconscious way of being that I learned from my family.

My second marriage is a good example of how the risk of incest can be carried on from generation to generation because it shows how I was carrying the family dysfunction forward into my marriage. Fortunately my husband was not an abuser. But I was so depleted I couldn't recognize the risk of abuse when it presented itself elsewhere.

The Progress of Depletion

I was under a lot of pressure at work. I had an executive-level job At home, I had a desperate, frantic need to take care of my daughter, to keep her safe. I hated leaving her every day, and I agonized over her safety. When I got home every afternoon, all I wanted to do was hold her, just hold her.

I was breast-feeding, so I would stay up at night and nurse three or four times a night, then express milk after nursing to leave with the sitter for the next day. As a result, I never got more than three or four hours' sleep and never more than an hour-and-a-half at one time. I think I did this because of my desperation and feelings of inadequacy.

During this time, my husband would disappear for days, back to his own apartment. He did everything he could to show his hatred for me. I was overwhelmed, just surviving from day to day, feeling desperately afraid for my baby. I had phobias about disasters happening with no warning on an ordinary day—fires, massacres, tornados, accidents. I was constantly anticipating the tragedy I thought was inevitable and from which I despaired of ever protecting her.

Ignoring the Truth to Preserve the Fantasy—Setting Up My Daughter

In this state of mind, I could not see the real dangers. I had denied them in my own experience, and now I denied them in hers. My husband found a babysitter for her, a family in his church. They were officials in his church and, in my depletion, I said, "Fine, we'll take her over there."

Those people did not feel right to me. I felt there was something seriously wrong with them, but I ignored those perceptions because of my own self-doubt and denial. I wanted so much to believe in my husband and keep the marriage together. I was like my mother, ignoring the truth for the sake of the fantasy. So I accepted my husband's judgment and allowed them to babysit my daughter.

But every time I took her there or picked her up, I had horrible fears of the house burning down, or some maniac coming in and killing them all, or someone abducting a child from the yard. My therapist later said this was the way I told myself something was wrong. Like my mother, I could not recognize the real risks. It came out in the form of exaggerated things. As a child, I was not allowed to recognize the real dangers and abuses in my family, I had been taught to deny them. So all I could do was find imaginary dangers in response to my perception of risk.

Facing the Real Dangers

Well, my daughter started doing all kinds of strange things from about 15 months to 18 months of age. I didn't put them all together until finally one day another mother who had taken her daughter out of the babysitter's called me up and said, "I just brought my daughter back from the pediatrician and he believes she was sexually abused at the babysitter's." Then she told me all the things that her daughter was doing, and they were the same things my daughter was doing.

I almost fainted. I remember holding onto the kitchen counter. I went numb; I went into shock. I went down into the basement and got a bottle of sherry and brought it upstairs and started drinking and I couldn't even feel it. I blamed myself for not using my own judgment and for letting it happen to her.

I called Protective Services and they investigated. Unfortunately, because of the ages of the children, there was nothing they could do. The children were not able to identify who did what, where, and when. The authorities said, "Forget it, you can't take these people to court; you can't do anything. We can't even shut them down, because we don't have enough evidence under the law." So I could do nothing. And they advised me that I shouldn't even confront them, because people like that can get very nasty and dangerous sometimes.

Recognizing the Cycle of Victimization

This event shattered me. I could not respond to it right away. It took about a year to absorb it and see how my denial of my own experiences as a child had made it hard for me to recognize what was happening to her.

At first, I took full responsibility and hated myself, wanted to kill myself for letting it happen to her. Then I turned on my husband, who had taken no responsibility. Finally, I could see how the whole situation, my marriage, my husband and I, with my background of incest and abuse, had all contributed.

I realized that as long as I allowed myself to be a victim without seeing it, my daughter would learn to be a victim too. I knew I had to face the incest, break my own denial, to see all the ways I was a victim, or I would be passing it on to her. I had to change my life, and I delivered the ultimatum to my husband, "This is changing. I'm changing, and you have to change too, or it's all over."

Well, he is no longer a member of that church, he has been in therapy a while, he is dealing with his problems, and things are much different now. I am learning to recognize abuse when it happens to me and to respond. It is very slow.

I'll never forget how I began to repeat my family of origin in my own marriage. I'll never forget that there was a direct line running through me, a direct line of tragedy running through me to my daughter.

Breaking the Cycle

But it is not going to be repeated in her life. It will not be repeated. There are big differences between my mother and me, and I will not have to be like her. There are big differences between my daughter and me, and she will not have to be like me. I am going to stay in therapy until this thing is taken care of. My child will not be devastated the way I was.

I am still trying to sort out how much of my victim behavior I learned from my mother, from experiencing her victimization, and how much of it came from my being victimized myself. I know that the "mother model" I turned to when I became a mother was constructed from the mothering I received from my own mother. And I know it was a very loving but desperately afraid mother I found when I turned to that model. I know that as a child I learned not to take care of myself, so I started out as a mother already depleted. The grand result was overwhelming feelings of fear, helplessness, and desperation.

I can see that the problems I have from incest are much more than just my father's sexual improprieties. They come from the whole complex of relationships in my family, of which incest was a part. I learned to ignore my needs and suffer. I learned to be a victim as a child, and I learned to dissociate to avoid reality. I learned to cover up legitimate fears and abuses with imaginary ones, because in our family, the real fears were unmentionable. They were not permitted because they implicated my father. So my mother and I were allowed only to recognize imaginary horrors to which there could be no effective response, keeping us from responding effectively to the real horrors: sexual abuse, emotional abuse, neglect, alcoholism. This is what I learned and what I have tried to overcome during eight years of therapy.

The Parentified Parent: Depletion Leads to Abuse

Being a parent to my parents left me with no real experience of nurturing. Having not been well nurtured myself, I don't have a strong sense of security and safety that I can bring to my children. You can't give what you don't have.

I can't tell if I'm giving too much or not enough, because I grew up without learning my legitimate rights. I have a problem distinguishing between discipline and abuse. I don't know where to draw the line between my rights and theirs. I never know if I'm doing too little or too much.

Overcontrolling or Not in Control

The daily problem is how to set limits, how to ask for what I need them to do, and wondering, "Is this right? What do I have a right to expect? What are their rights?" A million things a day: "Should I ask her to leave the contents of my desk alone? Can I tell her I don't want to read a story because my throat is so sore? Can I ask her to turn off her songs for a little while so I can play some of mine? Is it okay to insist on a nap? Can I tell her she has to have dinner when the rest of the family eats—and eat what we eat?" These little things were a source of agonizing tension.

I am better than I was before. After years of parenting, I think I finally have learned that I can say "no" without its being a horrible crisis. Before, I couldn't say "no" or set a limit until I was so angry and felt so abused by my kids that I would explode with rage. So they learned that "no" was usually an injustice, or that "no" meant "I hate you, you are bad and horrible." Either way, it destroyed their faith in me and destroyed their sense of worth. My daughter has had problems because of me but I know I can help her recover.

The Risk of Child Abuse

The daily incompetence I had as a parent blew up into a serious abuse problem when a lot of risk factors occurred together at one point in my life. I went through a very bad period in therapy when I encountered my grief for the incest, for the emotional loss of my father, and for the loss of my mother, who somehow went away from me emotionally around the time my father abused me.

During this period, I was pregnant and physically incapacitated. Also, my husband was on a temporary one-year assignment that required us to go live in a new area where I was totally isolated. I was cut off from my support systems, my friends, all my familiar rituals and activities. I began to crumble.

I believe that at this time I began to experience the fear and helplessness I had absorbed from my mother when I was abused and she was sick. As I became increasingly feeble and helpless, I couldn't cope with even little things. Little things became huge, intolerable things.

My two-year-old daughter became intolerable. The normal needs and demands of a two-year-old were so overwhelming, I hated her for having them. I felt abused and persecuted by my two-year-old. If she needed me to get her some juice, it was a physical crisis to get up to get it. Then if she decided she wanted a red cup, not a blue cup, I would explode because the exhaustion of just getting up to get it was too much and then to have her ask me to change the cup was intolerable. I would cry and scream at her.

I felt like an abused child. My own child was subsequently not a child to me but a threat, a demon. I felt that I was in a desperate battle for survival. She was the enemy.

After a bad day, she would not sleep at night from fear because Mommy had been such a monster. Also, I think she had absorbed my fears. She would come in crying, waking me up, begging for hugs, depriving me of sleep. Exhausted, I turned into a screaming horror. It escalated. I began to spank her, hard. I hated myself for being so out of control and abusive. I wanted to kill myself for what I was doing to her.

In lucid moments I could see that my screaming, spanking, and pushing her around were abusive and frightening to her. It was the ultimate devastation to know I was acting like my father. And I would experience a self-hatred that was total. I began to accumulate pills; I began to plan suicide. (My own mother had attempted suicide when I was a teenager.) The only thing that stopped me was the baby I carried. Then one night, I decided the baby would be better off dead rather than have me for a mother. I was going to take my pills when the baby's movements stopped me. I turned them over to my husband.

Help From Therapy

I had been going to a bad therapist. I had been telling him what was happening; I told him about my incest history, and he did not seem to believe how desperate I was. He even advised me to spank my daughter and lock her in the bathroom in the dark when she got up at night. That did not feel right to me. It was terrorism.

She was a wreck, I was a wreck. I needed to heal and to heal her. I decided to have her sleep with me. I needed to hold her, reassure her, and to feel that I was comforting her. I had to salvage some of my ability to mother. Every night that she snuggled up with me, I held her and felt us heal a little more. I found another therapist who understood the risk factors for abuse, who knew what I was struggling with. Gradually, things calmed down. The baby was born, I became physically well again, and things got back to normal. It took my daughter nine months to be able to sleep by herself again. It is taking her longer to repair her sense of self, her confidence, her self-esteem. But I can see progress. As I get to be more secure and less fearful, she does too. I am hopeful because I know I can help her to recover as I progress and recover.

No Cookbook Approach Will Work

There is no formula or method, no cookbook approach to parenting that will solve my problems as a parent. I read all the best available literature on parenting. I know more about developmental psychology than other mothers I know. And yet it doesn't fix anything.

I try the behavioral training steps recommended in a book, and it goes all wrong. The outcome is never in the book! The book says, "Use a quiet corner." So I put my daughter in the quiet corner, and she throws a fit and won't stay. The book says, "Use the bedroom." I say, "Go to your room." She refuses. I drag her upstairs to her room. She won't stay. The book says, "Lock the door, if necessary." So I lock the door. She goes totally hysterical and starts to kick down the door. There is *nothing* in the book on this. What next? Physical violence? I try a spanking. The hysteria merely escalates. The child has upped the ante on every single attempt I have made to limit her behavior, until I have a choice of either capitulating or committing serious physical violence. End result: Mom gives up. And then I would feel furious, resentful—because it wasn't supposed to come out this way! The book said it would work. Why doesn't anything work on this kid? What is wrong with her? What is wrong with me?

What I have learned is that the total relationship is the problem— it's me, all of me, and my daughter as a whole person. Books with techniques don't help—they just raise expectations and set me up for more anger and resentment. They make it look so logical, so easy— what kind of dummy are you if you can't do it?

Well, the truth is that the whole relationship is the problem. That has to change, and that can only come through my own growth and development over time. It will come somehow when I am healed inside, when I'm really a grownup in there, when I have a secure place my daughter can feel. When I have that solid place inside, my daughter will have security, and discipline won't feel like hatred, setting limits won't feel like abandonment. I'm getting better as fast as I can, but it takes so long.

Until then, I just have to love her and be open to her and try to respond to her the best I can. I have to be honest with her and with myself about my mistakes. I tell her I love her and tell her I'm sorry when I have behaved badly. And I stick with my therapy to try to grow up. I can see improvement every day.

MEGAN

We all can benefit from examining our own parents' childhoods and identifying the origins of our abuse. Megan has begun to recognize that her mother's history of parentification may have contributed something to the family dynamics associated with her own sexual abuse by a brother. It also helps her recognize many of her own problems with intimacy by seeing their origins in her family background. In Megan's family, parentification was characterized more by the emotional inaccessibility of her parents than by the children's assuming the parental roles. The result for Megan, however, is much the same, as we have seen in others who assumed more of a caretaking role toward their parents. It left her unable to recognize her needs or get them met, while she assumed responsibility for the needs of others. In this section we will see that parentification and its effects occur in varying degrees. While Megan does not experience the self-destructive, exploitative relationships that other parentified victims do, we still recognize in her some degree of self-impairment.

Her steps toward recovery are evident in the way she is starting to take care of her needs, as in the way she allows herself for the first time to depend on her friends during a period of unemployment, or in her conscious decision not to become involved with unavailable men. She shows us that change is possible, once we identify what we have to change.

For me, the whole issue of parentification has two parts. One is the way my parents treated me, the other is the way I see it in my life today in the way I relate to other people.

Taking Care of Mother

Looking back, I can see how I learned to take care of other people while disregarding my own needs. Periodically, children were the adults and my mom was the child. I became her sounding board, I would listen to her and she would talk about her concerns. My dad had a heart attack when I was 10, and she was concerned about his health. She was always concerned about someone else in the family, concerned about her friends, and I just plain listened to her. I became her sounding board; that is how she related to me. I always was the cheerful child in the family who did whatever she was told would do whatever she could to help out. I quite often took care of my mom because of that.

There were two positive things that came out of growing up in that family. My parents were very good about providing us with education. And the other positive was the spiritual part, their religious faith. When it came to emotions, my parents didn't know what to do with them, so they pretended like they didn't exist. You just learned from the time you were very, very little that if you needed help or wanted help emotionally, they were not the people you went to.

A History of Parentification and Abuse

Looking back at my mother, I've begun to wonder if somewhere in her history there was abuse. Because I see in her the signs of someone who could not take care of herself, and I see how when she married my father, in some ways he protected her. That is probably why it may have been difficult for her to express anger with him, because if she did she would lose her protection. So her anger all came out on us kids. Then, when my father got disabled by his heart attack, she could not survive without him. That was when my brother started abusing me, when my mother withdrew completely.

It just seems to me that there are so many classic symptoms of abuse in my mother, it makes me wonder if something wasn't passed on to me from her past. My mother came from this very strict Catholic family and had a strict disciplinarian father. She's the second oldest of five children. My grandmother was away a lot taking care of a younger child in the hospital, so my mother was left in charge of the house. I keep thinking about the fact that my grandmother was gone, and my mother was left in charge, the oldest girl, being asked to have all those responsibilities.

She was very, very protective of her sister, her only sister, who was 11 years younger. She was much better about protecting her sister than she was about any of her own children. I keep thinking that she didn't have to protect her own children from a father who may have sexually abused her—this is just a feeling I have—that she didn't have to worry about that, but she may have had to protect her sister.

MY MOTHER COULDN'T PROTECT HER CHILDREN

I see how my older sister, the oldest, is so incapable of taking responsibility for her own life. Maybe with her being the first child and my mother not knowing what to do, how to handle all the responsibility, maybe she abused her just by pushing her too hard, giving her too much responsibility too soon. And now she can't take care of herself.

I think of the way my mother couldn't protect her children. I think it was because she had never been protected. I don't think she knew how to protect. And my father, he didn't show emotions, so he was not very accessible. And my mother was withdrawn from us. They were both pretty much inaccessible to us. We just didn't get something, the nurturing, that we needed. I think it has a lot to do with the incest in our family.

The incest that happened with me, with my brother, was not the only case of abuse in the family. My older sister told me that an older brother approached her once, and he only tried it once and she punched him out. She was 12, he was 14, something like that. She was older, better able to defend herself, so he never approached her again. A younger brother also exposed himself to a younger sister—this was after my mother died and my father had been dead two years. The brother was 16 and my sister was 14; it was only a one-time thing. But something prompted that behavior. I mean, it was coming from our family dynamics.

Sometimes I think I see a whole trait of weird family dynamics going all the way back to my mother's family, and it makes me wonder if she also was sexually abused. My mother was a real shy person, painfully shy. I didn't realize it until I was a teenager. And now I can look back and see so many other signs that explain her personality, and maybe help me in some ways to forgive her for not being able to protect me from my brother.

As an Adult—Unable to Open Up

The other part of parentification in my life is in the way I relate to people now, as an adult. Since I've been in therapy, especially since being in a group, I have changed the way I relate to people. I allow people to get closer to me. One friend in particular has taught me more about how to be a friend than anybody else. She started it when we went to college. She told me one night that I was a lousy friend because I would let anybody come in and cry on my shoulder and I would listen to anybody, but I never once opened up to anyone else. She said, "Don't you realize how unequal that makes the friendship and how badly that makes me feel? It makes me feel like an emotional freeloader." Essentially, by me never opening up there wasn't really anything coming from my side. It was my way of saying, "Stay away, I don't trust you."

So, beginning with her and then through therapy, I began to let people get closer to me. It's been more of a process of me learning to open up to others, rather than always being the crutch to others. I've always been the type of person who really will listen to people. I'll do whatever I can to take care of them. I've always been that way with my family. I'm the only person in the family who makes sure I remember everyone's birthday, and I make sure that things are remembered for people. But I would never share my feelings. That's very different, that's still very tough.

Learning to Give and Take a Little

When I lost my job last year, one of the reasons why I became such an emotional basket case is that I really didn't talk to anybody about what I was going through, not even my best friends. I was only able to do that through therapy, by my therapist encouraging me to lean on my friends and reassuring me that it would be okay if I leaned on them, that they would support me. She said if I leaned too much, they'd tell me.

That has always been my fear, that I'm asking too much of people and imposing too much, so I end up giving more than they can give. I was afraid people just tolerated my presence, that they really didn't want me there, and if I asked anything of them, then I'd find out for sure that they don't really want me, because they'd reject me.

So, with my therapist encouraging me that it would be okay to lean on my friends, I leaned on them very heavily, emotionally, financially, and in every way possible. And they did help me, they were better to me than my family. Because last year when I was going through that, my brother and sister just essentially walked away. The family has never been there for me when I've needed them, but I've been very fortunate with these two friends.

Sexual Relationships—Avoiding My Needs

Another area where my inability to have reciprocal relationships really shows up is with men. Part of it is my fear of sex, because I always find myself in nonsexual friendships with men. That comes from the incest. But part of it is the way I only feel comfortable with men who are "safe" because they aren't in a position to give to me, so I don't have to feel the vulnerability of having my needs met. I think that comes partly from the incest, but also partly from the way I never got to acknowledge my needs while growing up.

One relationship that I had six years ago, the man turned out to be gay. I started the relationship around the time that I was starting therapy, and it was during that time that I remembered the incest and I remembered what happened. With this guy, the whole thing started more because I pursued him, I was the one controlling it. We started out as friends, and I pursued him a little bit more, calling him up to go out. But at the same time, he would call me up and go out. He never pushed me sexually, and that was okay with me, because at that time I couldn't have dealt with it, in no way, shape, or form.

I had always thought that the reason he had never approached me was my fault, because I wasn't sexually attractive enough. I had lived with those feelings all my life. Ever since I was 10 and my brother abused me, I thought I wasn't sexually attractive, and what man would want me, and I couldn't have it. But in therapy, I finally began to wonder if maybe it wasn't me, maybe it was something else. So when I pushed him on it, he said that he wasn't ready for an intense relationship, and we broke up for eight months.

Then we ran into each other again and he started calling me again. We started going out again, but this time there was a difference, this time there was definitely no sexual interest. Where before he would take two steps forward and one back, this time he was just definitely not interested. We would go out, but where before he was affectionate and would kiss me, this time there was just nothing there.

But I told myself this time, "I'm not going through this again," and one night I had him over for dinner, and I told him that he had to tell me what was going on, was he interested in me or not? He kept saying, "I can't tell you," but I just pushed him and pushed him until he told me that it was because he was gay.

I realized I had fallen in love with something impossible. Because that's the thing, I was madly in love with him. And I knew that if he was the only man I had ever met that I thought I would be willing to make the necessary compromises for, that I would want to marry, and that I had picked someone who was gay, then I was still not able to have a real relationship with a man. I was very sexually attracted to him, but it was only because he was so ambivalent about it.

But it wasn't just the sexual aspect, it was my emotional involvement. I was willing to be open to him, but obviously it was because at some level I knew the relationship was impossible.

Getting in Touch With Needs

There was a time last winter, in fact, in group, where I made the announcement that I didn't need men in my life, and then after that was when I remembered the thing about my father. I remembered a time in my life when I felt safe and cared for, before he had his heart attack, before I was abused by my brother, before my mother totally stopped being a mother. I got in touch with a lot of feelings then. I went through a long time with a nonobtrusive grieving process, grieving for the father I lost when I was 10, not the man who died when I was 15. It was like grieving for a whole different person, a person I had forgotten had existed.

I went through a terrible time with feeling confused and just angry. I wasn't interested in anything; I wouldn't want to talk to anybody. I just emotionally felt terrible.

Then as I came out of those feelings, I was so extraordinarily horny, I think I would have jumped the first thing that looked at me. And I felt ready for a relationship, for a real involvement. I'm still working on it. I feel like an adolescent, learning to relate to men for the first time, because for the first time for me, my feelings are all there. I'm not a child pretending to be all grown up and in control. Instead, I'm a grownup letting myself have those childish feelings and needs, knowing that I will be all right. Because I got in touch with a time in my life, before my father's heart attack, when I was all right, I was cared for.

It Is Better Than It Was

I can't say it's all better now, but I can say it is much better than it was. I still find myself attracted to "safe" men who are somehow unavailable. Just recently I started going out after work with some of the men I work with. One of them seems to be a favorite of my boss, who is also my close friend. The other man is married.

I started thinking about whether I wanted a relationship with one of them. Carl, the man who my boss seems to like a lot, is single and has no commitment to her. I know he is very interested in me. I pick up signals from him that it is a lot more than just friendship, whereas his attitude toward my boss is just a friendly one. The married man is also sending signals that he is attracted to me.

Now here's the kicker. I decided that I could not have a relationship with Carl, who is really available, and started concentrating more on the married man. My thinking was that I could not compro-

mise my friendship with my boss. Then I realized what I was doing—
I was again finding a pretext to have a relationship in which I could
have no rights, no legitimate needs could be met. The good news is
that this time I saw what I was doing.

PARENTIFICATION

DIDI

*Maternal illness, death, and incest are all mixed up in Didi's child-
hood, forming a desolate picture. The child who had to take care of
herself at age 11 when her mother died was also expected to take care
of her father. Taking care of his sexual needs was part of the same
abusive continuum as taking care of him after his heart attack. A distant and uninterested stepmother completes the picture. As Didi entered adulthood, the effects of parentification are evident in everything
from the casual presumptions of a neighbor to the intrusions of strangers in the supermarket.*

*In Didi's story, as in the others, her gradual realization that she has
rights, and that it is okay to assert them, is a sign of her recovery. In
the process of identifying her needs and asserting them, she will begin
to learn which ones can be fulfilled in the adult world, and which ones
are unmet needs from childhood that must be left in the past. It is a
long process that in the end helps to restore our self-possession, because for the first time we can do things for ourselves and feel good
about it. When Didi recognizes that her neighbor has violated her
rights, and decides not to send her daughter there again, she is not
only meeting her own needs but taking care of her daughter as well. By
taking care of ourselves, we become much more competent in every relationship.*

The Past Was Not So Perfect

I always thought I'd had a perfect childhood until my mother died.
But I've learned and remembered much denial and hatred and pain
and abandonment.

Everyone knew my mother was dying of cancer. Even me, I guess,
but I never realized what it meant. We never talked about it. Maybe
my parents did together, but not with us kids. When she did finally
die, I really didn't understand.

My mother, I feel, was in some way trying to protect us by not talking about her illness. It would mean admitting she was going to die.
I'll always be angry with her, though, for not saying good-bye to me.

She talked to my brother before she died in the hospital. But she never talked to my sister or me. That will always hurt me.

I remember my mother and sister never got along. They always fought—loud and long. My dad was always doing things with my brother (scouting and camping), and I remember once, lying in my bed crying, and wishing my dad would come home and stop them from fighting. I believe my mother was an alcoholic at one time before I was born when they were living overseas. That's what I think their (my sister's and mother's) problems stemmed from.

Thinking back, I also never had privacy as a child. My room, when I was about four, was an alcove at the top of the stairs, with three walls but completely open in the front. My next room was shared with my sister. In the house we moved to after that, my room was a normal one, but right next to the family room and, consequently, not private or quiet. Then I remember having a room my parents had to walk through to get to their room.

When my mother was very ill on our trip back to the States, my dad stayed in the hospital with my mother while my brother and sister and I fended for ourselves in an apartment or hotel. Then we went to my mother's home town where she was hospitalized, and we had aunts and uncles to care for us. But I've blocked most of that out. My dad told me about it. But I know it was a time when I wasn't taken care of.

Anyway, I thought my childhood was perfect and I guess it wasn't. But my mother and father must have done something right because I feel like I have some self-confidence and feelings of self-worth and self-esteem.

Taking Care of Everyone

After my mother died, I was pretty much expected to care for myself in ways my mother always had: laundry; taking care of my long hair; wearing and buying clothes; getting to school; and taking care of my breakfast, lunch, and helping with dinner and housekeeping; cleaning my room. I even remember making my own birthday cakes. And, of course, there was taking care of my dad, sexually and in other ways.

When my dad remarried, I thought my stepmother would take over my mother's role, but it never worked out that way. She didn't take care of me.

When I was 15, my father suffered a heart attack. I was extremely upset about it, of course. He was in the hospital a week or two weeks,

I don't remember. But when he came home from the hospital, he could not take care of himself. My stepmother, I don't know, I don't remember why, but she did not take care of him. It seems to me now, at this point, that it was extremely ridiculous that I stayed home from school to take care of my father, to bring him his lunch, his breakfast, to make dinners, to just help him up and get him around and bring him his medication. When I look back on it now, I think, my parents were not wealthy, but they certainly, certainly could have afforded a nurse to come and take care of him. I just fell into the role quite naturally, I suppose. I suppose everyone figured that quite naturally it was my responsibility.

Minimizing My Feelings to Spare Dad

Aside from becoming a parent for my own parents, I had to become my own parent for myself. I guess that's what's always made me so mature. I've always had to take care of my father. When I first told my father that I was remembering the incest, I did it in a way that minimized my own feelings so that he wouldn't feel quite so bad. I've done that before, lots of times, with people, taking the responsibility for something that is not your responsibility.

I remember when I talked to my father, he admitted that it had happened, but, I don't know how to explain it, he didn't remember it as anything important and he said it had only happened once, in his mind. I did stand up for myself and say that it went on for two years, which he couldn't believe, and I did tell him that it was important and it was incest, which he also couldn't believe. But I did not really tell him what it had done to me, how it had devastated me.

Always Looking Out for Others

I'm sure I have been the "parent" in adult relationships with other people, where their feelings have always meant more than mine. There were lots of relationships where I would have to listen to them talking about their problems and my needs would never be met. I've always been in relationships like that, and I still have relationships like that.

It's very painful because I feel as though I really don't have, aside from the group, a relationship in which my needs have been met. That's one reason why the group is so important to me. I've always been the one to meet the needs of the other person. It's very painful and it's no way to be an adult because you have a difficult time relating then to other people. You always have a feeling that you're not wanted. So, I don't feel as though I do have many friends that I'm close to and that I can deal with as an adult on an adult level.

Feeling Drained and Vulnerable

I wanted to talk more about what it's like being a mother and raising the girls through all of this. Besides being terribly, emotionally difficult, it was physically draining raising children. And then dealing with this incest problem too, being up nights, sometimes several nights in a row, crying and talking, or having an argument of sorts— I don't know, I don't know how I ever got through it. I was so exhausted all the time. I had so little left for myself, and the children needed so much.

Being pregnant was difficult; even getting up the emotional energy to go to the grocery store was difficult. I have a sister-in-law who is a normal person to me, and things like this happen to her too, because we talk about it, but I've found that people in the grocery store will come up and say the rudest things to me. I've been lots of places where people just come up and tell me how to raise my children, or I'm not doing something right, or, "Is that a pacifier in that baby's mouth?" or whatever. I never used to be able to say anything. I used to get so mad, just boiling, but I could never say anything. I always used to think it was just good manners on my part, I was just being well-mannered, but I wasn't. I was just being a wimp, and these people were walking on me and I just let them.

Learning to Stand Up for Myself

I went through a period in my life, ever since the abuse started, when people always would say or do things to me and I would just take it. Lately I've been at a point where I'm just not going to take it anymore. I'm not going to let people walk on me that way. I'm going to have that kind of an attitude. It just seems like people don't bother you so much if you ignore them in a cold kind of way, and then they realize what they've said was really rude. But when I was pregnant and just starting therapy, that was a really difficult time for me, because I can look back and pick out several instances of people just coming up and saying rude things to me. I didn't know how to stop it.

I've had to work at learning how to stand up for myself. I had a neighbor across the street who I was friendly with. I had to go to therapy one day during the week and I couldn't find a babysitter. So I asked her, would she watch my two-year-old, and she said, yes, she would. I went to my therapist, and she told me that day that I had to learn to start standing up for myself and standing up for my rights. She pointed out that I could do that for other people. I could stand up for my children and I could stand up for my husband, but when it came to myself, I couldn't. She suggested I think of various little exercises I could play during the day to learn how.

I got home that day and my neighbor had cut my daughter's hair, had washed it and cut it without even asking me. I was just terribly, terribly offended. It was more than that. I don't know really what it was, but I was really, really upset. I couldn't recognize my feelings and I couldn't say what I was feeling, and I didn't know if what I was feeling was appropriate. I had nothing to base it on, no one had ever done something like that to my child that really affected me.

The first thing that I said was, "Oh, you cut Shannon's hair," and she said, "Oh, you don't mind," or something. I said, "Well, I don't mind, but Danny sure is going to be mad." I could say something like that, but I couldn't say, "Damn it, no. I don't like it! What did you do something like that for?" I called her back about a week later and told her how I had felt, and she was very apologetic.

Recognizing My Rights

I would tell people this story and everybody thought that this woman was really offensive. Someone pointed out that possibly she could be one of those people who, if she thought that my daughter needed something else, she would do it, spank her or whatever, regardless of how I would feel about it. That really made me think and I thought, "Well, I'm just never going to take a chance of having my kid over there again," and I never did. Things have consequently been kind of cool. I do socialize with her a bit, but I'm never going to leave my kids alone with her, that's for sure.

But, at first, I really didn't understand that what she had done was a violation of my rights. It took a while before I could figure that out, that she didn't respect my rights to make decisions about my daughter. I grew up without any rights, so it was hard to know what was happening, to know what to do when they were violated, even where my daughter was concerned. But I did come around to it finally.

PARENTIFICATION

ANN-MARIE

Ann-Marie feels that she always has to pay a high price for meeting her own needs. "Why is it that I can't ever take care of my own needs without feeling that it is devastating for someone else?" she asks. The answer to this question is: incest and parentification. We enter adulthood with this feeling that asking anyone else to make an adjustment for our needs would devastate them, that we are not "allowed" to do this. It is hard to free ourselves from these self-imposed chains. We internalized that message as children, then as adults we ourselves project it into every relationship. As you read Ann-Marie, try to see the areas of her life where she does that, and you will probably recognize it in your own experience.

In reality we often attract people who like our not expressing any needs and who don't want to make any adjustments for us. Within this kind of relationship, is there any hope for love? Did we learn love as children, or obligation? Could we recognize and accept love when it is offered? Is our only concept of love a fantasy that can never be realized? What can we legitimately expect in an adult relationship? These are questions that we must address, with the reassurance that change is possible.

For me, parentification gets mixed up with the issue of control. Since my father was an alcoholic, and we had an emotionally chaotic household, I would do all I could to smooth things over. I am *very* uncomfortable when people around me are upset, and I have jumped right in trying to fix things and get everyone happy again. I've learned to recognize this, and I'm in the stage where my goal is simply to stay out of situations where I really have no responsibility, even if they want someone to fix things.

Taking Care of Mom

Making a cup of tea for me, lately, has become a very emotional, symbolic thing. My mom and I would always have a cup of tea together, after my father had fallen asleep on the living room couch, after he'd had a full meal, or after he'd been drinking. My mom or I cooked his meal for him. My mom would sometimes come home when he was eating, and then he would fall asleep. At the time I had a bedroom downstairs in what was the dining room. I would get up and go into the kitchen quietly to visit, to sit down with my mom and have a cup of tea with her and some cheese and crackers or snacks or something, and talk. I remember her talking about what was going on, the financial worries or problems with my father—things like that. I don't remember much talk about me at all. Looking back, I think she kind of gave stock answers to my emotional problems.

I don't remember especially wanting to tell my mom about the incest. If I did have a strong urge to tell her, I don't remember feeling it. My mother used me a lot as a confidante, and I became an adult very fast with all of this. I realize now that I had a lot of adult perceptions. As much as I think I might have wanted to tell her, I knew I couldn't, because I didn't think she could handle it. I felt very protective of her. I knew that she felt very burdened. She had a lot of the financial responsibility in our house because of my dad's drinking.

I don't remember. I don't know. I think I remember wanting to tell her. I remember my dad telling me it had to be a secret. I don't remember a specific conversation, but I do remember one time, standing up to him and saying, when I was 11 or 12, "Well Daddy, what would you do if I did tell?" My father had blue eyes, and he gave me one of the coldest blue-eyed stares I ever had, and he didn't say a word. It was kind of a deadly stare, just shook me to my roots. I think he knew that there was nothing he could really say, but that I wouldn't tell because I was the responsible one, and I was afraid.

Curing Daddy's Alcoholism

At one point I also tried to take responsibility for my dad's alcoholism. In high school I started learning about how alcohol was a poison, and what alcohol does to the brain cells. So I went right home thinking I had some information that would finally show my dad what he was doing. I guess I naively assumed he didn't know. I must have talked nonstop for a good half-hour, trying to convince my father of the physical harm that he was doing to himself. The whole family was home—my mother and my brother were there.

Finally, my father said that he was going to quit being an alcoholic for his kids. I was only 14 or 15 years old, and I said, "Daddy, we're going to be leaving. If you have to do it for anybody, you should be doing it for Mom." Mom just sort of sat there and said nothing. So, I've always had this protective thing, protecting everyone but myself.

In a lot of alcoholic families, there is a lot more physical responsibility, what I would call more routine chores and things. I did learn how to cook, because I did have to cook for my dad, but my mom did the shopping. For me, I think it was more of an emotional caretaking of the family.

My Mother—A Re-evaluation

My relationship with my mother has turned into such a complicated issue, especially since I've been looking at it in therapy.

I used to think I had emotional rapport with her. But now, over the last few years, it's all been one-sided. My mom has come to me on a number of occasions, as an adult, as recently as three or four years ago, when she and my stepfather were going through a very rocky time in the marriage, and the whole time I was relating to her on the same basis I would with any friend, a good friend whose marriage was in trouble.

It hurts now, because when I look back, I built up a myth in my own mind about how wonderful, loving, and supportive my mother's been. Then I wonder if she's even really been there for me all these years. I know she loves me in her own way. But it is very, very hard to accept her way. In her own way, I know she tried very hard.

Lately I'm reaching the conclusion that loving does not necessarily include caring for someone. My mom has professed love for me quite a lot over the years, but now I look back and I don't see much evidence of *caring*. Even now. This is very hard for me to accept—I'm still trying to keep my fantasy of her together.

One piece of parentification to me is protection. My mom protected my brother a great deal, lying to my dad to protect him from my father's totally out-of-proportion-to-the-"crime" anger. But I protected my mom and my whole family from the incest truth. No matter what my needs were, telling about it would blow the family apart, and I still feel that today.

Always Taking Care of Someone Else

Another need I have is to ask my mother about the incest. I think, at a minimum, I would like to at least know whether she knew or not, and if she didn't do anything about it, why? In her own words. I can make up all I want about it, but really I would just never know. I heard this tape, a talk given on incest, that says all this much better than I can, but basically it says that you have a right to know. I think that is true. But, it's not something I'm going to do in the next month, or maybe even in the next year. It's going to take a while.

I see my mother getting stronger in her own right because she's been going to Al-Anon a lot because of my stepfather. She is doing things on her own. Their marriage isn't real terrific, but she's learning, standing up as a person in her own right more and more than she ever used to. At some point, maybe I'll look at that and say, "Okay, I think it's time to take the chance."

Sometimes I think to myself it wouldn't surprise me that maybe she always knew but maybe she feels that if I've buried it and forgotten it, she doesn't want to bring me any pain, not realizing one can never forget things like this. She goes to Al-Anon, and many ACOA books are full of incest stories, so it's got to come up in the meetings she goes to. It's got to come up somewhere in those discussions. Doesn't she ever ask herself? But the point is, I am not able to even consider asking her about it without first worrying about what it would do to her. I'm always looking out for her, noticing her, even when it might not be good for me.

Confusion About Needs

I guess my own needs have been a mystery to me. I have felt very needy on occasion without actually knowing what it was I needed. Usually, I turned to the man in my life at the time, expecting him to know and fill it. Or I went shopping! I recall no sense of being conscious of my own needs until well after college graduation, when I was in my first marriage, and those needs to grow and be me blew the marriage apart.

In college, I almost totally sublimated my life and goals nurturing a young man with whom I fell in love my first weekend on campus. The relationship lasted three years, until he left a year early to go to medical school. I saw him once, about three years later, and he said he would never have made it through college without me. I was his constant companion and agreed usually to do whatever he wanted, most of which was study.

I've always got to consider what's right for everybody else. I can't just for once consider what's right for me and get something I need. Why is it that everything I need has to be so devastating to somebody else?

Marriage—Can I Have My Needs Met?

In group, we've talked about the pain and the problems with having children. My husband very much wants to have children. He's going to be, I think, an excellent father.

But I can see how much my husband wants children, and this is becoming an issue for me because I don't think I can deal with children right now. I need to take care of myself, to work out these incest problems. But then I have to feel that to do that, I might lose my husband, because he wants something I can't do right now. It is a high price. I have to pay such a high price emotionally for dealing with all this, to be able to turn and face it. Why is it I can't ever take care of my own needs, without feeling that it is devastating for someone else?

One of the problems with my marriage now is that I need a little bit of an emotional connection. I keep telling him I have to have some of that. It should be nothing new to him. We argued and discussed it long before we were married, to the point of late-night tears and big upsetting discussions. He would say yes, he'd do something, and make a lot of what I considered empty promises. I believe I had my choice as to whether to believe them or not, and I chose to believe them, and here I am married again and feeling trapped because I picked somebody who's not going to live up to his end of the bargain.

I feel trapped. This city is not an easy place to live by yourself, in terms of finances. I earn a good salary, but I definitely would have to give up the house if I wanted out of the marriage. It would be a major upheaval in my life again. So I don't want to leave him. But I don't have a real sense of love. I don't know what love is anymore.

Can I Call It Love?

The last time I really felt in love was with that man I was with for four-and-a-half years. Did you ever hear that song, "I'll Never Love That Way Again"? I remember lamenting to my friend, because the song would be on the radio at the time. And she asked, "Why would you want to?" because she knew how much pain I went through in that relationship. Now I'm asking myself, "Why does love always have to be painful for me? And can I really call it love?"

I'm beginning to realize that I don't know what it feels like to be in love. I don't know what it is. I read the books, but nothing is helping. I just make it day by day. At least we're still together, is kind of the way I look at it. We have fun together, we enjoy some of the same things, but he's no soulmate. That one man I was with four-and-a-half years ago, he was a soulmate. When I met him, we were both working for the same company, and we were both newly married. See, that is the pattern. My most exciting relationships were always with married men. In the end, I left my husband and, of course, the relationship lost its highly charged sexuality. In fact, it was pretty bad the last year. I don't know what it is, something happens.

I Can't Be Who I Am

Another important thing about the way I was brought up was to feel that my job is to let other people be who they are, but I'm not allowed to be who I am. One of the first major experiences I had still sticks with me all these years. I was a girl scout leader in my grade school, and I was a troop leader besides. We had some sort of a ceremony, and the woman who was our troop leader was the mother of one of my friends in school. Well, we're in the all-purpose room of my grade school. We're all sitting around, and we're celebrating. The other girls are taking their berets off and tossing them into the air. I wanted to do that, so I took my beret off and tossed it in the air. The troop leader came over to me and told me that I couldn't do that, to pick up my hat off the floor, and not to throw it in the air. All the girls, including her own daughter, were doing it, but she comes and singles me out. I was so hurt by that. Well, I tossed my hat up again, and she came over and reprimanded me again. That's the way I feel about my life. Ann-Marie has to be the good girl, she can't let her hair down. That's been the general feeling, and still is today.

I'm Not Allowed

At work, my ex-boss that I had so much trouble with is the same age I am. She's married, has two kids, and she talks fast like I do; she's very bright, energetic, some say aggressive. There are a lot of people who don't like her because she comes on very strong. She works for this manager who hired her and has been her friend for as long as she's been at the company.

People have told me how much I am like her, but they don't like me to be that way. They allow her to be a big mouth, but I'm not allowed to say what I think has to be said. When I'm aggressive and I want to do things and get the job done, I can't do that. I've got to be passive or I get shot down. They let her mouth off, and management doesn't do anything, she doesn't get shot down for these behaviors. I don't do any of that, and the few minor things that I do are misconstrued as "aggression" or whatever. I feel that I'm not allowed to do anything.

I Have a Right to Be Here

It's only very, very recently, especially where business is concerned, that I've realized that I don't have to do all the things that my company wants me to do. I've begun to see that I never had to do all the things that my parents wanted me to do to be a good girl or to be a responsible child. I realize I was a good child before I did any of that stuff. My parents definitely brought me up with a sense of "You're not allowed to be here."

There have been times when that has really been acute. I've never felt that I've had a right simply just to be here. I had to justify my existence. I have a problem now because of the things my husband has now started to do for me. I feel like I should be everlastingly grateful. I should jump into bed and start producing babies as quickly as I can out of gratitude that he has finally done something for me. I can't accept that he is doing it for me because I'm here and I deserve it. Regardless of what happens, I feel like anytime I get something good, I have to give back, that it is my job to be the giver, not his.

Self-Esteem

I know I have a problem with self-esteem. For the most part, it's probably the size of a quarter now; it was the size of maybe a pea when I started. It's because of that sense that people are always *taking* from me. I'm a giving person, and I'm not happy unless I am giving. For example, I got two cats, deliberately because I was living on my own and I was intending to stay that way, for a while anyway. I'd come home to nothing, so I got my two cats, and they've been wonderful. They have been such a tremendous source of comfort because they need me.

But with people I really feel used. Obviously, in my father's case, I was taken advantage of. But I feel like, all of my life, people have really taken advantage of me and my sense of goodness and obligation and always living up to responsibility.

"What Have I Done Wrong?"

For years, whenever something happened in a relationship, even a casual relationship at work, the question I asked myself was, "What have I done wrong?"

I can remember my earliest days, when I first started my career. I'd walk down the hall in the morning for coffee, and someone would come along and say "Hi!" Then, a couple of hours later, that person would pass by me in the hall and wouldn't say "Hi!" And I would go back to my office and literally rack my brain trying to find what I had done to cause that person to not say "Hi!" It took me years to realize that it may have been a memo they just got, or a phone call, and *had nothing to do with me.*

That's just a little thing. Big things can turn into a living nightmare. Just in the last nine months I've been working for a woman. And that relationship has been bringing up a lot of my issues. She's a very strong-willed woman. I was placed under her as head of a project. Someone above her did this. Even though she was originally a great champion of my career, even hired me into the company in the first place, ever since someone went over her head and forced her to accept me on one of her projects, she's been giving me problems.

She's done nothing but throw roadblocks in my way on the project, she's belittled me in meetings—not personally, but indirectly—in reference to my work, lots of things. I kept going to therapy and saying, "What am I doing wrong?" Then it hit me—she had her *own agenda*. It had nothing to do with me.

It has taken me an inordinate amount of time to figure out that I am not always responsible for everything. It has been agony.

PARENTIFICATION

BRENDA

The word "parentification" is too benign for the abuse Brenda suffered. What it does describe is her response to it—the way she accepted full responsibility for everything that happened to her, her brother, and even her mother. She is still struggling to relieve herself of the guilt, a primary effect of parentification, which teaches us we are responsible for everything.

Brenda's story is somewhat different because the sources of her parentified behavior include not only her mother and foster parents, but the child welfare institutions and schools as well. Even so, we still recognize the commonalities she shares with the other survivors. Her need to achieve, her tendency to get into one-way relationships, the difficulty she has in nurturing herself, and her problems maintaining intimacy with comfortable boundaries are familiar patterns.

Like Noelle, Brenda is aware of the intergenerational effects of parentification, which she discusses in part two of her story. A parentified child has difficulty establishing appropriate boundaries with her children, making it difficult to exercise discipline on the one hand, or to share love on the other. By examining the ways that our childhood experience is repeated in our parenting behavior, we can stop it from being passed on to our own children. As Brenda says, "It is never too late."

I Was Always an Adult

I never was a child. I remember being so envious of all the other girls at school because they could flirt with boys and they were so sure of themselves; I wanted so desperately to be like that, I wanted to experience what it was like. I always felt like an adult, even when I look back at my childhood, I could see the small child who was me, but she could think like an adult, and I just wanted to be a kid, desperately wanted to be a kid. I guess that was one of the hardest things for me, later on, to come to grips with, that I wasn't going to have a childhood, I was always an adult.

Growing up, I remember distinctly feeling I had absolutely no rights. I often wondered what right I even had to exist. I felt people could do whatever they wanted, and maybe that was another reason I didn't like to have associations and relationships with people or too many friends, because it left me open to be abused, to be told what to do and have to do that; I would have to. There were just no choices for me—never really experiencing any freedoms, but always a prisoner to what everybody else wanted. I was never asked to do anything, I was always told. Even now, sometimes, I get so angry when people order, it immediately causes reactions that I won't do it, I won't.

I've always been so much more concerned about other people's feelings, never taking care of myself, never protecting myself, never feeling I had the right to protect myself. Always making myself available to take care of someone else, in both of my marriages, trying to take care of husbands who were very needy. Trying to take care of my children. Trying to take care of my boss. Trying to take care of friends. Always my door was open to anyone who was needy. It gave me self-worth, I guess. It gave me a value, a purpose, plus, it was the only thing I had every known. I was put here to take care of somebody else.

Now I think very differently. I still feel that I'd like to help people whenever possible but I'm really trying to take care of myself; therapy is the one thing that allows me to do that.

Becoming a Parent at the Age of Three

I became a parent at the age of three, when my brother was born. I pretty much took care of all of his needs and any subsequent children my mother continued to give birth to. I remember my brother had convulsions as a young child, and being petrified that I was killing him, not understanding what was happening. Finding the strength to go call for an ambulance and, when they arrived, being horrified at the thought of them taking him away, that I had killed him, and taking full responsibility for that when my mother was drunk.

I took care of my mother. When she was drunk and couldn't walk to meet the johns, I'd walk with her and wait for her. In some ways it was good to be allowed to walk with her and wait because it meant that I would get something to eat, I could eat while I sat in the living room or outside the apartment, whatever. Sometimes I even got money.

As I said earlier, my first sexual experience was at three years old when my mother sold me to one of her friends; I remember that distinctly. It was oral sex. I remember being given potato chips to eat and not really knowing what was going on, but I was getting food to eat and that was so important. My mother was there, drunk, but again, even at that young age, not knowing the wrong that was being done, just knowing that if you did this, you got something to eat. There was a cause and effect for it.

Protecting My Brother

As I was growing up, I continued to take care of my brother, wouldn't let anybody hurt him, fought his battles, made sure he had what he wanted—what he needed, actually, not what he wanted. I continued to try and take care of my mother's psychological needs and physical needs as far as food, drink, and made sure that she got to bed or got to where she needed to be.

I remembered, when I lived with my mother, sleeping in the same bed where she was entertaining gentlemen, being exposed to that side, that sexual side again. Taking care to make sure that anyone who threatened to hurt my brother, that they would hurt me and not him. Taking the beatings for him. I remember leaning over him and cowering under tables so that when the belt lashes came they wouldn't hit him. Trying to take care of the other little ones. My mother would throw knives at us, beer bottles that would smash up on the walls. I would take my brother and run out into the street, we would cower either under stairwells or in hallways, or whatever. We moved constantly, we never stayed anywhere for more than a week or so. Probably when rent was due is when we would move. Always growing up and feeling that everything that went wrong was because I wasn't a good person, I didn't try hard enough.

I Let Something Happen to Him

After the incest, when I told, I ran away because I couldn't take it anymore. I suffered horrible guilt, because just about a year later, they also removed my brother and put him in places where he was beaten and, at some point, his nose was broken and they broke his arms. I remember feeling the guilt because I couldn't be there to protect him, and I blamed myself for not being able to take more of the sexual abuse, because if I had allowed it to continue, he would have been safe, he would have been with me. I still can't get over that guilt. I guess when I think back I could have suffered it, except knowing that he was hurt.

I Still Feel the Guilt

Even now when my brother and I get together (he lives out west) it's hard sometimes for me to look at him and realize that I let him down. Although when I talk to him about it, you know, he in no way holds me responsible. I think it's sad, a lot of the times, to know the guilt that I feel. I haven't quite reached a point where I can let go and realize that I had no control over that particular part. Otherwise, I can rationalize it. Mentally I can deal with it, it's emotion that I let something happen to him. That was another incentive that I would protect my children from physical harm—no matter what the cost, no one would ever hurt them.

I was so sad when my brother got into drugs and alcohol. I blamed myself because I wasn't there, I couldn't direct him. I never called, and I'd bail him out of jail and I'd send him money, and, I guess, finally I got so angry and we had such harsh words between us and he seemed to change after that. I'm not sure if he was afraid that I was going to let him go completely, because I was so angry with him. But, for whatever reasons, he did turn his life around.

Trying to Learn a Sister/Brother Relationship

Although I'm still very protective of him, I still don't understand a sister/brother relationship. I mean, I know he's my brother, but in many ways I'm still his mother. I hope that at some point with therapy I can gain an understanding of what a real sister/brother relationship is like, and what my role is, and that I have the right to possibly ask something of my brother, you know, that he can give to me. I think he would like that. I think many times he gets concerned about me and, for whatever reasons, I won't let him protect me. I always feel the guilt that I need to protect him, not vice versa.

But at least now I'm thinking about it and trying to figure out how it can become a balanced relationship. I know it's very unhealthy and has been for years. It's always me giving to him, which may have been one reason that he had low self-esteem. I never let him do anything for himself, never let him defend himself or take up for himself. I have such feelings of guilt for that.

Everything Was My Fault

Another one of the strong feelings that returns to me from my childhood is the rejection, the constant rejection from everyone it seemed I came in contact with. From my mother to my foster parents, my social worker, other kids, students, their parents, never did it seem, no matter how hard I tried that I obtained any acceptance, any consideration for who I was as a person, instead of where I had come from, or the areas in which I was still weak.

I remember when I was in foster homes or institutions for kids, there were visitations to my mother's home (or slum, as it is more clearly known) with her boyfriend, and always she held out the promise of a normal life and said she was getting her life together, that she was going to remarry, she was going to get her children back again, and she was going to get a job. None of these things having any chance of becoming reality, it didn't take me too long to realize that these were just false hopes. Now I look back and I know they were hopes of a destitute woman, things that she would probably have wanted but didn't know how to obtain.

However, at the time, each time a promise fell through, she accused me of being at fault, it was because I placed too many burdens on her, it was because she had too many responsibilities, it was because we weren't good kids and nobody wanted us to be around. Constantly I accepted that blame and was always apologizing to her for being a burden, for being born, for destroying her life. And each time that I apologized, it made me more aware of how nonexistent I really was and that I really was a burden to the world and I had no right to be alive. The only thing that really, the only thing, I guess, that kept me going, was the fact that I couldn't leave my brother.

Taking Responsibility for My Mother's Ego

There were times as a young girl, probably between the ages of 9 and 15, when my mother accused me of men in her life not liking her, liking me more, and who did I think I was taking her men. She was the pretty one, she was the woman, she was the most desirable. I was nothing, and who did I think I was, flirting with her boyfriends and coming on to them. Constantly accusing me of things of this nature, things that had sexual overtones, things that weren't really my responsibility.

Here again, I apologized profusely, reminding her that I wasn't pretty, I knew that. I was ugly. I couldn't figure out why the men wanted me and not her. That yes, she was the pretty one, she was the desirable one. Here again, reinforcing in myself, that, indeed, I had nothing to offer. In my own defense I had to constantly reassure her that yes, I was ugly, yes, I didn't have any attractions, no one should be attracted to me. Every time it happened, it just lowered my self-esteem, which was almost nonexistent anyway. The humiliation was that much greater.

Rejection

The rejection from peers at school and friends in the neighborhood was equally as destructive. No matter how hard I tried to be accepted, fit in, it never seemed to work. I tried everything from lying and being someone I'm not to trying to be myself, but always something came back to haunt me, so that I would lose a friend or people would make fun of me, or parents of a friend at school would find out what kind of background I came from and prohibit me from being friends with that person, once again lowering all chances for any kind of self-esteem as a child. It was really very devastating to me.

I remember back in junior high school, one particular teacher who was always trying to come on to me, and how fearful I was of this man. Always making inappropriate jokes to me or inappropriate mannerisms in my direction, making me feel that everyone in the class knew who I was, and that I was this horribly ugly person that people could do whatever they wanted to do to. I still have this feeling even now—with my children, my friends, and with men.

There Was No Consideration for My Feelings

Other forms of humiliation and shame: When I was living with the family where I had suffered the incest, I remember getting a bra for the first time. I was very young. Everybody humiliated me with jokes, having to look at my bra—just feeling so ashamed, that something that was so normal for a young girl to experience, getting a first bra, I was being turned into a sideshow. No one was respectful of my feelings, no one was respectful of what I was going through inside by being humiliated like this.

The same thing happened when I got my period, they were around the same time. I was very young, nine. The humiliation of everyone talking about something so personal. Here again, absolutely no caring for my feelings, only making fun so that they amuse themselves or the joke's on me again.

In gym class, one of the hardest things for me was to undress to take a shower, not that I didn't want to take a shower, but getting undressed and being exposed and thinking people could see through my skin to all the ugliness that was harbored inside of me. All the hurt. Feelings I didn't want anyone to know about. It was just extremely difficult for me to have to be in a room with nothing to protect myself, and, in some ways, clothing is protection.

The teachers didn't understand, and when I tried to talk to my foster parents, they thought it was just absolutely the most ridiculous thing they ever heard and why did I constantly continue to see it as harrassment? To be difficult? To not conform to the rules? If it was a rule to take a shower, well, you take a shower and don't make a big deal out of it. Here again, just reinforcing the fact that my feelings didn't mean anything. I didn't have a right to have those feelings. You conform to the rules and you get along; you do what people tell you. You have no rights.

Taking Responsibility for Everything

I always took responsibility for everything, blaming myself, assuming the guilt was mine. My first husband gave me a venereal disease. I remember when I found out in the doctor's office that I had the venereal disease feeling so humiliated, feeling so dirty, wondering why this was happening to me. Coming home, I remember feeling so much shame and wondering how would I tell my husband that I had a venereal disease, trying to figure out how it happened. Knowing full well that I had never been involved with another man, I had always been faithful to him. It never dawned on me that he had been unfaithful.

I remember coming home crying and turning to my foster mother, who's the psychologist, and asking her, "How do I handle this? How do I tell him? He's going to hate me." I remember her saying to me, "Did it ever dawn on you that he gave you the venereal disease?" It was like a light went on. It never dawned on me. I took full responsibility for something that didn't belong to me.

I remember confronting him with this, and him accusing me and blaming me and not accepting any responsibility for his own behaviors, let alone the responsibility for making me ill, giving me the infection, for making me be humiliated at the doctor's office, having to go in for the treatments and the shots, putting me through shame all over again. That was just—it was just miserable.

But what was important there was the fact that I accepted the responsibility without question, unconditional, not even thinking that it was his responsibility to accept the guilt and the shame and the blame. But it all goes back to the fact that I was so accustomed to accepting it. It just seemed natural to me that I should accept the blame.

Because of this infection, because of the incest, because of the early years of rape and molestation, by the time I was about 26, I had to have a total hysterectomy. I had a partial the first time and complete the second time. I remember the doctors being extremely concerned that my uterus was so torn up, I had holes eaten through it, and they couldn't figure out how I had managed to have two children without dying. Their emphasis was placed on the fact that I needed this hysterectomy because if I did get pregnant again, I would never make it through.

Here again, I was being punished for things that had happened to me, things that I had no control over, and the shame that went through me again, the guilt, accepting the responsibility, and wondering, "Why me?" And when did it end? When did I have to stop being abused? When would I stop feeling pain for things that people did to me? Thank God, I guess, that I had two children because after that, of course, I'd never have any.

Projecting the Pain

Because of all the pain and hurt that I've carried through all these years, one of the things I do is when I hear someone in pain or someone hurting, I assume that they are experiencing the same level I did, or would, which often makes me overcompensate. My therapists both warned me about that. To be sure and not to throw my own personal experiences onto someone and assume they are suffering the same as I would or have, which in turn becomes a form of protection for me.

I guess almost all abused people do that. They've known such great pain that when someone's experiencing normal pain, you give them a lot more or you feel they have a lot more pain underneath their problem than they really do. Therefore you want to compensate more than maybe is needed or wanted or even appropriate for that particular instance. I'm working real hard trying to make sure I understand what kind of pain a person is feeling, or how they're going to hear what I'm going to say.

One of the things I do with my kids is be cautious. I don't want to say anything negative, because when I was a kid, that's all that was said to me, and I know how much pain it caused me. I need to realize things are different for my children. When I say no to them, or when I won't do what they want me to do, or if I have to discipline them, they're not going to experience the same level of pain I did. That's a real tough one, because my first instincts are to avoid causing any suffering or pain.

Intergenerational Effect of Parentification

Brenda, like Noelle, experienced the cyclical nature of parentified behavior when she had children of her own. With little experience of nurturing, she had difficulty meeting the needs of her small children. It was particularly difficult for her to establish and maintain a gentle, effective discipline. This is a common problem for parents who never experienced a kind and loving discipline in their own childhoods.

The anguish, frustration, and helplessness Brenda experienced as a parent will be familiar to all parents who grew up without adequate parenting themselves. Her very positive message is that it is never too late to change. Many parents give up, and never address their mistakes after their children are grown, taking the attitude that it won't do any good, or that it is too late to change anything. The truth is that it is never too late. As Brenda says, "I'm working so hard trying to be a good mother even now when they are becoming young adults in the hope that they'll learn from my mistakes. They'll learn also about how I'm getting healthy and how they can be healthy, and when the time comes when they have children, maybe they will remember."

The cycle can be broken. It is never too late.

When I became a mother, I didn't know how to discipline. To me, all discipline was abuse. So I either did nothing or waited until things were so far along that I ended up being abusive—screaming, shouting, talking to them in a harsh, inappropriate way. But most of the time I did nothing. I was in no way going to hurt my children the way I had been hurt.

My Children Became Little Abusive People

People would tell me, you can say no to them, but say it in a way that says, "I care about you." But for me, no had always meant, "I hate you. I don't care about you. If you think you're going to get anything out of me, you're wrong." I never wanted to project that, so I never would say no. I would make excuses, or I might start out saying no but end up saying, "Okay, fine, you deserve it, I shouldn't have said no." I really did not understand what proper discipline is.

My oldest son, even now, when someone says no on the job or enforces some limit, he assumes they hate him. He's got a distorted idea of what discipline is. We did not have a balance, the children and me. They became little abusive people early on, in their own right. Because they knew that Mom was not going to spank or say no, they did what they wanted.

And that took a toll on me because, as they were growing up, I was feeling abused by my own children, and there was a time when I really hated them. I felt, "How can you abuse me when I take care of you and I don't abuse you? How can you do that to me?" And I started to feel like I did as a kid again—what is it about me that nobody likes, that they always try to take advantage of me? Now I know it was because I wasn't setting any boundaries, I wasn't protecting myself. I was just being a good old doormat: Come on in. Walk on me; do what you want.

Now that the kids are older and I can talk to them, I can reason with them. But I did a lot of things the wrong way for the right reasons. I gave them a lot more power than they could handle, and it was scary for them.

Give Everything, Then Feel Abused

My oldest son spent a lot of time in therapy, and the therapist would say, "Set guidelines, and stick to them." Well, I'd set guidelines, but I couldn't tell if they were reasonable or not, and I would feel so guilty when they didn't like it or felt unhappy. So then I'd drop it and we would be back where we started. The problem was that I was projecting on them the pain I had as a child, when they had no idea of the pain I suffered. I gave them all this pain that they didn't really have.

I go into relationships, promising everything, setting no limits, taking care of everything. But, after a while, you feel so resentful. This is the pattern with all my relationships—give everything, then feel abused. I did this in all my marriages and with my children.

I Did the Best Job I Could

With my own children, when they were young and demanding, I remember hating them sometimes. Why did I do this? Why did I have children? I can't be a mother. I don't know how to be a mother. Yet the other side was, I can't not be a mother. I have responsibilities. I have to take care of them. And not really knowing how, I did the best job I could, but building insecurities into them, my own unhealthy state became theirs.

There were times, periods of years, when I could put it all behind me and lock it back up, and we'd have some semblance of normalcy and some light. But I'm sure that my unhealthiness peeked out constantly.

With my son, with his low self-esteem and always wanting to be secluded, not fitting really into society anywhere, although he has not gotten into drugs or alcohol, he goes along at his own pace and kind of walks to the tune of a different drummer. But I think, had I been healthier, he would be a lot healthier.

He never had his father there. His father never participated in his childhood or in raising him, so another whole set of problems he had to deal with was constant rejection by his father. Even now he loves any attention his father happens to throw his way. Although he says he really doesn't think about his father and couldn't care less about him, I know that he still seeks his approval, and I've finally come to realize that there's nothing that I can do about that relationship. I tried to talk to him about it, be there when he needs to talk about his father, but I can't make his father be any different. I can only work on me being different, because for years I tried to be both, and not successfully probably at either.

Feeling Inadequate

I also remember times when the kids were crying, and the helplessness that I felt. The inadequacies that brought out in me—that I didn't know how to be a mother; I didn't know how to take care of their emotional needs. It brought back memories of my inadequacies as a child, my inabilities to be in control and many, many times I would just sit and be so depressed and maybe yell at the kids, or scream at them, or wish that they would disappear just because I didn't know what to do. Then, later, the guilt that would come from feeling those things and placing blame on my own children for things that I just was inadequate at.

It was a time when there was a lot of sadness in my life, a lot of turmoil, just total inadequacy as a person, these poor helpless children dependent on me, looking for guidance, looking for love, and my inabilities to provide appropriate standards for them and to express my feelings to them. In the role as a mother, as a young woman, when the children were young, having all the responsibilities for the kids. Their father was not involved with them, there was no one to help in raising the children, or taking on some of the burdens and the work that is involved.

And, here again, feeling that I should be a superwoman and handle everything that came along, no matter what it was or how tired I was or how much effort or energy or money it would take. Once again reinforcing the fact that I was an inadequate person.

Recognizing the Child at Last

It's only been recently that I can look back and think about the little girl that I was, not the one I wished for in my fantasy world, but the real little girl that I was. For years I hated her. I hated everything she stood for—her weakness, her lack of ability to take control, to get herself out of the situations, protect herself, protect her brothers and sisters and do it better—not that I didn't try—but do a better job, do an adult job.

It's been only recently that I've been able to see it differently. A very close friend of mine has a daughter who is two years old, and I find myself watching this child and I love her a lot. She seems to be very much attracted to me. I sit and I watch her and I think of myself at two with all the responsibilities and the horror that was around me. I try to think of this little child, in such a helpless state—she's so dependent on her parents and people around her, she's so expecting of love that it comes naturally to her—and I try to think, how would that little girl react? What capabilities does she have? What control does she have? It's really beginning to help me put things in proper perspective.

As she grows older, I think it will help me also to look at the child I was in another light, a healthier light, and not be so condemning; not totally reject that child all the time. It's really been wonderful when I sit now and I look at this child.

It's sad, too, because I wish I had been able to do that with my own children. But, as I have said to the boys before, I'm working so hard trying to be a good mother even now when they're becoming young adults in the hopes that they'll learn from my mistakes. They'll learn also about how I'm getting healthy and how they can be healthy, and when the time comes when they have children, maybe they will remember.

PARENTIFICATION

ELLEN

Parentification in Ellen's life is evident in the lack of nurturing she received as a child and in the way she has become a caretaker in her adult life. She hates her caretaking role and feels trapped. Her story is somewhat different because at age 54 she is experiencing the inevitable role reversal that occurs as our parents age. Although her caretaking of her disabled mother is typical of the point she has reached in life, some of Ellen's responses to it are not. While taking care of her mother, Ellen feels abandoned and abused, feels guilty when she tries to assert her own needs, and hates the helpless invalid. These are similar to the feelings a parentified child has when she becomes a parent, as Noelle and Brenda describe them. The only difference is that Ellen has them about her invalid mother. This shows us how our inability to address our own needs ultimately leads to our feeling abused in every relationship.

I Was Better Off Not Existing

My parents did not nurture me. As far as particular incidents go, a few are outstanding. But beyond those, it was more the everyday absence of nurturing that I feel now.

After the neighbor boy performed sodomy—ejaculated in my mouth—I remember how I raced home. I ran through the woods and put dirt on my dress to cover his semen where I spit it out. I had dirt on my chin, and when my mother found me she called me dirty—dirty, bad girl—and spanked me and tried to wash me, but I would never be clean again.

When my father came home—the fear, the fear I feel in remembering—especially between my legs where he examined me and told me how bad I was. How could I have done this to him? How could I have been so stupid? And I knew then he was no longer my father because I didn't have one. And she was no longer my mother, because there wasn't a home anymore, because there was now no place to go. Then my Nana, my grandmother, died—without telling me she loved me, without telling me it was not my fault. I was better off not existing.

Recently, after 44 years of not remembering my Nana, I began to remember her—her soft lap, the hugs, the feeling, "Yes, you are loved." The only time I ever had that was with her.

I Felt I Was to Blame

My mother fought my grandfather to the floor to keep him from sexually using me. I remembered this recently, too. But the way she told me—"You get out of here"—I felt, "She blames me, I'm dirty." I never got the chance to cry, to be held, to be protected.

And with Nana, the fear that she, too, would withhold her love.

And she did. The final withholding was her death. I blamed her for leaving me. Or was it my fault?

Now Everyone Needs Me

Now everyone needs me. I have gathered them all around me—my children, their families, my invalid mother, friends from my group. I feel trapped. But I escape to my boat on weekends.

My good friend Leigh was terribly, horribly, unspeakably abused by her father: When I hold her so she can cry on my shoulder, I tell her it will be all right. I feel strong; I can protect. I can feel maybe I'll be okay, too.

With Brett, before we broke up, I hated his little-boy number. He was a child—he wasn't thinking of a future together—he was abusive. He cared, but not really—it was hard for him to love me. He never came to me and held me close and loved me. It was always a hand up my crotch or a cheap remark. He was degrading me. (Of course he was insecure—why else would I choose him?) And yet I thought there might be hope for the relationship. But did I even want to hope? I'm not sure. I look at his pictures and realize it was his looks I loved; his potential, not his reality. His reality was that of a little boy. And I hated that in him. But aren't we all babies at times? Why did I hate him so when he did that?

Guilty About Mother

And my mother. She is so old and wrinkled. My mother is now an invalid. She was living with a housekeeper, a woman from Trinidad. The house was full of roaches. It was a terrible environment—and I felt so guilty that she was there. I kept her at my house for almost a year, and at one point she said of a good friend who is also a survivor and was living with me—she said, "That woman is disgusting. I wouldn't let her touch my dead body!"

I was trying at that time to bring my mother into the therapy process. I wanted her validation. I wanted her to remember the name of the boy who raped me. And she says, "I don't remember anything about it. I don't want to hear anything about it, and you shouldn't be talking about it either." And then she pulled this hatred thing on my best friend. Also, she decided she hates my eldest granddaughter. It's real weird. My mother must have had some very strange things happen to her when she was a child.

The upshot of this is, I took her over to my brother's house and dropped her off. Three months later, he sent her away because he had a similar experience with her. She got real critical. She couldn't stand his wife, and so on and so on—so he finally took her to this place with the housekeeper. It's like each place she goes, she alienates everybody and ends up in progressively worse environments. It's almost like I'm watching the things happen to my mother that I'm afraid are going to happen to me.

I felt like I should run and get her; gather her up and take her home and take care of her. I know that is crazy. Finally I brought her here to live with me until an opening is available in the nursing home.

I Still Feel Abused and Used

My father died at age 63. He was alcoholic and I never confronted him. I don't know how to deal with my mother. I think what is happening with my mother is that each time she pulls one of those critical things, it's a rerun of the early stuff. It's like it's not me she's concerned about. I'm feeling that again. And that's why I don't want to go near her. She has put herself in that position.

She didn't protect me, she didn't save me, she didn't even let me be okay—she made me bad. She put the seal of disapproval on me, which I wear so loudly, which I protect so carefully. "Yes, Mom, I'm coming. Straighten your pillow. Sure, Mom. You're cold? Just a minute, I'll turn up the heat. Did you take your medicine at lunchtime? No? I'll get it for you now." There's nothing you can give me now, Mom.

I have to sell her house, put her in a nursing home. Now I have other lives to consider—now I'll have to grow up. And my mother's wrinkled voice: "Where have you been, Ellen? I've been worried, Ellen. Don't you want to stay here, Ellen? You aren't going out, are you, Ellen? You con, Ellen, you're going to put me away and sell my home. I hate you, Ellen."

She is not able to help me with my grandfather's legacy—the half-remembered sexual abuse. Yet she fought him to the floor to keep him off me.

"Dramatizing—that's all," Mom said. I'm so good at dramatizing—hurts, oh, that hurts. And it's not all right to feel the hurt. I even have to turn that off. Oh, how I hate her sometimes. My hatred is so *very big*.

My mother said, "Why dwell on this? Put it behind you, it's all over." She will never understand—they rarely do. But, I don't much care now—I don't need her now. Especially now. I must go to work now, for me.

"I feel *so guilty*," I told my friend. "I am not doing enough," I said. Her instant rejoinder was, "Haven't you been totally responsible for your mother for six months now? Haven't you sacrificed evenings, weekends, literally every free moment for being with her?"

I wonder why I have given so much of myself to this woman who hates me. Am I afraid of the ultimate abandonment?

Looking at Mother Realistically

I have heard it said that "The secret you seek is that there is no secret." This, right here, right now, is all there is. So make the best of it—you won't get another chance. Unhook from her I must. And unhook I did. My mother became someone I'm ultimately not responsible to help, protect, or do anything for. She became a bent, gray-haired, nasty, little old woman in my living room. I became me—describing simply to her the rules of my home. Rules she must comply with, like myself and everyone else in my household.

She will no longer be allowed to abuse anyone verbally including herself. She must try to express her feelings directly, and she will not be allowed sarcasm or innuendo. Her goal is to hold out her arthritic arms and hug me before she dies.

And her first statement in response to these directives was, "I feel sorry for you because you've been brainwashed by this group of self-pitying individuals who call themselves an incest support group."

May she someday learn to rest in peace.

CHAPTER 5—FOOTNOTES

1. All descriptions of parentification are paraphrased or quoted from Gelinas, Denise J., "The Persisting Negative Effects of Incest," *Psychiatry* 46 (November 1983): 319–325, with the exception of comments on victims' susceptibility to exploitative jobs and their being underpaid and overworked, which originate with the author. Role-reversal is well known and discussed in many other excellent sources. I chose to refer to the Gelinas article because she discusses parentification specifically in terms of the incest trauma, both as a contributing factor and as an effect.

6

Specific Effects of Incest Trauma: "Am I Crazy or Does Everybody See Lizards Dining Out in Washington, DC?"

Chronic traumatic neuroses with "secondary elaborations" resulting from lack of treatment are characterized first by denial, with "repetitive intrusions" of certain elements of the trauma. "Total denial . . . is infrequent. Most common is denial of the significance of the event. It is also common to repress elements associated with the experiences such as the time period, the emotional content, or the place." The "repetitive intrusions" will be the recurrence of some aspect of the repressed trauma. It may be cognitive—such as nightmares, hallucinations, recurrent images, or obsessive ideas . . . Or they may be emotional recurrences—uncontrollable weeping, fear or panic without any awareness of the relationship between the event and the incest trauma. . . The recurrence could be behavioral, such as compulsive talking about the trauma, bodily reenactments or artistic renderings. "When the recurrences occur," Gelinas warns, "the individual's memory and affect in relation to the original trauma may be so vivid, intense and unmodified as to constitute flashbacks, and they can be triggered by circumstances similar to the original trauma or by therapy itself. . ." Dissociation is another characteristic of traumatic neuroses . . . often reported as confusion, disorientation, "freezing" of thought processes or total amnesia.[1]

SPECIFIC EFFECTS OF INCEST TRAUMA

It is difficult to know when our responses are "normal" and when they are distorted by incest. To recover, we have to work on identifying the feelings that originate in the past and deal with them, rather than letting them intrude inappropriately in our lives. When they intrude unexpectedly and inappropriately in our lives, we call these intrusions "recurrences."

For many of us, it is hard to identify recurrences because they happen so frequently they become a part of our lives. Unable to connect the recurrence with the incest trauma, we decide we are "just crazy" sometimes, or that it "runs in the family." "It's a chemical imbalance," or "female trouble" are other explanations we hear.

It is usually a great relief to find out that our fits of rage, "irrational" fears, and episodes of crying or panic are a predictable result of the repressed incest trauma. They begin to make sense. They aren't so frightening. We aren't so crazy. In fact, these recurrences aren't even neurotic. For that reason, some practitioners prefer to call these symptoms "post-traumatic stress disorder" rather than "chronic traumatic neuroses."

Recurrences appear to be related to denial, because when the trauma cannot find direct expression, it will find indirect expression. For some of us, this means hallucinating spiders the size of bushel baskets. Until recently, the conventional wisdom in psychology was that hallucinations were psychoses. Now it appears that hallucinations in a nonpsychotic person are an indicator of a physical trauma such as incest. Even though in traditional theory it is still contradictory to talk about hallucinations in a nonpsychotic person, experienced practitioners are recognizing the phenomenon and becoming aware that it originates in a physical trauma such as incest.

For those of us who don't remember the incest, even unpleasant recurrences such as hallucinations are a valuable pathway back to the trauma. Noelle's story in this chapter, and in the therapy chapter (7) will describe how recurrences can be an important therapeutic tool. Although it is *not necessary* to have recurrences in order to process the trauma, if they do unfortunately occur, they can be used in therapy. No therapist would willingly trigger a recurrence, however, because reliving the trauma can be a trauma of its own.

One type of recurrence I did not systematically include but I believe to be common is a "somatic" or physical recurrence. I have no hard data for this, but I have found that most survivors have some form of recurrent, intense pain. Headaches, menstrual pain, chest, back, and abdominal pain are common. Endometriosis, hypoglycemia, TMJ, and eating disorders also seem to occur with some frequency.[2] Without a statistical sample based on test and control groups it is not possible to determine if these symptoms occur with significantly greater frequency among incest survivors than in the general population.

This section should be useful in identifying some of the behavior that is specifically caused by the incest trauma. It is especially important for those who don't remember the incest. Recurrences can be very helpful to you, because once you trace them back to the original trauma, it is available for treatment. You can't heal the wound until you find it. Recurrences can take you there.

NOELLE

In this chapter, Noelle's story gives us a detailed account of the many ways repressed incest trauma intrudes into the life of the victim. Survivors who don't remember the incest have a different experience in some ways from those who do remember. In particular, they have a greater problem overcoming denial and recognizing the sources of their dysfunction, and they are more frequently traumatized by recurrences. Unable to make a connection between the recurrence and the original incest trauma, they attach various and usually self-destructive explanations to the recurrence. They begin to think of themselves as "crazy," or just incorporate the recurrence as simply one more degrading part of a self-image that is already poor.

For survivors who have no direct memory of incest, recurrences become pieces in a puzzle they must put together, first to break the denial and accept that it happened, and then to remember. This is a painful, agonizing process, and Noelle is the one survivor in this book who has gone through it. Although it is not necessary to relive the trauma to remember it, memories often occur as a reliving of the trauma in flashback, or they are accompanied by the emotions that were felt at the time of the original trauma. Noelle identifies the many forms a recurrence will take. Her experience will be a guide to all who are struggling to make sense of things that seem senseless and trying to remember something they spent years forgetting.

The Footprints Are There

I remember asking my therapist how he could think my father had sexually abused me when I didn't remember a thing. He said it was like walking through the woods after a snowfall and seeing the footprints of an animal that had passed. You don't have to see the animal to know it had been there. He said, "I can see the tracks throughout your life—the monster has been there."

Throughout my life, because I had no memory of the incest, the trauma asserted itself by breaking through in ways that didn't make any sense to me at the time. When elements in my present life in some way repeated some element in the incest experience, I would have a "recurrence." But since I didn't remember the incest, the recurrence would just seem like a crazy and unexplainable event, such as an episode of rage, or uncontrolled crying, or some weird fear that made no sense.

When my therapist identified the incest, I found the recurrences got worse! He must have stirred things up, but since I still didn't remember, the denial just intensified. So, for the first two years after the incest was identified in therapy, I had the most problems with recurring nightmares, hallucinations, fears and phobias, and flashbacks (intense episodes of crying, anger or panic). My therapist actually used these to help me get back to the incest trauma. It took years— about six years of intermittent therapy—to remember the incest.

Dissociation and Depersonalization—Habits of Survival

I dissociate wildly in all kinds of situations where I feel the slightest threat or stress or inadequacy. It is amazing to me how many and varied those situations are. I did it at work real badly. If I had any type of stressful confrontation or conflict situation at work with someone who I perceived to have power over me, I would dissociate. I would be sitting at the conference table and, all of a sudden, I wouldn't be able to argue, I would just sort of go mute. I'd just sort of smile and nod, agree with everything, not respond, and sweat. Then later, back at my desk, I'd get myself together and realize that I wasn't there. I was totally ineffective at my job in those situations. It was terribly distressing because I had a great deal of responsibility, and I felt, "This should not be happening to me, a grown woman."

The dissociation at work was very pronounced when I started a new career about 12 years ago. When I started this new career, all of a sudden I was thrown in with some powerful men who had a lot of authority. Often I would find myself in situations with a client where I would be one-on-one and I was expected to know something. I would be tense, and the next thing I knew I'd dissociate. It would take the form of being completely confused and not being able to understand what anyone was saying to me. It was awful.

I remember one of the partners in the firm once was going over a client problem with me. He kept going over it, over and over and over again, and I could not understand what he was saying. He might have been speaking another language, that's how bad it was This partner got really angry with me and said, "Are you stupid? You should know all this." I got more and more flustered and more and more confused, and I couldn't understand anything he said. Well, they took me off that job, and it hurt me real bad.

About two months later, a friend of mine, who had taken over that job for me, came in with the product, a management plan. I was supposed to review it as part of a routine peer review. When I read over the whole thing—the problem, the answers to the problem, the recommendations—it was very simple. I couldn't understand why I had not been able to understand it the first time. Why had I gotten so confused? That was a form of dissociation for me. In situations like that with a man in authority who expected me to know something, I would dissociate badly. Of course, the connection would be the abuse; it's real clear now. It was not at all clear until I remembered.

Dissociation would happen socially, not just at work. I would be with people who didn't know much about me, didn't know about the incest, didn't know how "bad" I was, only knew the superficial me, the "me" that had achieved some professional stature. It's amazing, I can see how I thought, "If they really knew about me." I would dissociate at parties, and I'd come home later that night and it would be like I had never gone. Someone else was at that party saying all the right things, smiling, nodding, and sweating from anxiety. The real me was a little girl who crawled off into a very dark place, put her head down on her knees, and just sat there waiting for it to be over, so that she could cry and grieve a little and not have to act happy.

I still dissociate badly during sex. I dissociate in any kind of power imbalance, though not as much as I used to. I thought I was getting better, but that's only because I've been home alone quite a bit, ever since I quit my job and became a consultant. Since the office was a place where dissociation was most common, I haven't had to face it since going out on my own.

There are so many situations in which I dissociate. I dissociate with my in-laws, with my parents, with neighbors.

I also depersonalize a lot. I think of myself as if I'm another person, a character in a movie or the subject of a newspaper article. I will see myself doing whatever I'm doing, as if I'm this character and not me. I'll construct and hear a running narrative about her: "Now she's rocking the baby. Now she's cooking dinner," and so on. Most of my fears take this form. I'll see myself being overcome by a horrible tragedy and hear people talking about it or commenting on it. I'll see myself struggling to escape or to protect myself and feel how pitiful and useless my efforts are, and feel the sadness and horror, but I'll be seeing myself as if from a distance, and part of me will be split away as the narrator. Sometimes I do this when I'm trying to be positive and reassure myself—I'll "talk" about myself positively as if I'm another person. I'll see myself as another person and hear myself discussed in positive terms by a narrator as in a book or movie or news article.

I know these dissociative habits are a big problem, but not as bad as they could have been. I never split away completely, so I'm not a classic multiple personality. But I understand very well how multiples can happen. I think I was dissociated for the first 20 years of my life, at least 20 years. But I remained one person.

Dissociative Recurrences

Another type of dissociation that happens is different. Instead of detaching from the present and letting *external* people or circumstances control my behavior, I detach from the present and let some inappropriate *internal* force from the past take control of my behavior. In both cases, I lose control. I'm gone.

This other type of dissociation happens when something in the present is similar in some way to the incest experience, although at the time I have no awareness of the connection. When it happens, I lose touch with the present and respond to it as if it is something that happened in the past. My behavior will be very intense and inappropriate. Later it all seems like a bad dream, and I am embarrassed and bewildered by my behavior.

The problem with this type of dissociation (or "recurrence," because it's a recurrence of something from the past) is that until I remembered the incest, they made absolutely no sense to me. I just felt that sometimes I went "crazy."

Most examples of this type of dissociation happened within the context of a relationship with a man. The man would say or do something pretty ordinary, but I would respond in a crazy way, very emotional and sometimes violent.

Once I was involved with a man who was younger than I, very emotionally inaccessible and distant, like all the men I picked. I was having the usual tortured relationship with him. One night when he was staying at my house, he was tired and did not want to have sex. This was before I remembered the incest and was still trying to enjoy sex.

His desire to sleep was not rejecting or hostile; he was simply exhausted. But something in me responded with a volcanic eruption of pain and rage. I felt he hated me and was rejecting me entirely; that I was being destroyed, annihilated by him—my self-worth, my self-ness totally wiped out by his rejection. I felt he loathed me, was disgusted by my sexuality; that I was a disgusting, repulsive creature to him.

I got totally out of control and attacked him physically. I remember throwing a lamp at him. Luckily I missed, and it hit the wall and shattered. He was terrified, and left. That was the end of that relationship. The next morning it all felt unreal, like a bad dream. I was ashamed and scared by my behavior.

These episodes stopped when I began through therapy to place those feelings on things that had happened in the past, rather than getting them confused with the present.

One thing I want to point out about those episodes that was important was the way I would be "split" at the time they were happening. Usually, a part of me, some fragment of myself, would be watching myself go out of control and do these crazy things, and know they were wrong, and not even want to do it, but be unable to stop it. That made it all the more upsetting and frustrating, because I felt I ought to be able to control it, and I hated myself for "letting" it happen.

As I progress in therapy and confront the abuse, these alien feelings become connected to my experiences in the past. They are no longer "loose" and no longer pop up unexpectedly to sabotage my life. And since I've put them where they belong, which is the past, they don't intrude now. They are relegated to an appropriate place.

Behavioral Recurrences
Artistic Renderings

At the point in my therapy when I knew in my gut that my therapist was right, that it had really happened, I was still denying it to myself. I started drawing little pictures. They were like ghosts, little ghosts with great, bleeding eyes, and instead of a mouth a huge gash right in the center of the body. When I look at them now, I can see clearly the sexual image. At the time, I could not. I also drew a woman kneeling, in a very defeated way, and I think that may have been another association.

Sexual

I think much of my compulsion to have secret sexual relationships was a recurrence. I was reenacting my relationship with my father and trying to get it to turn out differently. In the reenactment, I was trying to be the one in control. And I was trying to make him love me and accept me. The fantasy ending would be that I would be totally in command and he would want to take care of me. Of course it never happened. And if one of those men had ever actually done that, I would have dropped him immediately! I don't have any of that compulsion anymore.

Emotional Recurrences

Fainting

The onset of puberty started stirring up things, I guess, because a few things happened that I think were repetitions of some aspect of the incest. We discussed these in therapy. I remember them really clearly, though I didn't think anything of it until I started connecting to it in therapy. We were watching a movie on TV—it was *King Kong*. I was just watching it off and on. I thought it was pretty silly. I must have been 11 or 12. My mom and dad were there, I remember, and my brother. A part came on when King Kong picked up the woman and started flailing about, and she was really helpless, screaming. Well, I started shaking real bad, and my teeth were chattering, and I began to hyperventilate—my hands curled up. I almost passed out. I was very distressed and began to cry. My mom and dad helped me to bed, and my mom stayed with me. She was really worried. It was a real mystery as to why I did that. Now I think it's because of the association with the abuse—the big monster, little person, making strange noises and flailing about.

Another recurrence happened when I had first communion. I was kneeling at the altar taking communion. There I was on my knees, with my hands folded, and this man started coming toward me, and he was going to put something in my mouth, a wafer. I started getting dizzy; I had this funny feeling in my stomach, lines appeared before my eyes, and I couldn't hear. I remember saying, "Mommy," or something like that. Then apparently I flipped backwards and went head first down three steps right in front of the whole congregation, out cold, landed on my head with my dress over my head. I saw no connection with the abuse until I was in therapy.

It happened again when I was in my twenties. I have always avoided monster movies or movies with any violence, but once I went to what I thought was a wilderness movie and was taken completely by surprise. There was a scene where a man is in the woods and is attacked without warning by a bear. At the sight of the man being helpless and mauled by the bear, I passed out cold. My husband had to get an usher and drag me up the aisle to the lobby where I regained consciousness. It was embarrassing. I had wet my pants. I was old enough then to know that there should be some reason for this. I remember thinking it had something to do with my dad—but I thought it was because he was in the Middle East where there was violence! I went around telling people I could not stand any violence because I was afraid for my dad.

Panic

My therapist identified emotional recurrences in which I was acting out some part of the abuse in my personal life. I remember the first time a boyfriend wanted to have oral sex. I was 14, but we had been having sexual relations for quite a while. He wanted to do it to me, and he did. I became helpless and I dissociated real badly. I kind of went numb and kind of went into shock. I was in a state of numbness and panic. I couldn't talk, or anything.

I remember we got dressed, and we were driving somewhere to go to get something to eat, and, all of a sudden, I reacted with panic. I jumped out of the car and ran off. I don't even know where we were. We were in the middle of someplace, and I just started running blindly. I don't know what happened. It's kind of foggy to me. Somehow he found me, and I wouldn't get in the car with him; I was screaming hysterically at him. He got scared. He thought he was going to be arrested, and he forcibly got me into the car, and forcibly kept me in the car, and somehow drove me home. I went into my room for a couple of days. I was in real bad shape. That was when I was about 14; I had been having sex for years. I couldn't understand what was wrong.

Crying

One of the most significant recurrences I had happened regularly. I would grieve and cry after sex. This went on for years, ever since I first started having any type of sexual activity, when I was 12, until even now. After sex, I grieve. I feel overwhelmed with grief, and I cry. I never knew why. I thought it was normal for everyone to feel grief after sex, to feel real abandoned and cry.

I only did it if I experienced any sexual pleasure. When I was dissociated and felt nothing (which was most often), I didn't. I always thought it was a normal emotional release. My sexual partners would be upset and surprised about it. I would sort of say, "What's the big deal? I thought everybody did this." But everybody didn't do it.

When I had my memory dream, when I first remembered the incest, the overwhelming feeling associated with it was grief. It was the same feeling I had had after sex for all those years. In my memory dream, it was clear to me why I was having that feeling of grief. It was a really painful feeling. I'll know that I'm better when I don't have that feeling after sex anymore and I don't cry.

Flashbacks

Another recurrence I had was shortly after I remembered the incest. I was out with my husband and daughter, and it was a beautiful day. We had gone out for lunch, and on the way back, we had a coupon for a free car wash. So we said, "All right, let's take this old car to the car wash." I had never been through a car wash before.

I drove into the car wash, and here we were on this little track moving along, no control over where we were, and, all of a sudden, we were in this very dark enclosed place. All the windows were rolled up and things started happening. A blue cloth came down around the car, very quickly. The cloths were moving back and forth and hitting the car, and there was noise, confusion, and heat, and I was not in control. All of a sudden, I flipped out.

Later, I realized those blue cloths were like the blue curtain around the bathroom area in the basement where I was abused. Now, at that time, I had not remembered the blue curtain in the bathroom. But I started shaking uncontrollably. I started screaming and crying hysterically and babbling things I didn't understand. I was screaming and crying and saying, "Nobody can help me. Nobody's going to help me. Can't somebody help me? Nobody's going to help me." My husband had to take over, and he drove to a corner of the parking lot. I couldn't do anything.

I don't have much of a memory of what happened. Somehow he got me home. I lay on the bed for quite a long time. Then I went into a kind of shock. I couldn't seem to get in touch with where I was. I felt totally spaced out, and I threw up. I also remember opening the car door to throw up on the way home. It took me about ten hours to come back. I believe I relived some of the trauma. Later I remembered that the curtain around the toilet in the basement where I was abused was blue.

Physical Sensations

There is an aspect of these recurrences that is very upsetting and confusing for me and very shameful for me. When I had my first memory dream, when I first remembered the incest and knew it was real, aside from being astonished by the feelings of love I had for my father, another strange and upsetting part of the memory was that I experienced some sexual arousal with it. Also, when I had the recurrence in the car wash, what accompanied all those emotions was a strong feeling of sexual arousal, along with nausea and physical pain. That made me feel crazy and ashamed. Here this horrible thing had happened to me, but I had had some physical response to what he did to me. I think that contributes a lot to the sense of shame. As if, by feeling sexually aroused, I was responsible. I feel I should not have had those feelings, that by having them I had accepted his actions. I know it isn't true, but I still have the feeling.

Phobias and Fears

All my life, I have had problems with phobias, and the fears I have are of everything. It's not just a fear of this or that. My first therapist called it agoraphobia, which is fear of leaving the house. I was afraid many times to leave the house when I first went into therapy. After my baby was born, it got worse. I was afraid of everything.

Here's how it worked: there would be days when I could not answer the phone, because I couldn't stand the fear and anxiety of what was going to be on the other end. I could not open my mail because I thought, "I can't deal with the mail. I'm afraid of what's in the mail." I would stay in my house and not go out because I couldn't deal with what was out there. I couldn't deal with driving. There were cars out there that could hit me. I couldn't deal with the high tension wires that could fall on my car. A bridge could collapse, somebody could shoot me, there could be some maniac out there shooting, ready to shoot me.

Just my general fear of everything probably came from being badly abused at such an early age, before I had developed a good solid basis of reality. I had no secure boundaries, everything could get to me. Most children grow up and learn that bad things happen, but in general, the world is a pretty reliable place. I grew up feeling the world is a totally unreliable place, where sometimes good things happen. That's a completely different orientation.

The phobias intensified right before my daughter was born, then after she was born they skyrocketed. I remember the day before she was born I had to have some work done in my basement, and the plumbers were going to come. I had a vivid image of a plumber, or a man in a uniform, coming up the stairs from the basement with a horrible look on his face, and I knew he was going to kill me. I had to have a neighbor come over and sit with me while the plumbers were there because I was so sure they were going to kill me.

At that time, I had not yet remembered the incest, but I had this thing about basements. I was terrified of them. When I would go down into my basement, I would be doing whatever I had planned to do, and suddenly I would get spooked. A panic would overcome me and I would just rush up the stairs terrified, and I didn't know why. All basements did that to me. Later on, when I remembered the incest, I remembered it happened in the basement, so no wonder I had these waves of panic come over me in basements. After I started remembering the incest, all this began to make sense, but until I remembered it, all I knew was I had these crazy episodes in basements, and that I had crazy fears in general of going anywhere or leaving the house.

I developed a very odd phobia at one point in my therapy. Although we were talking about the incest, I had not yet remembered. I had been having a clandestine sexual relationship, which was about the only kind I knew how to have, with a man at work who was living with a Chinese girl. He told me he was going to marry her and would never leave her, so I knew what his situation was. Somehow in my subconscious or whatever, the Chinese girl he was living with became representative of my mother, I guess. He was father and she was my mother, somehow. This is what we kicked around in therapy—later.

Anyway, I was very emotionally involved with this guy in a sick way. At his father's funeral, I found out that he had decided to get engaged and was going to marry her, in fact she walked up to me and shoved her hand with a ring on it in my face, and said, "Look, we finally decided to get married."

It was like the bottom fell out of my world. What I think was happening was somehow I was reexperiencing the feelings of betrayal and rejection I had as a child. Somehow I was now a bad person. I was no good, and she was his perfect little queen.

After that, if I saw a Chinese female I would go into a panic and run, involuntarily, no matter where I was. The first time it happened was a couple of days after the funeral. I was in a department store buying a baby present for a friend of mine. I was standing at the counter getting out my credit card to pay for it when some people came in behind me. I turned around and looked at them, and they were Chinese. At the head of this crowd was a Chinese woman, with long black hair.

I went into a panic and lost all control. I dropped my credit card and ran out of that department and through the store, totally out of control. I left my purse there. I left all my belongings and purchases there; I was in a total panic. Then I was out on the street, and I didn't know where I was going. After running a short distance, I finally got my mind back and I realized what I had done. I was so embarrassed; I was crying.

I waited a couple of minutes, and then I sort of sneaked back to the store and went up to the department where I had left my purse. The sales girl was there. She said, "What happened to you?" I said, "I started feeling real sick, so I had to run to the bathroom," and she believed me.

It happened again. I was at a friend's house, and it's real funny, because she's a therapist. I was leaving her house, and I was standing outside at my car talking to her. I was telling her about how I had this trouble with Chinese people. All of a sudden, a carload of Chinese pulled up at the house next door and started getting out of the car. I had this feeling of unreality, and the next thing I knew I was running down the street.

I stopped after a couple of blocks. I just sat down on the sidewalk, crying and laughing at the same time. I felt so ridiculous. I waited a while for the Chinese people to go away and I went back to the car. My friend was standing there looking at me, and she said, "You know, Noelle, you've really got a problem here. You really have to get some help on this." It took a long time for my phobia of Chinese people to go away, but it did go away.

Depression, Suicide

I was depressed and suicidal most of my life, off and on. I tried to commit suicide for the first time when I was 15. I took bottles of pills—aspirin and all kinds of stuff. Then I lay down on the couch and decided I would just die there. I passed out. Apparently I slept on that couch totally unconscious and unmoving for 16 hours and my parents did not notice. That shows something about what was wrong with my family. It was a combination of abuse and neglect.

When I finally did come to, I couldn't go to school or anything. I couldn't hear very well—apparently the drugs I took impaired my nerves. I was dizzy. I never told them I tried to commit suicide. They didn't ask; I didn't tell them. I was disappointed I had awakened, but I decided not to bother to try again. It seemed as pointless and futile as everything else.

Actually that was the only time I really tried to commit suicide explicitly. Other ways I tried to do it were really stupid, like driving at a 120 miles per hour in traffic, and stuff like that. Those were kind of impulsive acts I did that were very dangerous and self-destructive.

Cognitive Recurrences

Hallucinations

I started hallucinating spiders when I was 18. I would be awake; it would often be at night when I was getting ready for bed, or early in the morning when I just woke up. That's how it started. I would see large spiders on the wall or coming down at me from the ceiling. I wouldn't be asleep. I would be awake and these would be quite clear. They would be so clear I would scream and hit at them, or run away. So, it wasn't anything fuzzy or imaginary or vague; they were real clear spiders.

Then, as time went on, I saw them more and more. I would see them at various times. For example, sometimes I would go down in the basement and open the basement door, and I would see a spider about as big as a bushel basket. It would kind of breathe or pulsate. It would have this pulsating motion. I'd slam the door and get myself together and open the door again and see if it was still there.

My first husband got so accustomed to me seeing spiders at night that when I'd start screaming and pointing at the wall, he'd go over and calmly kill the spider, or knock it off, or do something to remove the spider. That seemed to satisfy me. As time went by, the spiders changed too. When I got into therapy and I started dealing with the incest, even before I remembered it, the spiders acquired red legs that looked like penises. I didn't make that connection until much later.

Anyway, the spiders were a recurring and continuous type of hallucination that I had all the time. Even now, I have them on rare occasions. When things are real bad, I might see one. If I go down in the basement when it's dark, I'll see one, pulsating in the dark. It hardly ever happens anymore.

Another hallucination I had that was a real scary and frightening one was when I first started therapy and I was first getting into the incest. Things were real tough in my life at that time, but when I had the hallucination I was having a great evening, actually. I was out with two friends of mine, a couple I know, and we were at a lovely Italian restaurant downtown. I was having one of my favorite Italian dinners, calamari in marinara sauce. I was not drinking, because I hardly ever drank at that time anyway.

We were talking, and I looked up as some people were leaving a table near us. I happened to glance up as they walked by our table, and I saw a woman who was very well dressed, with a hat; impeccably dressed, but she had the face of a lizard. It wasn't a human face, it was a really awful looking lizard face. Her skin looked like inhuman skin. There was strange pink tissue forming a ridge across her eyes, and the same weird pink tissue formed striped-like things going up into her forehead. She had a nose that was two holes, and a slit-like mouth like a lizard has, and then this strange pink tissue going down from the corners of her mouth to her throat and hanging down in folds on her throat. It was a lizard face. It was shocking.

I looked up, saw this face, and I just froze. She walked by the table and went out the door with her friends. It happened in just a few seconds. I looked at my friends to see if they had noticed, and they didn't seem to have noticed; they went on talking. I pointed at her and stood up, and I started going, "Uh, uh, uh, did you see that?" They didn't seem to have any reaction at all. I said, "Did you see that woman?" and they said, "No." I said, "She looked like a lizard," and they just laughed. They thought I was joking; they had no idea.

I'll tell you the truth, for a long time I didn't recognize that as an hallucination. I thought I had really seen a lizard or a human being that somehow had a deformity to make her look like a lizard, or even someone disguised as a lizard. It took me a long time to accept the fact that it really was an hallucination. That was the most difficult hallucination I had to deal with, because it was so bizarre.

Nightmares

The first recurring dream I remember started when I was in my late teens, early twenties. It was a dream of being pursued by a man in a dark and closed place. The outcome was always the same. I would run up some stairs to get away, but he would always catch me and kill me. I could never get away from this dark, faceless man.

There would always be confusion about who he was. Sometimes I would think I knew him, but then I would think, no, it can't be him. Then, later, as my therapy progressed, this dream recurred again. Sometimes it would be my father, but then he would change and not be my father. I felt real confused, like, "Could this be my father? No, it couldn't be my father."

One day, I remember it was the spring of 1972, I had this dream, and as he was pursuing me up these stairs, I realized I could kill him, and I did. I turned around and pushed him, and he went crashing down the stairs and landed at the bottom dead. I ran down the stairs in my dream and stood over the body exulting. I had this incredible feeling of relief and liberation and freedom and joy. I woke up from that dream exultant. I remember going around elated for the rest of the day. I was so happy. I felt so free, and, you know, that sense of freedom and liberation lasted. That was my first step toward getting better and I hadn't even known what that dream was about. But that's a point of my life when I decided, "I'm going to live my life," and I did.

That same night I had another wonderful dream. It was a beautiful dream, in color, of all these beautiful, colorful birds flitting around and chirping happily. They were real funny, cute little birds; they landed on skis. That was a joy dream, I think. It was a dream about the joy of life—that night I had recaptured some of that joy of life by killing my pursuer. I think at that point I was on my way to getting better. It was going to be a fifteen-year process, but I was going to get better. The dream of being chased by a man came back later when I was in therapy with more details and with variations.

After that, I did have other significant dreams, but I didn't know they were significant. I had two dreams that were recurrent. One was about my contact lenses, and I had it whenever I went into a stressful situation like a change in my life.

In my dream, I wore contacts, and I knew I was helpless and couldn't see without them. I would be wearing my contacts, and, all of a sudden, I would have to take one of them out because something was in my eye, hurting me, and I'd have to put it in my mouth. When I put my contact in my mouth, all of a sudden it would get big. I would feel it get bigger and bigger and bigger, and finally I would pull this thing, it was huge, out of my mouth, and here would be a contact lens that was as big as a saucer. I'd be terrified. And I'd be thinking, how did it get that big? What am I going to do now? I'll never be able to get this thing back in my eye. I would be terrified, knowing I was helpless. I can't get it back in my mouth. How is it going to get back in my eye? How will it ever get small again? This dream was terrifying. I would wake up sweating and trying to scream.

Well, you know, I had that dream over and over and over again and I never knew what it meant, until, of course, I had my first memory, and then I realized that that's what my father had done. He had forced me to perform oral sex, and that dream was a reccurence of the sexual act, but of course it took me years and years to know that. (While editing this, I had a flashback when I went over the words "because something was in my eye, hurting me" of my father trying to push the penis into me and hurting me. I had intense vaginal and lower pelvic pain that lasted two days. This was a new memory for me.)

Another recurring dream I had that was really important, was a bathroom dream. I would often have terrifying, fearful dreams where I would be in a bathroom sitting on the toilet, and I'd be real aware that my genitals were exposed and there was no door to this bathroom, and people could come in and see me, and they'd be able to touch me, and I'd be terrified. In another version of this, I would have to urinate badly but could not find a bathroom that wasn't exposed, that had a door. I wanted to go to the bathroom as fast as I could and get out of there, but I couldn't urinate because someone was coming. It was usually a man, and the terror I had and this feeling of being exposed, that my genitals were exposed, it was just an awful dream.

That's what happened when I was little—the bathroom in the basement where I was abused didn't have a door. Actually, it was just a toilet and a curtain around it, and that's where my father abused me. I couldn't keep him out. I couldn't. There was no door to close; I could not be safe in the bathroom. That's what that dream was about. But, of course, I didn't know that until ten years later.

Finally, the incest became known to me through a dream. I had it at five o'clock in the morning, and it was about me as a little girl. I was in the bathroom in the basement, and my father came to me. He came through a curtain, a very young man, and he was saying "It's all right, don't worry. It's just a game." He was so nervous and tense, and the look on his face was so strange, I knew it was serious and this was a bad thing. But I wanted so badly to believe him, so I did what he told me to do. He made me sit on the toilet (which looked huge, because I was little) a certain way, then he did some sexual things, oral-genital, while he was watching the door at the top of the stairs. All the while I was afraid, I was terrified, but kept telling myself it was all right; it really was a game. This was the part of the dream that was a memory.

Then there was a whole bunch of jumbled other things that were not actual memories. I was trying to hide him, because they were going to come and take him away and kill him—I knew he was in great danger and I loved him terribly. So I hid him under my bed. Then the bed turned into a boardwalk at the beach, and they were coming after him, and they were going to take him away. And the next thing I knew I was lying on the floor at my grandfather's house next to a baby, and I was in a lot of pain in the vagina and lower pelvis. I said to my mother, "Oh I'm going to have a baby, but it's all right. I did it all by myself; there is no father." Then my mother picked up the phone. Then there was a part where my grandfather was looking for my father. The whole dream was very stressful.

Anyway, when I woke up, I was screaming and crying hysterically and I could not stop crying or get myself composed for six hours. The pelvic pain lasted all day. The feeling that something in the present was unreal lasted several days. I went to my therapist, who for five years had been working on getting me to recognize the sexual abuse by trying to show me the ways in which my current experiences contained elements of the abuse. I went to him and I said, "You can break out the champagne now, you were right." I said, "I never believed you. I wanted you to be wrong, but I can't deny it anymore. You were right. It really happened, and I hope you are happy." I was heartbroken. I grieved and grieved and grieved, but then I started making real progress in therapy, and it was because my dream broke the denial.

I had other dreams that were related to the incest. I had more bathroom dreams that involved a blue bathroom curtain. I also had a dream about my father pointing to pictures in a book and accusing me of doing sexual things, and feeling totally, helplessly confused, because I couldn't understand why my father was angry and screaming at me and accusing me of doing bad things when he knew he had done them to me himself.

Then, when I saw the pictures in the book, I was terrified, because I thought, "Oh, my God, it's in a book. Now everybody knows. I'm really in trouble now." I was terrified because I was so little that I thought we were the only people in the world who ever did those things, and if there were pictures of it in a book then it had to be us, and now everybody would know, and, boy, was I in trouble now. This was a real important dream, because, again, I was a three-year-old in this dream. I had the thoughts, feelings, and perspective of a three-year-old. It was coming back to me, the feelings of betrayal, grief; the fear of punishment, of discovery. It was all there.

I had another dream that was a healing dream. In it I was only about two years old. I ran to my daddy, and he picked me up and he kind of held me up, threw me up in the air, and then caught me and gave me a huge hug. And the feeling of this dream was, "I love you and you love me, and everything's all right. I didn't do a bad thing. I'm a good little girl." This must have been a dream about feelings that dated back to before the abuse. It was me getting in touch with a happier time, before I was abused, when everything was all right, and that was a real important dream.

That dream preceded a period of my life when everything got worse. Because that was the stage at which I got in touch with some incredible grief and pain, which I had not been able to access before. I had to have a feeling for what I had lost before I could process the pain and grief of losing it. I had to go that far back in time, and that dream represented me reaching back into myself and finding the feelings of love and peace and contentment I had lost. There followed then a really bad period of months, when I just hit bottom. While I was at the bottom, I had another important dream.

In the dream, I was at a beach house. My whole family had been at this house, and it was a very old house. I was in a room, and I was looking out a window. The wood and the boards around the window were kind of bleached and silvery grey, like wood gets when it's exposed to the weather. The light in this dream was very bright and illuminating like light is when it's reflected off water. There was a breeze, and it was just so bright.

I was at this house, and my whole family had been there, but they were all gone now. I was the last one to leave this house. I had a sleeping bag sort of laid out on the shelf, and I was rolling it up and putting it away. There were some books on a shelf, and I was putting those away, too. I picked one up and I looked at it and I opened it, and I realized that this was the book of my parents' life.

I leafed through this book, and it was a tragic, sad book. Here they were: there were happy pictures of them as this beautiful, young, happy couple with everything in the world to look forward to. Then, page after page, there was grief and pain and loss and tragedy, just the terrible tragedy of our family. I was overwhelmed with feelings of sadness and loss. Suddenly, my mother came and appeared beside me. She looked at me, and her eyes were very understanding and very sad, and she said, "Oh, I see you've found the book," and I said, "Yes, I found the book." And she said, "That is the saddest book you'll ever read," and then she was gone.

I looked at the book, and I realized there was a part missing. The last chapter was missing, and I had to write that chapter. I knew then that the book was sadder than even she would ever know. It was sadder than anyone had ever known, because I had to write the last chapter, and it was mine. They would never know how sad it really was.

That was a hard dream. It marked the beginning of my realization of how horrible the devastation had been for me, for my family. How we had lost so much to alcoholism, abuse, and denial. I had lost my parents at an early age. I had pretty much left home emotionally at the age of three and lost my mother and father, lost my childhood, lost everything, and that's what the dream was about. I had to face up to that, had to leave that house, and I had to write that chapter. Then the book would be finished; it would be over. That was one of the last dreams I had that was significant about incest.

I had a dream that was a detachment dream in which I confronted my father with what he did, and he just said, "Oh well, so what. I'm not going to let you make a big deal out of it. I've paid my dues, and so what, it never happened anyway." That was a detachment dream. It sort of indicated I had reached a point now where nothing he said mattered anymore. Nothing he did mattered anymore.

Dreams are important; nightmares are important. They're part of the trauma, but they can also be used as a tool to get better. I wonder if I would have been able to break through my denial if I had not remembered the incest in a dream. I don't know.

Megan

Many of us have problems with sex. Megan did not remember her rape by a brother, but her body did. She avoided sex carefully, but when she finally had her first sexual experience, her physical response constituted a type of recurrence that may be familiar to you.

Recurrences

Physical

Before I ever had any memory of my brother raping me, I had a funny thing happen that was related to it. I had known a man as a friend for years and years, and then we started dating. I was 26, and so was he. He is the only one of three men I have had sex with in my 35 years. But the sex was very difficult. I did not know why, but I could not stand having him on top of me. I found it unbearable, and I told him we had to find another way.

So we tried every position you can imagine, anything other than him on top. Nothing worked. It took him two weeks to penetrate me, two weeks of trying every single night. When he finally did, he had to force it. By that time, I had reached the point where I was saying, "I don't care what it takes, let's just get it over with." He kept saying to me, "Are you sure this is worth it? Are you sure this is enjoyable?" And I kept saying, "People have been doing this for thousands of years, so it can't be this hard or I would never have been born." I kept saying, "I can't believe my parents had any children, I don't know why anyone would do this." It was just horrible. So finally I said, "Just do whatever it takes, I don't care."

Well, as a result, I ended up ripped and torn. I was bleeding like hell. I went to the gynecologist the next day, and he just kept saying, "I don't understand why you're torn so badly." I was very honest with him. I told him it was the first time I had had sex, but he kept saying, "I don't understand, there isn't anything physiologically to account for it." Later, when I was in therapy, my therapist explained that there is a spasm that happens when you experience sex as a trauma. And that's what my body was doing; it was saying, "Don't do this to me." Also, when I remembered my brother raping me, I remembered being powerless with him on top of me. That was why I couldn't stand having a man on top.

Nightmares

I had a terrible nightmare, an absolutely horrible nightmare, that I still can remember—very, very Freudian. It happened the night he finally did penetrate me. In my dream, I dreamt that there were men breaking into my house, and they all were carrying pistols and dressed in black, and they robbed my jewels. The therapist kept saying, "You're classic, you're classic."

Dissociation

I did not remember my brother raping me until I had been in therapy for years. I started remembering when I went with a group. First, I started by just having the thought—it just came to me that he raped me. It didn't have any feelings or emotions attached; it was just a thought. I did not remember any details, and the thought didn't have any other content. Then one night, after group, I remembered him doing it. I remembered where and when. It came very quickly, all at once, in a flash. I was calm, and I still did not have the actual reexperience of it. But after that, I became terrified that I would remember all the details, that the whole experience would come back. I was especially afraid that if I ever had sex again, I would remember everything. But I talked about it in group, and everyone agreed that if I ever started to remember and felt that I was going to have a crisis, I would call members of the group and they would come over immediately.

For a few weeks, I was terrified every night that I would be alone and remember. I had the phone numbers and held onto them. But then it passed. I never remembered the rape in detail, and I never had the crisis. I got through that fear of it with the help of the group. I think that just knowing I had people who would be there when I needed them helped it pass.

A recurrence can be a direct re-experience of the incest trauma. When this happens we call it a "flashback." It feels as if you are suddenly transported back to a different time and experience, but you are here. That feeling of being there but also here is very disorienting. It also frightens us to be so vulnerable to the past. It helps to remember that these experiences stop happening when we address the incest trauma directly.

Recurrences

Physical

The sexual dysfunction I felt was what sent me into therapy. Before we were married, sex was not a problem. After we were first married it never was right. I guess it went on for two years where I was uncomfortable making love. I would always end up doing it to please Danny. We never discussed it, really, until it just got absolutely too, too bad to not talk about. That was when I went into the Women's Center. It was the morning when we hadn't made love in a long time because whenever he would touch me I would recoil.

I look back and I believe what kept me from having sex with him was not necessarily flashbacks in my mind, but in my body. I couldn't help them. I don't know how to explain it, but it wasn't in the mind. It was a remembering, my body remembering a touch that was inappropriate. My body would remember and it would respond with repulsive feelings. I guess in a way my subconscious was saying, "No, it's not right. I'm not going to allow this again." I would recoil. I would hate it. If we did make love I would never enjoy it.

I went to doctors and kept telling them that it was painful to have sex. They would examine me and tell me, "I can find nothing wrong; there is no physical reason for sex to be painful for you." Then I found out later that there is a spasm that happens when your body or your mind does not want to have sex, and that was what was happening.

This was very painful for the two of us, because we had gone through periods where sex was very, very good, before we were married. No problems at all. Then this sexual dysfunction went on for about two years. That was when I was afraid I was going to lose my husband. Here I was, I was pregnant and had one young child already, and the idea of losing my husband was absolutely intolerable. What was I going to do? He had always been the person I could count on, that I could lean on, and who truly loved me, although I really didn't know it at the time. But I told him about it, and he was upset and that was when I went into therapy. I went into therapy, but even after I started therapy, when we did make love, it was always a very, very difficult thing.

Flashbacks

Anyway, we got to a certain point, I don't exactly remember when it was, but I had a terrible, terrible flashback in my mind. It was extremely painful and I was terribly upset by it. Danny and I would always play around, we'd always fool around in a sexual way and a joking way. I suppose that's what makes us healthy sexually, is that we play around together at home. I guess I was flirting with him, but he touched my breast and I couldn't get away fast enough. I pushed him away, I pushed his hand away and grabbed my clothes, and I just ran.

I was so shocked by what I had felt and what I had seen. I had seen my father touching me and grabbing me. It was terribly, terribly upsetting. I know that you would understand a feeling like that. It was no longer my husband and myself, it was my father and the child I was, and it was a real feeling. It was like I was back to being ten years old. The only thing that was different this time was that it stopped when I told him to stop. He stopped and I left. It was horrible; I was just devastated.

You know how you feel when you can barely function and yet you have to? You have to go on with the dinner and the groceries, and I just was thinking, "My God, I just can't go on with this." If I ever have something like this happen to me again I think I would just die, it was so horrible. Thank God I've never had this again or been that way. I've had remembrances, but that was definitely, definitely the worst.

ANN-MARIE

Recurrences can be very subtle. As I collected material for this section, I found that many survivors have frequent episodes of intense pain in their lives, but little of what I would classify as an emotional or cognitive (nightmares, hallucinations) recurrence. Although I do not have any sound statistical data on what I would call "somatic" or physical recurrences, I suspect that intense recurrent pain may be common in incest survivors. Ann-Marie's headaches struck me as significant, particularly because she is such a highly controlled person. Recurrences will be different for everyone, and they may very well take the form of physical phenomena.

Emotional Recurrences

Fears

Two things here: I have a fear that my stepfather wants to put the moves on me. He and my mom almost separated last October, and through the emotional turmoil that followed, he and I talked about his alcoholism, which had been an open secret and never discussed, and his recovery. He and Mom have lots of problems communicating, and he and I talk a fair amount over the phone. I'm afraid my mom is going to resent that he and I might get close, while he and she have a rough time of it. It feels like a replay of when I was a kid—I sensed my mom's jealousy often, because it was openly acknowledged that I was Daddy's favorite, the apple of his eye, and so on.

I'm afraid my stepfather will mistake my caring for an interest in a different kind of relationship—I don't know how to be emotionally close to him without having to maintain my guard against inappropriate moves he might make. Sometimes my alarm bells go off when he hugs or kisses me—nothing obvious, just the alarm bells go off. Sometimes I wonder if I'm being paranoid, or are my instincts right on? I have learned to pay attention to my instincts. but here that means someone who purports to care for me wants to use me. Who knows? I only see them a couple of times a year, so it doesn't come up often.

Cognitive Recurrences

Nightmares

For years, well back into the time of the incest, I have had two types of recurring nightmares. I can recall one specific dream as an example of one type: I'm in my small home town, walking from my house to the downtown area a short distance away. I'm only a few blocks from downtown (I'm about seven or eight), and I suddenly realize I'm wearing nothing but a sleeveless tank-top style T-shirt that barely covers the front of me. Just then, a male adult who lives two doors from me appears in his car and offers me a ride home. (I vividly remember that car—'60s, white, Chevy Impala with bright red, vinyl interior.) He totally ignores my state of undress as I climb in the car, feeling ashamed and exposed. Then he takes me home. I often had similar dreams of being a young child covered with very little clothing in public with absolutely no erotic intentions, though I don't recall any in the last year.

I've had another recurring nightmare over the years that usually awakens me. I'm being chased by someone evil, and as I try to make my escape, I'm in a building where I go down staircases, through doors, farther and farther into the interior. I usually wake up when I realize that I'm about to run out of places to go. I still have this one occasionally.

Recurrences

Dissociation

The only thing I can say for sure about dissociation is that I think I just shut down, or whatever, when my father was abusing me. As I said, I don't remember him actually raping me, although he did try to have intercourse and I moved him away from the vagina. I don't think I ever really felt any emotions at all while he was doing it. I just don't remember any feelings. There is just nothing. I can only remember sometimes, afterwards, having this feeling that I was special, that I was meant for something.

I'm not aware of dissociation happening to me now. If it does, I don't know it. I mean, it may be happening, but I haven't identified it yet.

Behavioral

I see specific cases where my behavior was influenced by the incest. When I look back, it seems the best sexual relationships I've had were with married men, when I was single. In both cases, they were separated from their wives at the time and both eventually were divorced. I've never had an exciting, fulfilling sex life with any man I was "supposed" to be with or was "allowed" to be with—regular, single boyfriends unattached to anyone—including my husband, although our sex life is the best among those in this category. Recently, I cried out my heartache in group, feeling that my father completely robbed me of a normal sex life as well as the ability to feel worthwhile in my own right. It also turns out that those married men were very skilled in making love to a woman, and the others much less so.

Physical Recurrences

Headaches

My headaches started in high school, early high school. I had such severe headaches, my mother thought it was caused by school. Being a conscientious student, I was taking a full academic schedule. I never got to take art or some of those extra courses because I was carrying math, science, history, English, whatever—five courses, a foreign language. One night at group, we talked about how all of us, in one form or another, have had an extreme amount of physical pain somewhere. So now I think it is related to the incest.

My headaches were close to being migraines. I've never gone to a doctor or had them happen when someone could examine me, but they were the kind where sometimes they would wake me up out of a sound sleep. All I'd want to do is cut off the top of my head. If I could I would just cut it off and set it aside for a while because it's this huge, physical, pounding pain. Up until the last couple of years, they always happened in the hours when I was away from work. The last couple of years they started happening at work as well.

I remember one day, this was like three days before I was getting married, I got one at work in the middle of the day and I took a couple of aspirin. I had a comfy chair in my office, and I tried sitting there and closing my eyes and saying, "I've got to get home while I can still drive." It almost goes behind the eyes and it doesn't cause weird lights or anything, but it really hurts. Well, don't you know I got a speeding ticket on the way home. I was so mad, but I finally got home. I just took aspirin and tried to find a comfortable position where the pain abated somewhat so I could drop off. Eventually I'd drop off asleep, and I'd still feel exhausted.

BRENDA

Some of the more disturbing recurrences are those that leave us feeling a loss of control. Episodes of dissociation in which we can't function properly make us feel vulnerable. Episodes in which we lose physical control of our bodies feel humiliating. It helps to remember that these episodes are no different from the headaches, nightmares, or other intrusions of the incest trauma. They too will pass.

Recurrences

Dissociation

One of the remembrances I had was when I was married to my second husband, when I was entering the deep depression where I was becoming suicidal. I remember going into a somewhat semi-conscious state one evening and not really knowing where I was or what I was doing. Later on, my husband said to me that not only did it scare him to death, but one of the things I kept repeating during this time was, "I'll be good" over and over. I was talking to my mother, expressing how sorry I was that I was such a bad girl and that I would try desperately to be good, and would she love me, things like that. It must have lasted for about an hour. As far as I know, that's the only time that ever happened to me. Like I said, I was really in an extreme state of depression.

I remember as a young child, I was probably about ten or eleven, coming home from church one Sunday and sitting on a bus, with the man sitting across the aisle from me masturbating, and being absolutely horrified. We were the only two people on the bus. I was so terrified I couldn't get up and go to another seat or signal the bus driver, just paralyzed. I'm sure if he had approached me or something, maybe I would have done something, I don't know, but I was terrified into a state in which I couldn't move. When I came home, I remember telling my foster mother about this, and she was making light of it and almost not believing me. I got the distinct impression that she thought I was making all this up.

Physical Recurrences

Headaches

In referring back to the hallucinations and the phobias and fears, what have you. I do remember years of suffering with extreme migrane headaches—headaches so bad I could hardly see. Anyone walking in the room around me would just send pain shooting through my head. Going to numerous doctors, neurologists, having CAT scans done. Thinking for sure I was going to die from some sort of brain tumor, and always tests came back negative, nothing there. Doctors wouldn't understand why I had these kinds of headaches. They were written off as probably stress. In my mind I see it as probably being a suffocating of emotions trying to get out and my not wanting them to come out.

Enuresis

Recently, I went through a somewhat bad depression where I wanted to commit suicide because I thought people didn't love me, no one cared about me. That was followed by a period where I would wet the bed. I did this a couple of times. The shame involved was just tremendous. I remember rushing out and buying a plastic shower curtain to put on the bed so when it happened it wouldn't destroy the mattress. Just the shame of knowing this was happening to me, that I was losing control of my bodily functions.

Like I said, it only happened twice, but it took me about three months to get over it. Even now I still sleep with the shower curtain under the sheets for fear that if something happens, I'll wake up and the bed will be destroyed, or whatever. As my therapist explained it to me later, if you don't let the emotions out, the stress has to come out somewhere. I guess I have now exchanged the headaches for the bedwetting. Like I say, it may have subsided because I don't feel nearly the stress levels that I used to experience.

I know my therapist has told the group a couple of different times that people who cry alleviate some of the stress and poisons from their body. Being a person who does not allow herself to cry, bedwetting has become my way of releasing those stresses and tensions and emotions that can't come out. It's the only way, I guess, my body knows how to cleanse itself. I still find crying a form of weakness, and will do everything within my power not to cry. It also represents a form of humiliation to me, which is indicative of my being out of control. I hope one of these days I'll be able to cry about all the things I need to cry about.

Emotional Recurrences

Fears

When I think back, as a young woman, I remember being petrified of being alone. This all goes back to be alone so much as a small child. Either my mother would be out with one of her johns and we'd be left unprotected, or she'd be out cold, drunk, and we'd be unprotected. She never took care of any of our needs, and as an adult I felt so unprotected when I was by myself. I was afraid to be in the house alone, even when the children were asleep. Many, many nights I'd sleep at the top of the stairs or stay up all night. I guess this helped me develop a need for very little sleep. Even now I survive on four to five hours sleep.

I think I pretty much overcame the fear of being alone. I still don't like it, but I don't suffer the anxieties and the powerful scares of being in the house and being a victim again. What if somebody broke in? What if someone knocked on the door late at night? What would I do? Just so afraid. I'd be unable to function sometimes the next day because I had been up all night. Then I'd probably be not understanding at all with the children when they got up in the morning and feel terribly, terribly put upon to have to get up and function with them, when really what I wanted to do was to go to sleep after being up all night and stressed with fear. I remember that distinctly—sleeping in front of the door in a sitting-up position, so if someone tried to break in I would hear it. Always putting locks on doors; just horrifying fear of being a victim again.

The other fear that I remembered distinctly was going on a date and being petrified that the person would take advantage of me, especially on the car ride. Always in a car with a man I feel like a victim, not knowing what's going to happen, not knowing if I can get out of it. Always on the alert. Dates became nightmares almost. Just afraid, and no matter how many times I went on a date and nothing happened, the next time it was just a new fear all over again. Never trusting. I had a roommate for years, and when she would go away on vacation or a trip or something I remember just being horrified that I would be left alone in the house. Of course, never expressing any of this to anyone, telling anyone about it, because I was afraid they'd laugh at me or think I was some sort of abnormal person, or crazy or something.

Years after being with friends and expressing some of my fears I found that many women are afraid to be alone or afraid of being a rape victim, of someone breaking into their home. That helped me, really helped me not to be afraid so much—knowing that other women suffered the same things I did and they hadn't been victimized. It was one of the things I felt was leading me towards normal.

Cognitive Recurrences

Hallucinations

I remember hallucinating about spiders; it was in cars. Here again, a car is where the incest took place between myself and my foster father. I would be driving down the road and nearly crashing because the gigantic spider landed on the windshield; it would try to claw through the driver's side. Or I would see things out of the side of my eyes like little spiders crawling at the windows. I would be hallucinating when I was driving through downtown traffic. Also, sometimes the buildings would be collapsing around me, and feeling like I was almost in an earthquake. I would be just petrified and be sweating, and my heart just ready to jump out of my chest, and I'd have extreme headaches. Then the hallucinations with buildings collapsing around me would begin, and when I would get to work, I'd be exhausted already.

Nightmares

I remember a continuing dream I had after the incest had stopped. It would recur, not every night, but it recurred until I got into probably my thirties, of a man chasing me, exposing himself, and running through a fog, not getting any assistance, people passing me and not helping me, and always he was just right behind me. I'd wake up, here again, terrified, afraid to go back to sleep, afraid that somewhere in the dream he would catch up with me. The man had no face, he wore a hat, but clearly was exposed, I couldn't figure out why other people couldn't see that.

I don't give myself enough credit for my own knowledge, my own ability, my own experience. I don't know what I know. I assume someone else knows more than I know. That has been one of the hardest things for me, to give myself value. I've always functioned either on automatic, where I did things because I knew I had to or was supposed to, or if someone said to do something, I did it because I didn't have a choice, I had to do it. That comes from my upbringing, because when I was growing up in foster homes, you didn't have a choice, you just did what you were told to do. I carried that forward into my adult years. It's only recently that I've started to say to myself, "Now wait a minute, I'm not stupid!" and started to follow some of my gut reactions.

One of the things that happens to me is when I don't do what is right for me, I start to get confused. My therapist says that should be a trigger for me. When I feel that confusion, I'm doing something that isn't right for me and that is how I'll know it, even though I won't have a clear idea of what it is at first.

ELLEN

Ellen is just starting to identify the effects of incest in her life. With her extreme denial, it is difficult for her. Some of the more obvious signs of the trauma she has recognized, such as her memory loss. She also re-

alizes that dissociation began to happen to her at work. Emotional re-
currences are more difficult for her to identify. Also, although they are
not included in this chapter, her dissociative episodes described in
Chapter 4 (which led to her hospitalization) are a form of recurrence.
It will be useful to go back and re-read her part of Chapter 4 from that
perspective and note that 30 years ago recurrences like these were con-
sidered to be psychotic. We are fortunate to have a better understand-
ing of our problems today.

Recurrences

Dissociation

The first nine years of my life, I don't remember them at all; it has
always been a sort of family joke. My grandmother was apparently a
very loving person to me. She died when I was eight, just after I was
raped, and I cannot remember. My mother always says, "Oh, I think
it's really comical that you can't remember your grandmother." So
I've been working on that, but in my mind, something inside me
wants to say, "This is a hobby, this is a sideline. This isn't real important, this remembering stuff."

After I was raped, my father said, "How could you have done this to
me?" And I think that then and there, I decided that because I had
hurt my father, I had lost him. My mother turned me over to him, so
I figured I had lost her too. My grandmother died shortly after, and I
figured it was because of what I had done. So I think the sum total of
all this in my little-girl mind was that I would be better off not existing. So I just repressed it all.

My dad was the type of person who told us over and over again
when we were children that we were worthless. He'd say, "Do this,
even though I know you can't do it right." So he reinforced those
early experiences over and over again. Now, whenever anybody I love
or start to feel trust for tells me they love me or care about me, I just
lose any feeling I have. It just dissolves completely and I just want to
get away from them.

Another thing, I started dissociating as an adult. I became very
successful in my work, I was giving international papers, and people
were very interested in my work. And something started happening
that frightened me, so I don't go to meetings anymore and I work
alone. What happened was, I started going to meetings and my mind
would go blank. I would see a person, know they were familiar, have
no idea who they were, what work they had done. I couldn't associate

them. Someone would come up to talk to me about their work, and I would be desperately trying to figure out who they were, and it would turn out I had been talking to them the month before.

Emotional

I think my repression of my grandfather's abuse has been total. The recent memories I've had of my mother fighting him off of me are the closest I've come to anything. There have been short flashes—my grandfather's erection, his drooling tobacco juice on the bed—not much. Just enough to make me afraid. Do I want to remember?

And yet, I keep having images come up, and I started having nightmares recently. I've had some reactions that are a little weird. The first one that really shocked me was about six months after I'd been in the incest group. I tried to take the disgusting feelings I had towards the man I was going with, and put them in my grandfather. I had to actually almost physically do it.

Brett (the man I was involved with) and I were driving to the boat for the weekend, and on the way there I was doing this. When we got into the boat, he wanted me to come and sit on his lap. Something in me just said, "No, I'm going to say 'no' to him." He had a way of wanting sex that made it feel like abuse. I didn't feel that he wanted me as a person. It was like I was an ice cream cone or something.

So I pushed him away, and I said "No." As I did, I started crying hysterically. It's never happened like that to me before. It just came out. Every time I said "no" in my mind, I just burst out with more and more tears. I cried for 45 minutes, uncontrollably. He was there. He didn't go anywhere, or tell me I was crazy. He didn't offer much support, and when it was over, I just felt completely removed. If my mother is right, and I'm making all this stuff up, then I'm doing a real good job of it, because I had no control at all over those tears.

CHAPTER 6—FOOTNOTES

1. Description of chronic traumatic neurosis is paraphrased from Gelinas, Denise J., "The Persisting Negative Effects of Incest," *Psychiatry* 46 (November 1983):315–319.
2. Darlene Davis, administrator of Parkside Lodge of Salt Lake City Utah, identified many of these physical symptoms in sexually abused patients. Other practitioners have related similar observations.

7

Therapy: A Series of Small Nuclear Explosions

"The effects of the relational imbalances are usually the symptoms that compel the victim to seek treatment . . . Victims will report family and marital problems, sexual dysfunction, ask for help in dealing with disobedient children, talk about depression, and discuss suicide . . . alcohol and other substance abuse . . . job difficulties . . . anxiety, fears and low self-esteem. Such symptoms are merely a presenting part of the long-term negative effects of incest that often emerge as a result of . . . a developmental trigger, which is . . . any new developmental stage involving some functional area that has been damaged by the incest . . . In therapy . . . discussion of the incest is usually accompanied by very intense emotions as the repressed memories are released[1] . . . The intensity of the affect during this process can be disconcerting for both patient and therapist, and it can easily be mistaken as psychotic decompensation, which it is not.[2] The often painful details of the abuse and its aftereffects can test both the therapist's ability to handle such material, and therapeutic conviction that it is essential and curative to do so. Many therapists have perhaps understandably shied away from this disturbing and painful material and have preferred not to treat these issues[3] . . . [However], psychotherapy directed at the original trauma is very successful."[4]

THERAPY

Therapy is often a confusing and frustrating experience. The stories in this section should convey some of the realities of the therapy process and prepare you for what to expect. Half of the survivors in this book did not find good therapists right away. The point is that each person has the responsibility for finding a competent therapist. Take care of yourself. You deserve it.

How do you find a good therapist? There are two sets of criteria. One is objective; the other subjective. Both are important. You are looking for someone who will be a guide in a very difficult journey you are going to make. Choose your guide carefully.

Objective Criteria

1. *Education:* Look for a person who has credentials from an accredited institution. The degrees you will look for will be M D. (psychiatrist); Ph.D. in Clinical Psychology; M.S.W. (Master of Social Work), or B.S.W. (Bachelor of Social Work), and various counseling degrees. Also, L.C.S.W. (Licensed Clinical Social Worker) is another frequently used term. Don't be shy about calling a therapist and asking about credentials. A qualified therapist will respect your concerns.

2. *State Licensing:* Every state has different education and experience standards for licensing. In most states, anyone can hang out a shingle as a counselor or therapist, without any background or training. But to get a license the practitioner has to meet state standards. The only way of protecting yourself from incompetence is to insist on a licensed practitioner. That way you are at least assured that your therapist has met some education and training requirements.

3. *Insurance:* Your insurance company will have specific descriptions of the type of psychological care it will cover. Most companies will provide coverage for treatment provided by an M.D. psychiatrist or a Ph.D. clinical psychologist. Other types of licensed providers may or may not be eligible for insurance reimbursement. Check your policy. No insurance company will cover care by an unlicensed practitioner. However, many clinics employ counselors who are not licensed, but by providing a minimum amount of supervision by a licensed practitioner, they meet insurance industry requirements for coverage. Be careful if you are placed in the care of an unlicensed but supervised practitioner. Sometimes the supervision is not really there. Ask about it. Assure yourself that you are getting the quality of care you need.

4. *Experience:* Licensed practitioners are required to have a minimum amount of experience. Unfortunately, this does not mean that your caregiver knows anything about incest. Many qualified practitioners know very little about the long-term effects of incest in the adult survivor and are not prepared for the presenting symptoms. Try to find a therapist with experience in treating in-

cest survivors. If you cannot find someone with experience, discuss incest on your first visit and see if the therapist is willing to listen to you and work in this area. If you feel any resentment or hostility when you raise this issue, or if the therapist tries to dismiss it as unimportant, find someone else. When you find a therapist willing to address your needs, share this book with her or him. It will help your therapist learn to help *you* better.

Subjective Criteria

1. *Comfort:* You have to feel comfortable with your therapist. For those of us who have been taught all our lives to ignore our feelings, it is sometimes hard to know when we're uncomfortable. Sometimes it takes a few sessions to realize we don't feel right about our therapist. When this happens, change therapists. But be careful—don't confuse your uncomfortable feelings about the incest with uncomfortable feelings about the therapist. It is difficult to make that distinction, but one way of doing it is to see how you feel about the therapist when you are not discussing incest. If you find that the uneasiness only comes up when you bring up the incest issues, then you may be feeling your own discomfort about incest. But be careful—you may also be feeling your therapist's discomfort about incest!

   Some of the factors you should consider when choosing a therapist are age, gender, and ethnic background. By picking someone who is compatible in general categories, you have a better chance of success. The gender of your therapist can make a big difference. Many female survivors can do well with a male therapist up to a point, then have to switch to a female when they start accessing their feelings associated with incest. Many survivors cannot work with men at all, and many male therapists cannot work with incest survivors. The sexual issues are too close. Conversely, many survivors who have been abused by women are not comfortable with a female therapist and make better progress with a male. About the only guideline available is your own sense of comfort—follow it!

2. *Nurturing:* The old style of psychoanalysis in which your therapist is totally detached in the therapy relationship is not good for us. We need a more interactive therapy in which we receive therapeutic validation and nurturing. If you don't feel you are getting that, find another therapist. If you hear your therapist say, "What really happened? Are you sure?" or "You've got to stop dwelling on

it, there is nothing wrong with you," or if you feel your incest issues are being dismissed in any way, those are red flags that tell you to leave. What you should hear from your therapist are things like, "It wasn't your fault." "You were hurt and now we need to make it better." "You will learn to be cared for; you deserve it." Many survivors have found that female therapists are better at this because in our culture nurturing is associated (but not guaranteed) with the female role.

3. *Respect for Boundaries:* A therapist should respect your personal boundaries. The nurturing should not exceed standards of propriety. More important, your therapist has to understand that your boundaries have been violated repeatedly and should be extra sensitive to your need to have them respected. Your therapist should not touch you without asking you if it is okay. Your therapist should respect your emotional balance and make no attempt at a storm-trooper assault on your psyche. Any therapist who deliberately triggers a recurrence is not taking care of you. Role-playing and encounter group techniques that are commonly used with patients who have not suffered a traumatic physical violation are not good for us. They can turn into flashbacks or recurrences that are often mistaken for psychotic decompensation. Look for a therapist who respects your need for secure boundaries and who will not traumatize you further with aggressive therapy techniques.

   A respect for boundaries is especially important in group situations. We have experienced boundary violations all our lives, and we need to have controls that will protect us from that in a group. Insist that group members make a commitment to the group, a minimum of six months, so that each person can trust that the group will be there. In this way members can learn to trust and develop therapeutic relationships. Insist that no new members be admitted without consent of the group. All our lives we've had to make adjustments to other people whether we wanted to or not. In our therapy group, we need to be able to say no. The group also needs a sensitive leader, a therapist who will keep the group from becoming overwhelming while helping the individuals in it learn to establish their boundaries themselves. A group can only be therapeutic if we have in it the security we need to develop.

The other important consideration in therapy is readiness. You simply won't make progress unless you are ready. Most survivors are compelled to seek therapy by a crisis that they don't consciously connect with the incest—sexual dysfunction, marital problems, a suicidal or depressive episode. Survivors who don't remember the incest often start to have recurrences and memories after a child is born, and they seek therapy for what they believe is their "craziness." We rarely enter therapy specifically for incest, because our denial prevents us from recognizing it as a source of our problems. But with a good therapist, it is soon recognized.

Each person will have a different reaction, but for therapy to be successful there must be a readiness to address the incest. If you go to therapy at someone else's suggestion, as Ellen did, chances are it won't be very successful. When the incest is recognized, it takes a strong commitment to stick with the therapy, because it is not easy.

Described theoretically, it sounds easy. The purpose of therapy is to confront the incest trauma and its long-term complications in a controlled and guided manner. In the process we learn new, healthy coping skills. We have to unlearn the dysfunctional coping mechanisms we acquired when we weren't allowed to respond to incest directly. The first step is to respond to incest directly—and this usually means experiencing some disturbing emotions—pain, grief, anger, fear.

What sounds so easy when described objectively becomes the challenge of a lifetime when experienced subjectively. We grew up without learning how to deal with these intense emotions. Denial was the primary response in our families. In therapy our feelings are validated, we break the denial and learn how to experience our feelings without letting them overwhelm us. We learn how to respond to our feelings in a healing, self-nurturing way. For example, Noelle learns to focus on the good things in her daily life to alleviate the pain from the past, Megan learns to share her feelings with others, and Brenda learns to accept care from others.

The intensity of the emotions will vary from person to person, depending on the pace at which they are accessed. Some people are very controlled and move slowly, or let themselves experience their feelings about the incest indirectly through books, movies, or other people. Others might have flashbacks that constitute a "direct hit" and can be frightening. Either way, the experience is painful and difficult. One thing to remember is that you should always move at your own pace. You will learn to respect the way your mind only lets you handle what you are ready for. Any psychological techniques that assault your natural defenses to break them down traumatically are harmful and should not be used. This includes aggressive role-playing and group encounter exercises.

Survivors who don't remember the incest have to work harder at overcoming denial, and they may find that recurrences will be a primary source of information about the incest. They will also find their lives disrupted when memories start to emerge, as they often do, during the therapy process. The emergence of memories can take the form of flashbacks of great intensity. These will not be so frightening if you know what they are.

Even knowing what they are, the emergence of memories is traumatic for survivors who forgot the incest, because it means they have to completely revise their mental construct of reality. Having lived a life that didn't include incest in their conscious experience, they suddenly acquire a piece of information that shatters their mental construct of themselves and their world. This new piece of information feels like an anomaly, as if it can't possibly fit into the picture without destroying it. As Noelle says, "If this [the incest] was real, then nothing else can be real." Noelle talks of the "unreal" or "surreal" feeling that lasts for days after the emergence of a memory. She is describing the jarring effect of trying to adjust her mental construct of reality that simply didn't include incest. Part of the therapy process for Noelle and others who don't remember is to examine themselves and their lives very carefully to identify the trail of dysfunction left by the incest, as we did in Chapters 4, 5, and 6. By recognizing that it was there but unseen all the time, we can alleviate the "unreal" feeling, the "craziness" Noelle describes when a new memory presents itself. We can accept it and begin to deal with it.

Noelle's story is most valuable to survivors who are remembering, or trying to remember, a repressed incest trauma. It might also be helpful to go back and review the Noelle section in Chapter 6 where she discusses the role of dreams and other recurrences in the process of remembering.

Survivors who do remember the incest also go through a period of feeling confused and shattered. This happens when we start to break through the distorted images of ourselves and our personal world that were forced on us by denial. The breakthrough is initiated when we begin to recognize and accept feelings and thoughts we have long denied. For a period of time, when the old images of denial start to break apart, we will not yet have a completed replacement based on our own feelings and perceptions. This is a precarious time for us. We feel uncertain, confused, behave erratically, experience rapidly changing points of view, and generally feel uncomfortable with ourselves and others. It feels as if we are getting worse, not better. Many of us want to give up and drop out of recovery at this stage. We want to go back to the way we were, where at least we knew what to expect. It is very important at this stage to have a therapist you trust, who can give you desperately needed support while you put your "new" self back together. This is a painful and difficult stage, but with competent professional help we do get through it.

Therapy is an uneven process. This can frustrate us at times, especially when we feel that we are making no progress. Invariably we will feel even worse when we start to dredge up the old pain we stuffed away for years. Pain is the given condition of our therapy. We feel incapacitated by it at times. It also feels humiliating for us, as adults, to be reduced to an emotional baseline we associate with children. But that is what we have to do. We return to the condition we were left in as children and respond to it appropriately for the first time with self-nurturing, self-love, self-acceptance, and self-respect. We learn to care for ourselves and to accept care.

In therapy our feelings receive the validation they never got, and slowly we learn that we will survive them, and we grow. We feel as though we fall apart for what seems like an eternity, until we put ourselves back together properly for the first time.

My therapist said he often felt like we were digging up an old, rotten, half-buried corpse so we could bury it properly. That was how unpleasant it felt. Everyone reports the same thing: you have to feel worse before you start to feel better. For a while, incest will dominate your life. You will feel it acutely, all the time. You have to feel the pain, so that you can respond to it properly and finally grow beyond it. Sometimes you will feel that it will never end, but it will. If you have confidence in your therapist, you will get through it easier, if not faster. And if you have a therapy group, you will have other people who can be there when you need them, people uniquely qualified to help! Only you can do it, but you don't have to do it alone.

NOELLE

Noelle's therapy was different from the others' because she had no memory of the incest. Even though her therapist recognized it quickly, it took her years of working backwards through dreams and recurrences to finally accept it. Her contribution to this section is of special value to other survivors who are struggling with an incest trauma they can't even remember and don't want to believe. Noelle discusses the difficulties and discouragement she had to overcome in her lengthy process of recovery. The reassuring part is that you don't have to remember everything to recover. A few tiny fragments will do. Or if you can just recognize the presence of the incest trauma in your life, in recurrences, that can be enough for you to process the emotions and learn to respond to them in a healing way. Noelle finds that she can "come back" from the past and focus on the good things in her daily life.

Among the other issues Noelle raises are self-disclosure and changes in her relationships. Her point on self-disclosure is well made. Many of us go through a period in which we talk about incest compulsively. It looms so large and dominates us so completely while we deal with it that it is for a while a major part of our lives. At this stage we are vulnerable to inappropriate self-disclosure. Some of us tell everyone. Unfortunately, people often identify us primarily as incest victims and never get beyond that. It makes it hard for us when, after our therapy is completed and incest is not a part of our lives anymore, other people persist in thinking of us that way. We need to protect ourselves and carefully choose the people with whom we will share this part of our experience.

STARTING THERAPY—FINDING A THERAPIST

I started therapy after my first marriage because I never wanted to repeat that relationship again. I needed help dealing with my relationships with men. I knew something was terribly wrong and I didn't know what to do about it. So I shopped around for a therapist. I went to one guy who was a psychiatrist who was just awful. He was very old and hostile and asked me questions that were designed to demean me. I talked to him for 20 minutes and realized that would never work.

I went to another therapist, a man again, who was very touchy-feely. He was into the hugs, he was just too California, the nouveau Rolfing type. I couldn't deal with that. I'm real suspicious of the "new psychology." There are all kinds of weird things going on in the field—primal scream, get in touch with your toes, bio-this and that. I was nervous around someone who wanted to touch me, for obvious reasons.

Then I went to a family therapy clinic and I found a psychologist who I really liked; he just kept a comfortable distance from me. I'm so glad I found this guy, because he knew how to keep his distance. He must have known or felt or somehow been intuitive or schooled well enough to know I couldn't deal with somebody overwhelming me. He kept enough distance that I could be comfortable with him.

The Dog-and-Pony Show

I would go in there once a week and tell him all about myself, mostly my fantasy self, and he would nod his head and listen. After a while,

I stopped putting on the dog-and-pony show. I had presented myself as this character, playing up all my adventures and outrageous behavior. I was very entertaining and amusing. I was also avoiding all the real feelings. I figure it took me about six months to get through all the bullshit I had constructed about myself and start getting into real stuff. When we got into the real stuff, it's funny how everything changed. I started seeing the contradictions and inconsistencies in everything I told him. I started hearing myself give a lot of "Yes—No— I don't know" answers to his questions.

I was really lucky I found this guy. I think any other therapist would have got caught up in addressing my work problems and my marital problems. The normal garden-type variety abuse I suffered at home was enough to keep any therapist occupied. But I really lucked out. I found one who spotted the disguised presentation.

Stumbling Upon Incest

I was terribly shocked about six months after I started therapy. I came in one day, and my therapist said, "I would like you to talk more about your problems with men, and particularly your sexual problems." I said, "I don't have a problem with sex," because at that time, I was really sexy, my whole identity was that I was a sex kitten, couldn't keep the guys away I was so alluring, all that stuff. When I said, "I don't have a problem with sex," he said, "Yes, you do, you're afraid of it," and I knew in my gut he was right. I started feeling this funny kind of tension in my body, and I started to cry. Then he said, "I think you were sexually abused as a child, and I think you know who did it, too." It was like a bomb going off inside me.

I felt my mind start spinning wildly around. I became overwhelmed with the feeling of grief and fear. I started crying, and all the muscles in my body knotted up, and my stomach tied up in knots; I sort of curled up in a little ball. I remember repeating over and over, "That's not true, that's not true. Don't tell me that. That can't be true." He said, "Well, if it's not true, then why is it upsetting you so much?" It was funny, because there were two levels, one level was saying, "It's not true, you can't believe this. You must not believe this," and then the other level was saying, "It's true, and you know it's true."

I drove home in my car screaming and crying. I got home and I just got in the shower with all my clothes on and screamed. Then I got out and took off my clothes and got into bed and screamed into the pillow. What I was feeling was unbelievable. It was relief, pain, grief, and fear. I felt crazy because here, after thirty-some years, how could that be real? I thought, "Well, if that's real, then nothing else can be real, and I don't know what is real."

Hiding From the Truth

My mind was spinning, and I could not focus. Every time I went into therapy after that I was afraid he was going to want me to talk about sex or my father. My whole body would tense up, my muscles would be in knots. I would hold my breath. It got harder and harder for me to go. I kept finding reasons not to go, and finally I called him up and I said, "I can't go to therapy anymore. I'm having trouble at work and I'm just going to have to stop." I actually dropped out. I dropped out for quite a while, for about six or nine months.

Then when I went back, I said, "I can go back to therapy, but I don't want to talk about incest or sex. I'm not going to talk about that," and he said, "Okay, you don't have to talk about it." So for about another year I made no progress, my relationships just continued to repeat the abuse over and over again. It was a waste. I got myself into so much trouble at work, having stupid, secret sexual relationships. I lost one job because of it, then started a new job and promptly began to start another series of secret relationships with the men I reported to. I could not stop.

Let's Pretend

This went on for a while. Finally, one day in therapy, I said, "You know, I keep talking around sex and I keep talking around the incest," and he said, "I know you're doing that." I said, "Well, maybe we should talk about it. If it did happen, I mean it's all hypothetical now . . . I don't think it happened, but *if* it happened . . ."

So then we started talking about it hypothetically, about how things in my life would indicate that it had happened. I could not talk about it all the time, just when I felt exceptionally secure. At this stage, my therapist and I started trying to relate what I now know are "recurrences" to the original incest trauma. When things happened to me that seemed "crazy" or "weird," we would talk about them in terms of how they might be an expression of the incest. We especially worked on my dreams, because I had quite a few recurring dreams, and all of them were representing the incest.

I made little progress because I resisted it, but it did prepare me for the way I would feel when I did remember. Because even though I did not believe the incest had happened, when we would discuss a dream in terms of incest, I would have intense, painful, emotional episodes.

It seems to me I would start to cry at the beginning of the session and cry for hours afterwards. Or I would go through the session repressing my tears and cry all the way home and for the rest of the day.

I began to repress my emotions more and more when I was with my therapist because I did not want him to see it. I knew he would think my emotional response was "proof" that he was "right," and I was determined that he would be "wrong."

Working With Recurrences

Other things we talked about as indications of the incest were my spider hallucinations, the unexplained fainting episodes and panic attacks, my fears, and my sexual relationships. I knew they all indicated some sexual trauma. I could not accept that it was incest.

We made the most progress with the dreams. The recurring dreams were of a man doing something terrifying to me in a basement. I would sometimes be grown, sometimes be little. I would feel confused and wonder, "This couldn't be my daddy—it must be someone else, but I thought it was my daddy." I would awaken screaming and soaked with sweat.

Although the meaning of my dreams is clear now that I have recognized the incest, it was much, much harder for me to see it then, because I could not let myself recognize the subject of the dreams. I also spent years in therapy without any significant behavior change because I could not recognize the incest, and therefore could not recognize how it was directing my life.

Denial—What It Feels Like

I want to talk about denial because it is something I didn't understand, and I think it is hard for other people to understand too.

Denial is not a conscious act. It's not like you say to yourself, "I'm going to refuse to believe this." There were all kinds of carefully constructed reasons that I had for not believing the incest had happened.

I had a particularly difficult problem because I did not remember the specific acts of incest. That is another thing that I think I should address—what it feels like to not remember.

The Emotional, Intellectual, and Intuitive Wars

Over the months, as we tried unsuccessfully to approach it in therapy, I could only deal with it from the position, "It isn't true—my therapist just thinks it is true." But then, alone at home after therapy, I would curl up and cry for hours about it. But I would cry over and over again, "It can't be true, it can't be true." While feeling the pain and grief on an emotional level, I was resisting it on an intellectual level. To explain my emotional disruption, I decided I may have at one time fantasized to myself that my father molested me, in a projection of my own desires for him as a child—the old Freudian interpretation. This was the way I rationalized it, while I experienced the emotional reality of it.

There was yet another level that I was aware of as a sort of background noise that knew it was true. But the intellectual level fought that, saying, "But you have no memory." So these three responses, the emotional, the intellectual, and the intuitive, all were going at the same time and were at war with each other.

The fact that I remembered nothing was important for me, because if the part of me that knew it was true started gaining, it would be overcome by the rational part that said, "How can it be true—you don't remember it!" And then I would feel crazy and ashamed for even thinking it could be true.

And if it were true, I felt I could never live through the realization. How could I live, knowing he had done that to me when I was so little?

How Could He Have Done That to Me?

My feelings of unreality were especially bad because of my long period of denial, during which I had forced on me an image of my father in which incest was impossible. I wasn't allowed to acknowledge his cruelty and abusiveness, so my image of my father was of a very idealistic, high-minded man. He was unbelievably pure. Hearing him rage for years about the vices and corruptions and injustices of the world, I naturally acquired the idea that he was more pure than anyone in the world. We never had any cheap novels or men's magazines in our house, either. I felt his purity extended to sex as well. Here was a man whose personal and professional life looked exemplary. How could he have done that to me? It took a long, long time to reconcile.

I had to break down the fantasy father and see the real man. The "crack" in the facade that I worked on was his abusive behavior toward my mother and me. I began to see that his self-centered, infantile self-absorption was an indication of much deeper and more destructive developmental defects. Gradually I could perceive that the capability was there. Now I feel that, given the way he is, incest was almost inevitable. I say *almost*. I don't believe in complete determinism.

But until I could see through the facade-father, I couldn't fit incest into the picture. It wasn't just his image, either. I had my own image that didn't include incest, and it took more years of looking back and examining my behavior to see the signs before I could accept the possibility on an intellectual level.

Remembering—Five Ways

The process of remembering is also something I should talk about. I've had people ask, "How will I know when I remember?" Well, everyone knows the difference between real and unreal. All I can say is that, right away, you know. But for me the process of remembering has been more than just simple memories—it is a complicated process.

I remember in five ways. One is emotional. At first I did not accept the idea that my emotions about the incest were a form of remembering, but now it is clearer to me. The intense outburst I had when my therapist first mentioned incest was a form of remembering. I was having all of the feelings associated with the event. It was terrifying.

Another way is through my body. The first introduction of the incest in therapy caused me physical pain. My stomach and back muscles tensed, my hands and legs started to tingle and go numb, I found it hard to breathe, and I experienced lower pelvic pain. Later, when I had my dream and other memories, they were preceded by or accompanied by lower pelvic, lower back, and vaginal pain, as well as nausea. A part that made me feel ashamed was the sensation of sexual stimulation.

Memories also come back as thoughts, images, or dreams. The thoughts are just a sudden formulation, a sort of understanding that occurs without any visual image. "Oh, yes—so that's what he did" type of thing. Images are visual flashes—I just see very suddenly what I saw at the time. Dreams show me events with myself pictured in them as if I am watching a movie. Only it is real. Sometimes they occur together. In my first dream, I saw my father position me on the toilet, and I experienced every tiny detail of that event. Then suddenly there was an unexpected change that I experienced as the feeling of being thrown back. Although I didn't "see" what happened, I knew I was experiencing oral sex.

The last memory occurred while I was editing my section on dreams for this book. I've always thought all the sexual activities were oral, and as I read the transcript of my tape on my contact lens dream, I was going on that assumption, that it was about the oral sex. When I came to the part where I said I had to take out my lens because "something was sticking in my eye and hurting me," I didn't like it. Without any thought and just on a recoil, I crossed it out. My feeling was discomfort. I didn't want that in there.

Later, when I went back to it after a few weeks, I read that sentence and thought, "No, that belongs there, it's true," and I began to pencil it back in. As I did, I had a flash in my mind, an image of looking down between my legs as I sat on the toilet and seeing a penis sticking into me. I instantly had severe pelvic, back and vaginal pain, which lasted three days, and I had some very intense emotions about it which also lasted quite a while. The depression lasted for weeks.

Getting Back to the Past—A Process

Even though that particular memory came to me as a sudden image while I was writing down the dream-words associated with it, the process of arriving at that memory is more complicated. It actually took quite a while to get to it.

I believe that I started to open up the door to that memory weeks before in therapy. I have known for several years that the incest took place in a basement. I also knew that my spider hallucinations were related to the incest. Because of their penis-like legs, I've always thought they were representations of the male genitals I saw while being abused. Then, in a therapy session, my therapist suggested that maybe, since I was abused in the basement, and spiders tend to live in the basement, perhaps I really saw spiders while I was sexually abused. At the time, that made a lot of sense to me, but it was no sudden revelation.

Then, a few days later, I suddenly had two memories of the basement where I was abused. I remembered standing at the top of the stairs, needing to go down to the bathroom, yet terrified to go alone. I felt agonizing conflict, ready to wet my pants, but too scared to move. Then my mother, in great irritation, said, "Well, Daddy can take you down." And then I felt horrible, overwhelming panic—and conflict—I was afraid to go alone and yet I was terrified to go with him, and how could she do that to me?

Then I had another memory of my brother taking me downstairs and leaving me there, and me running between the toilet and the steps, desperate to go potty, crying with terror at being left as he walked up the stairs.

It seems that identifying the spiders with the basement got me back to the basement. The next memory was of my mother putting me on the toilet and me jumping off, crying, sure that a snake was going to come up and bite my genitals. In this memory I'm going from the basement to the specific events that happened to me there. The "snake" is an erection.

Then, about a week or two later, I had the memory of attempted intercourse on the toilet in the basement triggered by the association with my contact lens dream image of "something sticking in my eye and hurting me."

My therapist, when we discussed this, suggested that my father may have told me to close my eyes. But when I was hurt, I looked down and saw the penis sticking into me. And that is exactly the image I had—of looking down at myself and seeing it happen.

This last memory was bad, but not as bad as earlier memories. For one thing, the series of memories leading up to it meant it was a more gradual release of emotions. I think I cried more over the memory of my mother sending me into the basement with my father. Also, I feel I was ready for this latest revelation. The fact that he tried sexual intercourse seems to be a last detail. I had already dealt with most of the feelings of being sexually abused through my memories of oral-genital contacts. I doubt if there is more to remember.

The Reaction to a Memory—Denial

Even though I have been working on this for years, this latest memory brought out denial, shame, and feelings of craziness. Shortly after I had it, when the crying and pain and grief had subsided, I started to feel that it couldn't be real. It was an active feeling of resistance. I began to think of reasons why everything must be a big mistake. I began to construct an elaborate theory that an operation I had ten years ago had caused me to imagine that my father had sexually abused me. I imagined calling up my therapist and saying, "There is nothing wrong—it's all a mistake!" And I imagined the relief I would feel if I could do that.

At the same time, I knew I was rationalizing and knew it was wrong. I knew the incest really happened, but I wished it hadn't.

I also had feelings that if the most recent memory was not true, then I must be crazy, really crazy, to think it. And if it was true, then how could anything else be real? The apparent normality of my routine, daily life couldn't be real if something that horrible had really happened. This was the same feeling of unreality I had eight years ago when the subject of incest had first come up. This time I went through the whole series of responses until, finally, after two or three weeks, I was adjusted to this new memory. This was an improvement—it used to take months.

A basic issue for me was a question of truth. I was so afraid that if these memories were not true, then I was a bad, sick, horrible person to believe them. I was afraid to have them, and then when they came, I was afraid to believe them. But when they came, I was compelled by the reality of them to accept them. Their reality prevailed. If not, I really would be crazy!

Dealing With Memories—Keeping Myself Together

I had my memory dream at five o'clock in the morning. I woke up overwhelmed by the emotions and the intensity of it. I was very disoriented, very dysfunctional. I just lay in bed and my husband held me while I went through an intense emotional episode, but I couldn't stop crying. I was in a bad bind because we had rented a cabin in the mountains that weekend with two other couples. It was something we were committed to, and, for some reason, I felt that we had to go. I wanted everything to be normal.

So all morning I walked around the house crying and trying to get organized to go up to the cabin. I walked around the house putting things in my bags and getting my daughter's toys together. The whole time I was crying; I couldn't stop crying. Finally, we got out of the house and into the car, and we started driving. All the way there in the car, for about a two-and-a-half hour drive, I cried. I could not stop crying.

Then I started getting scared. I thought, "Oh, we're going to get to the cabin, and I'm going to be in just terrible shape. People are going to notice." So as we got closer to the cabin, I stopped the car, and I put my sun glasses on, and I thought of some credible explanation.

We got to the cabin and we started bringing in our stuff. Everybody said, "Well, what's wrong?" I looked really bad. My nose was red, my eyes were red, and I sounded congested from all the crying. I said, "I must be having some allergies or something. I woke up this morning like this." That's what I told people all day. I'd sit there with tears running down my face, my nose running and my sunglasses on. People just thought it was my allergy attack; that's how I covered up for myself. When things got too hard to cover up, when I would have some overwhelming feelings coming again, I'd go into the bedroom in the cabin, lie down and cry in the pillow, or I'd go out into the woods for a walk. I'd leave my daughter with my husband and go off into the woods. That's how I got through the weekend.

Learning That I Will Survive

It was one of those situations when you feel so strange because, on the one hand, you're with people and you're trying to make it look like everything's all right, and, on the other hand, inside you're fragmenting. But I got through it. I'm glad we went to the cabin because it forced me to hold myself together. It forced me to be in the present, more than I would have if I had stayed home. It meant that I wasn't overwhelmed, I was able to keep things relatively under control. I think it is very important to learn that there is control, because those emotions are going to keep coming out for a long time.

One Small Nuclear Explosion After Another

Once I started accessing the emotions related to the incest, it was very painful. It's a stop-and-start process. I'd go through one set of emotions and feel real bad for a while. Then I'd start feeling better, and I'd feel like I was dealing with life. I wouldn't walk around crying all the time, I could keep myself together at work and things would be on an even keel, and then something else would come out. I'd have to face it, I'd have the emotions again. It's a process, little by little, one little bomb after another. One small nuclear explosion after another going off in your life, and each time it happens, you have to weather it, you have to let the feelings go through you. You have to adjust to them and cope with them, and then gradually they fade away and you start feeling normal again. Then, "boom," another one goes off.

My Children Absorb My Emotions

Even though I do everything possible to act normal around my children, somehow they can pick up on my distressed condition when I have to deal with a memory. I don't know how they can tell. It must be my tone of voice, my body language, my face. Whatever it is that gives it away, somehow they know when my inner self is in distress.

They show symptoms immediately and dramatically. The three-year-old will have sleep disturbances, wet the bed, be afraid to stay in a room without me, "shadow" me around the house, and come into my bedroom in the middle of the night for a kiss and a hug, become fearful of the wind, lose her appetite. The baby will wake up every hour during the night, cry more, eat less, generally lose interest in play, and want to be held all the time. This will go on for weeks, until I feel better.

Seeing my children reflect my fear and insecurity is just about the most painful part of all this. I would give anything to spare them this. I'm getting better as fast as I can, but it is not fast enough. I hate doing this to them, and it is hard not to despair and lose sight of my purpose, which is to get over my trauma. I have to keep going, because even though I see them suffer the effects of the therapy, I know it would be worse to see them suffer the effects of the incest.

At Work—Concentrate on the Present

Some of the biggest problems were at work. Let's say I had a really tough therapy session and I'd have to go to work the next day. I'd cry at every little thing. I'd have to go in the bathroom and close the door and cry. Or I'd be sitting at my desk, and, all of a sudden, I'd start weeping uncontrollably. People look at you, "Oh God, there she goes again." You are allowed to say, "Oh, my mother just died." or you are allowed to say, "Oh, I'm feeling sick today, it's my arthritis," but you are not allowed to say, "Oh, my incest is bothering me today, please forgive me." You can't say that. There is no explanation you can give. It's very humiliating.

Putting It in Its Place

Just going through that process repeatedly of pulling myself back together and forcing myself to focus on the present was therapeutic and it has helped me a lot. Because gradually what has happened is the incest has assumed a smaller and smaller and smaller part in my life. I've begun to see myself as much more than that. I have so much more. For example, I'd have to focus on my daughter; I'd have to focus on my job, my home, my husband, my other relationships. And really, in perspective, the incest, even though it pervades all those things, it is just a small part of my life. I have much, much more going for me.

My Father Is Out of My Life

I have been very lucky in one respect. My parents are far away and I don't have to see my father. Other survivors who have to go through this and still see their abuser have a totally different story to tell. The issue of confrontation hasn't come up for me, because my father is simply not a part of my life today. It might be different if I had to see him regularly. I don't think it's an accident that he is not around. I believe at some level of awareness he is avoiding this issue. I know that if I confronted him, I would never see my mother again. He would reject me completely, and my mother, with no other choice, would have to stand with him. I know how things stack up, and I see no need to bring things to that point. I can recover without them, and I am.

My Mother—Fear and Anger

In working through the incest, I had to go through some new feelings about my mother. Before I remembered the incest, but while I was having a lot of recurrences in nightmares, my mother started to emerge as a player in the trauma. I started having dreams in which I was running from my father, and I would try to escape out a window, only to find my mother waiting outside for me, aiming a gun at me and smiling. So I knew if I tried to get away from him, she would force me back in. And the feelings I had in these dreams were terror, grief, abandonment, betrayal. I remember the first time I had it, I screamed over and over, *"She knows! She knows! And she's helping him!"* I was heartbroken. Recently I remembered my mother sending me to the potty in the basement with my daddy. I had those same feelings. I think that was the origin of the dream of her with the gun.

For a long time I struggled with the feelings about my mother. I had always seen her as a helpless but loving mother. I got angry— "How could she have let that happen?" but also I grieved for the loss I felt—I had lost her. My progress over the years was to see her as a prisoner of her own limitations, doing her best. She loved me. That's all she could do.

Sex—A Thing of the Past

Like other people in my incest support group, I went from being very sexually compulsive to being sexually dysfunctional. Before I started dealing with the incest directly, I wanted to have sex and I told myself I had a very good sexual relationship with my husband. Before my marriage, the way I experienced sex was usually in the context of an exploitive or abusive relationship. By abusive, I don't mean physically abusive. I never went out with men who were violent. My sexual dysfunction took the form of having secret sexual relationships with men in a position of power at work. They had no commitment to me, were always involved in some way with someone else. My big thing was to go through this tortured relationship in which I wanted them to commit to me and they wouldn't. We always had very passionate sex, and I would alternate between feeling elated and worthless. That stopped when I got married.

Sex Feels Like Abuse to Me

When I found out about the incest and started identifying my feelings of being abused, the link between sex and abuse became apparent to me. It is still a problem to me; sex of any kind still feels like abuse. I haven't been able to break that association. I'm working on it, but I think it's going to take a long time.

I feel I'm sexually dead. I feel as if that part of my life is over. I can't ever imagine experiencing sex again and liking it. To me it's just something that I have to go through from time to time. I dissociate badly when I'm having sex. I can't help it, it's involuntary. If I try to have sex, no matter what I do, my mind goes away. I go away; I check out. I go off on journeys; I decorate the house. I think about this or that or my work or the kids. I just go off somewhere until it's over. I can't help that.

I look back on the days when I had really strong sexual desires and I think of my sexual behavior, how there were times when I really wanted sex and how overwhelmed I was by physical desire, and I wonder how I could have ever felt that way. It seems really stupid and alien. I feel sex is degrading and ridiculous, and I can't. I just can't get in touch with any sexual feelings at all.

I Even Look Different Now

All I feel is this sense that I should not feel this way, that somehow sex should be a part of my life. I'm trying to make it a part of my life again, but it's taking a long time. I don't think of myself as a sexual person. I feel that I have no sexuality at all, none. Physically, my appearance has changed. I think I used to look very desirable and attractive, and men noticed me wherever I went. Now, I don't look desirable, I don't look sexual, I don't look attractive, I don't think men ever notice me, and I'm quite comfortable that way. Aside from just a little qualm about losing a whole part of human functioning, I really don't care.

I Need Help to Change

All the other women I've talked to in my group, we all have the same problem. We need help from our husbands to work on it. I guess what I would like my husband to do is somehow be sensitive and understanding, which he is. But I also need him to try and foster and nurture in me some sort of feelings of sexuality that are not intrusive or threatening. I need him to be very affectionate and loving and caring and help me learn how to experience sex a different way. He doesn't know how to do that. Eventually, I think we should go into counseling and work on this, but I don't care. I'm not ready to, and he's not pushing it. So I don't think we are going to do anything very soon.

Self-Disclosure—A Considered Decision

Another issue that comes up for me a lot is the question of disclosure—who do we tell? Everybody seems to have to struggle with the idea of feeling like a fraud because everybody doesn't know about the incest. I think there is a reasonable way of approaching it. One way of approaching it is to respect that this is very private material. It's a very private, very traumatic experience. It's hard enough for me to handle it, and I grew up with it, I lived with it. For people who have never been exposed to this sort of thing, they just don't know how to act or how to respond, and they just don't handle it well. It's devastating to the relationship when you tell them, because they don't know how to think about you after that. What happens is, all of a sudden, you become one thing: You become an INCEST VICTIM and they forget about all the other parts of you. It just looms up, dominates your whole image, and, after that, they don't ever think of you the same. I am, as a person, far more than an incest victim. In one tiny part of my life I was a victim, but in the rest I accomplished a lot. Those are the things most of my friends know about and I don't see anything wrong with that.

I have found it's really not necessary to tell people. It's often destructive to tell people. It may be too much to ask to expect others to deal with this. I have an old-fashioned point of view. There is a private world, a personal world. There should be a respect for some privacy and that people have a right to have some reserve. It's presumptuous to just lay all this stuff on everybody around you when they can't respond to it appropriately. There's no way that most people are going to be able to respond properly. It's hard enough for *me* to deal with.

Beware of the Initial Compulsion to Tell Everyone

It's true that being isolated with your feelings is hard, but to alleviate that, there are people I can tell—my husband, one or two very close friends—female friends, I might add, because men have a harder time dealing with it. Then there's my therapy group of other incest survivors whom I love. They are the women who share this part of my experience in the way that nobody else can. We can even sit around and crack jokes about it!

I think some of us go through a period, I know I did, at the time I first started discovering the incest in therapy, when I compulsively talked about it to everybody. I couldn't stop. It was always on my mind day and night. It always came up in conversation. I was sort of running around saying, "God, I think this happened to me," because it was so unreal to me. It's almost as if I was telling everybody in an effort to assimilate it into my life.

A Bad Experience With a Friend

Later on, I got through that compulsive stage and became very selective about who I told. Even then, I did have a bad experience telling someone, a business associate, a man I worked pretty closely with in my field for about seven years.

He and I got along real well and I thought we were close, because he had told me things about himself that made me feel we had a close friendship. One time we were out having lunch, and I don't know how it came up, but incest did come up. He said, "I just don't know how people can do that." He said, "That's just beyond my comprehension." So I told him about my father and how it happened and the family dysfunction and how it affected my life. And the whole time I was telling him, he sat there just kind of not looking at me.

Then he said, when I was done explaining all this to him, "Are you sure that you just didn't make all this up?" That just shattered me. I've never been so hurt by a friend in my life. Because who would make up something like this? Why? Why would anyone want to make up something like this? I mean, life is bad enough without inventing awful things. What kind of person would I be to make up something like that?

Later on, I realized that it was not my problem, it was *his* problem. I mean, I still felt bad because I lost a friendship. But, it's not me, it's him. I think that's a good example of what we should keep in mind about self-disclosure. Protect yourself; you deserve it.

Changes in Relationships

The process of therapy has been hard and very demanding. I've had to re-evaluate so many things, like my marriage. When I confronted the incest in therapy, finally accepted that it happened, it was like a switch in my mind was flipped and, all of a sudden, things that never have been clear to me before were very clear. Things that had been acceptable to me before would never be acceptable again. I had finally been able to connect my feelings with the abuse, and now I could recognize abuse when it was happening. When I had those feelings, I could now know that I was being abused.

The most important thing was that an abusive relationship would never be acceptable again, and that included my marriage. It's almost like a light went on and illuminated this landscape within me and I could see how abusive my marriage was, and it looked like insanity for me to put up with it.

I confronted my husband, "Look, I make more than enough to support the family, I don't need you living with me. You get the hell out if you're not going to change." It was wonderful. All of a sudden, I could say that because I could see so clearly how abusive it was and how unnecessary it was for me to do that.

Facing the incest gave me a chance to live, to take control of my life. I couldn't do it until I faced it. Because until I faced it, I could not see what it was doing to me. I couldn't see how it had made every relationship I had abusive.

It also changed my attitude towards my work. Up until then, I had been the sort of person who would just give everything to my job and not have any expectation of getting much in return. All of a sudden, I realized that I could bill twice as much as I was billing and that I could pick and choose my clients. I saw how incredibly qualified I was in my field.

All of a sudden, I saw a glimpse of myself as I really was. I wasn't that little abused child anymore; I was a grown-up woman. I saw the abused child clearly and I no longer confused her with me so much. Until I could see her clearly and accept her and recognize her, I got her confused with the grown-up me a lot.

I think of therapy as a few small nuclear explosions going off, one after the other, and your whole life changes. I don't want to exaggerate the amount of change. It doesn't have to change dramatically or overnight. The changes are slower. They are slow to achieve. But one thing that did change dramatically with me was that I recognized abuse when it happened to me. I still could not respond, but at least I could recognize it. Before, I had not been able to recognize abuse when it happened to me. It just felt natural to me. Then, all of a sudden, it wasn't natural anymore.

Heading Toward Resolution

Things are starting to feel resolved now. The problems of sex and love are still to be worked out in my therapy. I found that my male therapist worked out fine until after I remembered the incest. Then, suddenly, I was very aware that he was male. I was ashamed to talk to him about the sex, my feelings about my dad, and about what happened. I thought he felt I was disgusting. Now I see that I was projecting that. But at the time I couldn't. After a year or so, I had to switch to a female therapist. Another need I had was to address my mother's role, and I needed a woman to help me with that.

I thank God that I had a therapist who knew what he was doing, who was there for years and years when I was in denial, and who knew a disguised presentation when he saw it. I hate to think what would have happened to me if I hadn't had him. I still might be in therapy getting nowhere.

MEGAN

Like so many of us, Megan went into therapy for something other than incest. She was fortunate to have a therapist who could respond appropriately to her casual mention of her brother's "molestation." Megan's progress in therapy is very typical—a period of dealing with peripheral issues, a period of feeling worse while addressing the incest, a period of feeling better, then a discovery of more incest-related problems to resolve. After eight years, Megan has gone the whole gamut. Her progress in therapy is evidenced by two things. One is the way most painful problems are spoken of in the past tense. The other is the way she is able to deal with problems—not necessarily having answers, but having a positive feeling that she will be able to resolve them. Therapy doesn't solve all our problems, but it helps us learn how to do it.

STARTING THERAPY FOR DEPRESSION

I started therapy because my depressions were happening more often. I decided whatever therapy was had to be better than the pain of the depressions. There was another reason, too—the family jokes about the women in our family being flakey. They just take it for granted that we are all flakey. Everyone talked about how Grandma was flakey. My mother was on tranquilizers the last ten years of life; she lived on valium. I did know when I was growing up that every once in a while my father would just take her away for the weekend, but as I got older, I began to realize that she went away because she was on the verge of falling apart. My mother's sister, her only sister, had one nervous breakdown at 38, and the year I went into therapy, she was hospitalized the second time at the age of 50. My sister had a breakdown at 27 and was hospitalized. Another sister suffered from depression, I suffered from depression, and I was terrified I was going to end up like the other women in the family.

My mother was angry her entire life. I could remember her screaming and yelling at us. I can see now it came from the ways the marriage worked and that she never liked it. My parents never argued, never—at least not in front of us kids. As a child I kept thinking married people didn't argue. She didn't argue with him, but she took all that anger out on us.

I Mentioned My Brother Molesting Me

So I really started to get into my family and our relationships. And within a few weeks I told her about my fear of men. Somewhere, within those first few months, I mentioned that my brother Kevin had molested me when I was ten but insisted that it hadn't affected me.

I had told her it was no big deal, and I was only ten when it happened; it really didn't have any impact on me. Right then and there, she said it had everything to do with my fear of men, but she also said maybe because my denial was so strong that that was not the time to push me on it. I wouldn't believe it, that's why we started dealing with my relationships with parents and with the family first. And, as we worked through those dynamics, it came down to the relationships between my brothers and sisters.

"Because of What He Did to Me!"

The way it all finally even started to come out was that, around the time of my twenty-eighth birthday, I went over to Kevin's to celebrate my birthday with his wife, whose birthday was within a few days of mine. That day, Kevin was giving me all these instructions on what I should do to meet men, where I should go to meet them, and how I should be conducting my life. This is how Kevin deals with everybody. He doesn't know anything about any particular subject, but he is an expert on everything. This time he was an expert on the single life and what I should do to become married, now that he was married.

Anyhow, when I saw my therapist, which was like two days later, I was ranting and raving. I went on and on about how angry I was, and she said she couldn't understand why I was so angry that Kevin would presume to tell me about men. Finally I just screamed back at her, "Because of what he did to me." Even then I still couldn't spell out what he had done to me. I would just use euphemisms for the longest time.

But, from there, I started to remember bits and pieces, and what came back was an incredible terror. When I started remembering, the fear was always present; I suffered anxiety attacks where my entire body ached, my legs and arms hurt, and there was this fear that was indefinable and overwhelming. I got through it because my therapist scheduled my sessions for the end of the day and gave me open-ended sessions that would last up to two hours sometimes, usually for 90 minutes. I saw her two and three times a week. All of my energy went into therapy. I went to work and went to therapy, that was all I had energy for. I read everything I could get my hands on. I cried and couldn't eat or sleep. I was terrified, and hated remembering, and was afraid I would never feel well again.

Remembering—A Lot of Terror

Anything and everything could trigger a memory. I can remember now trying to explain to my therapist—I was at work and I was drinking coffee, and I just started to shake uncontrollably and started to cry, and I just had to go sit in the bathroom for like a half an hour. The only thing I could think of was the stick in the coffee reminding me of his penis. I have no idea what the connection was there, but it made some connection.

That happened to me repeatedly, and as each memory came back, every single time the reaction was physical, I would start to shake, and I would start to cry, and I would have to go sit somewhere and get back into control. I kept telling my therapist I didn't want to remember, I just wanted to take away the memories, I didn't want them. She kept telling me that was the only way to get over them.

She also told me what was happening to me physically; it was as if my body was physically regurgitating at remembering what happened. So she recommended hypnosis, which until that time I thought was a radical hocus-pocus. I didn't want anything to do with it. But it reached a point where I was terrified. I was afraid I was going to lose my job, because I would just disappear for half an hour at a time. I thought for sure that they were going to end up disciplining me or something. I couldn't function. I couldn't eat, which is unusual for me, I can eat anytime, anywhere, anything. I went three weeks when I could not eat, nothing tasted good to me. I went without sleeping. So finally I called, and I said all right, I'll try hocus-pocus. I'll try hypnosis because, I said, if I have to remember, then I want to remember in a controlled atmosphere, not just anywhere and lose control. So we did try hypnosis. It worked for me exceedingly well, because when the memories came back, there was a lot of terror.

Hypnosis—Lets You Remember What You Will

I went on a Saturday for two or three hours the first time she tried hypnosis. We were going to try and find out how long the abuse lasted. She said that she was going to count off numbers, and each one of those numbers would be a month. I was just to raise an arm when I got to the number of months that it lasted. I always told her that I thought it lasted about a year, from the time I was 10 'til I was 11. Anyway, when she hit the number 13, my arm shot up involuntarily. I don't know where it came from, but I knew that was right. That's how it coincided with everything else that I had remembered in bits and pieces.

My therapist was convinced that there must have been intercourse, but I couldn't remember it. In one of the hypnosis sessions she did try to trigger that memory. I was lying back in one of those lazy boy chairs, and my whole body got stiff, my arms and legs, and I couldn't respond. I couldn't do anything. My body was just tense from head to toe. She stopped and said, it may or may not have happened, but if it did, you are blocking it so thoroughly I should not push you on it. You will remember it when it's right.

Confrontation—Placing the Responsibility on the Abuser

I was doing a lot of reading about incest, and one of the things that stuck with me in one of the books was that when other women had confronted their abuser, the guy never took responsibility for it. They made the confrontation for themselves; they went through it for themselves. On one hand, they would be upset that the abuser wouldn't accept responsibility, but on the other hand, they just knew that for their own growth they had to do it. They had to place the responsibility on him.

That stuck with me, this idea, and I thought, well, I don't know how Kevin will respond, but I talked to my therapist about it. Her suggestion was that since we only lived 90 miles away from each other, that maybe Kevin could come down and go through a session with me and maybe help me. Maybe he might remember things that might help me, because some of my memories were so cloudy.

So when I called him, it was with that intention, would he be willing to come to a session with me for that purpose. Kevin's reaction was "I don't understand, and if you're going to have a therapist there, then my wife has to be there." He looked at this as a very adversarial approach rather than he trying to help me. He immediately became defensive.

"There Wasn't Any Sex"

Like I said, he never denied what happened, he just denied the extent of it. The conversation started out very calmly, but when I called it incest is when it got ugly, when I put that label on it. Even calling it a sexual encounter didn't bother him, it was the label "incest" that just pushed him right over the edge, and he got very ugly. The very first thing he said was, "There's no harm done, there's no harm. Why are you concerned? There was no harm done. You weren't hurt." And I said, "Well, Kevin, yes, I was hurt. Maybe not the way you think it was, but it was still a violation of my body." Kevin said, "I didn't violate your body, there wasn't any sex."

And, you see, that was the only reason why it took me so long to remember the rape. He completely denies that it happened. He said, "You weren't hurt, and there was no intercourse, so there is nothing." Then I mentioned incest, and he had hysterics when I said that. He said it was not incest. I said, "Kevin, incest is defined as sexual relations between two people who are related. We are related; we are brother and sister. It is incest."

He Was of No Use to the Therapy Process

Then when I had identified it as incest, he called me a liar, and said that my whole problem is not that it happened. My whole problem was that I was 50 pounds overweight, and if I lost weight then I would be okay. Well, at the time that we had this conversation, to put this into perspective, I weighed forty pounds less than I do now. I was maybe ten pounds overweight at the time of this conversation. He told me, "Your whole problem is that you're fat, and if you were to lose weight, you'd be okay." Then he said it was my therapist's fault, that she was putting the ideas into my head. Then he went on to say that my whole problem was that I was still dependent on Mom and Dad, and I had to accept that they were dead. I couldn't be a reflection of them anymore. He just ranted and raved for the longest time, and then I got hysterical. It was the one and only time in my life I could understand how someone could commit an act of violence. I swear, if he had been standing there and I had had a gun, he would be dead.

After that conversation, he told his wife about why I had called, and he insisted that if I did want him to come down, my therapist had to call him. So my therapist called him. I asked her why, and she said she just felt that something had started, so she should finish it. When we met the next time, after she talked to him, she walked in and said, "I shouldn't be saying this, I am a professional, but your brother is crazy." She said it was the most bizarre conversation she has ever had in her entire life. And she said he would not be of any use whatsoever to our therapy process. So I didn't go any further as far as Kevin participating in therapy.

He Never Has Accepted the Truth

Kevin told his wife, his wife told my younger sister who lived in California, so she called me up and wanted to know why I was picking on Kevin and acting so mean to him. Kevin also called my older sister and told her that I needed a new therapist. My older sister said, "No, I think she is doing very well." I did try to talk to my oldest sister about what had happened with Kevin, but she took the attitude of, "I have my relationship with Kevin, and you have your relationship with Kevin, and I don't want to get involved. This is between you and Kevin." She wouldn't listen to me, she couldn't. She never has been able to listen to me. So essentially I got shut out by two of the people in my family. One, my younger sister, blamed me, and my oldest sister said I can't listen. So, consequently, I've never ever talked to anybody else in my family.

Well, when Kevin moved, I took over his apartment, and then he only lasted six weeks at his new job and came back. When he moved back, he wanted me to help him out, and I told him that I wouldn't. He told me that I owed him money from the apartment, and I told him I had given him precisely what the amount was for those weeks. So he started telling me that he was going to tell the entire family what I had accused him of. I said, "Fine, be my guest. It makes no difference to me what you tell the family." He said, "It means a lot. They don't know about the lies that you've made up about me." He never has accepted the truth.

Coping With It Alone—Go With the Tide

There were times when I wanted to tell my family, but I won't. I would like them to know me for the person I am. I think that they have a very unrealistic image of who I am, where I'm at. But I fear that they'll just tear at me. What I'm more concerned about now is not my brothers and sisters. I have 15 nieces and nephews, and I'm afraid that my brothers and sisters will react in such a way that it will interfere with my relationship to them. So I've talked to no one in my family.

During all this time of confusion and fear and loneliness and anger and hatred for what I had been asked to endure, my therapist used a wonderful analogy to get me through—she said it was like being caught in a riptide, and if you fought the current, you would drown. But if you moved with the current, you could swim through it and come out of it. So she encouraged me to move through the pain, to allow myself to feel it, and in doing so, I could move past the pain. She was right, and I always remember it whenever I face extremely painful experiences. It is not that it makes it easier to feel the pain, it just keeps alive the feelings of hope which are essential to the process. Without hope that things will get better, there is no purpose to the exercise of therapy.

I Thought I Was Okay

After three years of full-time therapy, I felt that I had come through the worst. I had dealt with the deaths of my parents, and my brother's abuse, and was ready to face the world. I dropped out of therapy, and for the next three years I appeared to be okay. I still did not date (following the fiasco with the man who turned out to be gay, I have not been involved with anyone). Oh, there are men to whom I am attracted, but nothing ever happens. I knew I was stagnating, and went back and saw my therapist, but it was as if she and I had come as far as we could. So I stumbled on. Because other parts of my life were okay, I thought I was okay.

What I did was to throw myself into work. I worked 60 and 70 hours a week; I belonged to two different volunteer groups. With all of that I did not have to face my dateless life. I made friends again with other women who did not date (namely, my cousins). I did very well at work, and was promoted three times and doubled my salary in less than three years. So I thought, all in all, I was doing quite well. So what if I did not date, I thought, you can't have everything.

Then I turned my life upside down by transferring to another city. I did my usual thing—I threw myself into working 60 and 70 hours a week at the office; went in on weekends. At one point, I worked 48 straight days in a row. With my spare time I did volunteer work. And eight months after I arrived, I found myself out of work because of a political situation over which I had no control. There I was, alone in a city without family, friends, or contacts. I was devastated, and felt absolutely betrayed by my employers—it was two men who had used me as a political football and then tossed me out.

Entering Group Therapy—Everyone Looked So Normal!

I tried for a few months on my own, not getting anywhere, when I found the Women's Center. I went in for career counseling, and then mentioned maybe I might want psychological counseling. Because of having been through it before, it didn't take long to get back into the process, and early on I told the therapist that I was an incest victim. She said she had guessed because of how betrayed I felt by the men who had used me at work. Evidently something in the depth of my feeling of betrayal was too much to be attached to losing a job.

Anyway, the therapist recommended a group, and I thought okay, I'll try anything, but I was terrified. I had never talked to another incest victim. And I was afraid that when the other victims heard it was my brother and that there was only molestation (this was before I remembered the rape) that they would ask me, what's the big deal? I had always thought what I went through was nothing compared to others, so what was the big deal?

And then Monique, the group therapist, interviewed me and told me that it wasn't true that the other members would think I was making too big a deal out of it, and that one of the members had been abused by her brother, too. Needless to say, Monique made me feel better. And so I went.

I will never forget that first meeting. I was terrified, and almost did not go in. If I had not already met Monique, I would have turned around and gone home. What shocked me first was how normal everyone looked. I guess I was expecting women with three heads or something. What shocked me even more was to hear that there were members who had married and had children. I could not imagine it. How could women with our histories marry and have children? It was the first time I realized that I believed other women could have marriage and children, but not me, and it was because I was an incest victim. The one thing that bothered me about the group was calling us incest *survivors*. I didn't feel like a survivor, I felt like a victim and resented the word *survivor*.

I Now Feel Like a Survivor

Well, after a year, I now feel like a survivor. I can feel the difference in the words. Victim feels to me like someone who is presently hurting; survivor feels like someone who has come through the worst and will be okay. I now feel like I will be okay. I still have a ways to go, but it no longer seems hopeless. As scary as it is to face these last few demons (and I am praying that these are the last demons), I know from past experience that the pain of facing the demons is not as bad as living with the demons for the rest of my life. Maybe I will stop being tripped from out of nowhere.

I only hope there is something useful in all of this. I realize why it is so difficult for me to give simple answers—there are none. Incest is complex and insidious and takes a long time to heal. I have been in the healing stage for nearly eight years now. I guess it is a sign of how well I have healed that so much of my experience has jelled and it is hard to go back and sort it all out. What I do know, though, is that I get through most days by trying not to think about it except on the days when I have group or therapy. I get through those events by coming home and being by myself and writing or thinking but not by being with anyone. I could only be with someone if they knew and understood and could just sit and listen. I know no one can fix it for me now—I can now accept that I must fix it for myself.

Aloneness—Better or Worse?

One thing we talk about a lot in group is whether it is better to go through this process alone or with a spouse. When I went through the period of grieving for my loss of my father, all I wanted to do was be by myself. I didn't really want to be with anybody. It was a feeling that no one would understand, and I guess I was fortunate that I could be alone. Within our group of seven, four are married and one is living with her boyfriend, one dates. I'm the only one who is unattached and has been for years. Within our group, I'm the only one who's ever shut down like that.

Anyhow, one of the married women turned to me, and she said that sometimes she envies me, the fact that I'm alone, because I don't have to worry about anybody else. I can just take care of myself and I don't have to worry about being called selfish by somebody for wanting to take care of myself. I said, "Well, on one hand, you're very right, but there is a trade-off. I have gone through this entirely by myself and there were times when I would not want to have been by myself. I would have given anything, I would have sold my soul, just to have someone there to hug me. Even if they couldn't always understand, I wouldn't have cared about that, I would have just been happy for their presence." The idea of having another person there who cared about me at any level, who cared what happened to me when I was going through this, was wonderful. And I didn't have that. So that's a trade-off for all this.

I was trying to explain, because one of the other women Brenda, is living with her boyfriend in a very crummy, crummy relationship. She said something to the effect that just having somebody there doesn't mean that they're going to be of any help. I said, "I still think that sometimes it just must help to know that there is someone there, physically."

My aloneness, that's the thing that's been the hardest to deal with. I think that is why, even in group, it takes a lot for me *not* to detach, *not* to intellectualize. It is hard to talk about my feelings. I am so used to doing it all by myself and not having anyone to listen. The isolation has become part of it. It's an accepted part of it. But it has become a habit not to interact with people on an emotional level. My usual reaction when I hit something loaded with emotion is just to want to be by myself, unless I can be guaranteed that the person who is with me is going to understand. But you never can be guaranteed, so then it's not worth the risk. But then I feel this need for someone there, to be there. I haven't worked this out yet.

I'm Ready to Believe Now

I still have a ways to go, because, on one hand, I would very much like a relationship or like to get married; I would like to have children. But all my life I've lived with the feeling that I can't have those things. Those are things that I cannot have. Other people can have them, but not me. So, to even believe that I can have those things is probably the first step. I've got to believe that that's okay for me. And I'm ready to believe that now.

DIDI

Like many of us, Didi went into therapy because of marital problems— in her case, it was her sexual dysfunction that was the problem. Then she found herself confronting the incest. One thing to keep in mind as you read Didi's and other stories in this section is that it is often true that you feel worse before you feel better. But it is bearable if you can remember that when it is over you really are going to feel better than you did when you started.

Other issues she addresses are the problems of coping with children while trying to address incest, and the stress on her marriage.

We all have to learn to place responsibility for the incest on the abuser, either by direct confrontation with the abuser, or by shifting the responsibility in our own hearts and minds. Didi's experience with her father in joint therapy is especially useful as an example of a successful confrontation. Abusers rarely prove to be so helpful. But even as willing as he was to take responsibility, we can still see the strength of his denial in the way he tries to minimize the trauma. Confrontation is something we must prepare for, and we have to be ready to accept the consequences, including total denial. Each survivor must make an individual decision based on what she thinks will help her the most, and a realistic assessment of the outcome. Many survivors are able to place responsibility for the abuse on the abuser not by actual confrontation, but by writing unsent letters or by role-playing with their therapist. There is only one rule for confronting your abuser: Never do anything that will hurt you.

THERAPY

I Went in for One Session Expecting to Walk Out Cured

The first thing I have to acknowledge is that my incest experience affected my sex life with my husband. If it hadn't, I might never have sought therapy. Sex is so important to Danny, and before we were married it was great. But after we were married, I got so I couldn't stand it. For about two years it was painful for me to make love. I was going to doctors who were saying there was nothing wrong, but it was never right. Then we reached a point where I couldn't do it anymore, not even to please him. That was when I had to do something, and I called the Women's Center.

The first time I went to see someone, I knew right from the beginning what it was that I wanted to talk about, and I went and talked to her for an hour. I called the Center, I told them that I wanted to speak with someone, asked what were the fees, and she told me about different fees for the psychiatrists and the social workers. I told her I would talk to a social worker. She said a social worker could help me if I had a problem, but if I just wanted to talk, she could help me, too.

I thought at that time, well, all I want to do is talk to someone and it's only going to be one time. I think it was funny—I thought I could go in one time, tell the whole story, and walk out cured! So I went and talked to her and told her from the very beginning, very matter of factly, with very few tears, what had happened with my father and my sexual problems.

Finding a Group

She was impressed with my forthright approach, that I could come right out and tell her what I was dealing with and what had happened to me. She told me right then the first thing that they try to do with an incest survivor is place them in a group and that it was proven that the best method of dealing with your own problems is to meet other people.

I think everyone who's been a victim of abuse feels that isolation from other people, and once you are put into a group with other people who have been abused, your feelings of isolation dissipate. I felt more at ease talking with these people, especially when they began to share some of the same feelings and the pain.

Two Therapists Who Cared

I was lucky to get a therapist who was concerned about me. She is not the best therapist; I believe she is pretty new. I don't even think she had her master's in social work when I started. I always used to feel that when I left therapy for the day, she would run and look me up in the book somewhere and read about my case. I think she was concerned I would elude her, her first incest victim, her first survivor. She was good with me in that she really cared about me; she was a very caring woman. It was all new to me, so I was a little bit on edge about it. I would be very upset and concerned when I left, and before I went, I would be anxious. But I really believe that the best thing that ever happened to me was that she put me in the group with Monique.

It's kind of funny because I remember her saying, "Well, you know, this woman is going to call you, and you have to go interview with her to be in this group," and I thought, "I'm not going to join any group and I don't need that. That's stupid." One time was all I wanted; that's all I needed. I had no idea the amount of work, I would have to go through, that lay ahead of me.

Getting Better and Worse

I first went into therapy because of my sexual dysfunction. When I began to deal with the incest, I thought everything would be fine again. What a blow to my head! Every night I would go to bed tense, wondering, "Is he going to come to me? Want me? What will I do?" My own husband, who was going through a difficult time also, and I couldn't stand his touch. No, I couldn't even stand the thought of his touch. I sobbed and cried, felt my heart break into many pieces. I needed him, wanted and loved him. He was as understanding as he could be, but he needed so much that I couldn't give.

I lived every day feeling incompetent as a wife and a woman. Danny could not leave me alone. I would be angry. I'd express my needs, and his first response would be, "Well, what about me and my needs?" I really didn't care, but I couldn't tell him that. I really only wanted to think of myself, but I couldn't. He and I battled back and forth for a long time, talking and crying, getting better and then getting worse again.

It was real difficult being a mother at home with two little kids and trying to deal with incest in therapy. I was pregnant with Megan at first, and at some points, she was the only reason that I kept from killing myself, because I couldn't hurt my baby. I knew that if I killed myself, I would probably kill the baby. Or if I didn't kill myself and I only tried, the baby still might be hurt, and I didn't want to hurt her. But the pain of remembering the incest and the problems that it was causing in my life at the time and the problems that it had caused all my life made me really, really want to die. I was so depressed. I constantly just dreaded living, and I wanted to kill myself. I guess being pregnant, I felt as though it wasn't something I would be able to do, be able to carry out.

Trying to Care for My Family

Dealing with my oldest daughter was hard, too. I didn't abuse her, but I was not there for her. I didn't respond to her the way she needed me to respond. I spent a lot of time on the sofa, lying on the sofa in the living room, just being depressed. It was hard for me to get up, get out, get dressed, do things, even to make a meal or to do laundry. It was just too much, too overwhelming.

I don't know how I got through it; I just did. I just did everyday a little bit more. The most painful feeling was feeling like I was getting ahead and getting better and then sliding back. Two steps forward, one step back. Two steps forward, one step back, and the going back was so incredibly painful. I would feel like I was getting better and have some sort of a setback, a phone call from my father, or a visit. I'd have to visit my sister or I would see her for some reason. It was unbearable. That was really the most painful thing, the feeling like I was getting better and then not getting better. I was getting better, but I wasn't getting better as fast as I wanted to, and that was also very difficult.

I guess, in a way, I dissociated myself from my everyday tasks. No matter what I was going through emotionally, I still had to clean house, change diapers, plan meals, shop for groceries, talk to people, as if my life was fine. And I do not know how I did it. I remember Danny saying once, "You're not there for us." I cried and cried because I thought by carrying out my daily chores, I was taking care of my family. But I couldn't take care of them. I could barely keep myself alive, and I had the added responsibility of being pregnant.

Dealing With Other People

We live so close to our families that dealing with them was not uncommon. I had to see my father, stepmother, sister, her husband, and their two kids. I lived every day hating them all. The outright favoritism that he displayed for my sister and her two children hurt so much. My daughter sensed it—she knew he was not interested in her; in fact, she referred to him as "your dad"—not "Grandpa," but "your dad."

Danny's family was close by, too. But they provided a haven of "normal" people that I could hide in. I felt accepted and loved for what I was. My daughter Shannon was spoiled by aunts and uncles, and my parents-in-law were generous with love and attention to her (and the baby inside of me), but with no favoritism.

Sometimes keeping up the front for other people is the most difficult thing to bear. I felt cynical and angry when people told me I had a perfect life. I wanted to scream, "No! It's been awful. It's been painful. Feel sorry for me!" But, of course, I couldn't. I couldn't even say it to people who loved me. I still have never told my best friend—using the excuse I can't talk over the phone about it. I'm sure you know the lengths one will go to in order to keep the charade going.

Feeling Weak While Growing Stronger

Another problem I had to learn to deal with was feeling weak. It was bad enough feeling inadequate in my roles of wife, mother, lover, friend. I also felt completely unable to cope with life. Little did I realize at the time, but I was using inner strengths and supports of my own every day. At the time I felt weak and not in control. Every day, commonplace things were justifications of my victim-self. A burned finger, a bounced check, my cat being hit by a car, my child's illness (a cold), the uncomfortableness of pregnancy.

I would never wish this on anyone, but I feel that I'm a much stronger and healthier person emotionally because I dealt with it. It was never easy. It was always hard. Sometimes my heart ached so bad I wanted to die. My little family means so much to me that when I realized I was dragging them down with me, I couldn't bear it. I would rather have died than ruin them, too. If I had not had unfailing love and support from my husband, I don't know what would have become of me.

I just want to say, too, that the partner of an incest survivor has a tough time. They have the hurt, hate, anger, revengeful feelings, too. But Danny told me once, after I was over my first part of therapy, that even if he knew about what our marriage would be like during therapy and what dealing with the incest would be like, he still would have married me. And in therapy I did make progress. Gradually I started feeling better.

The Second Round—Dealing With Dad

I left therapy after I had been in for about ten months. I left therapy because I was doing very well, and Danny and I were back in sync. We had no problems for about eight months, and then things started to come back. I guess I had enough of a rest, and things started to come back, bad feelings, remembrances. My father would do small, very minute things but they would hurt me. I noticed things he would do for my sister that made me feel left out, things he would say about my sister, things he would give to my sister. I would feel terribly hurt.

I guess it was on my birthday when Danny told me I had to deal with Dad, that he either had to go into therapy with me or I had to tell him no, I can't see him again. It had to come to a head for us.

It had reached a point where I could not deal with my dad. I remember one time when he called me, Danny answered the phone. When he said it was my dad, I just got up and said, "Tell him I'm in the shower," and I went in the bathroom, took off all my clothes and got in the shower. Danny didn't like that. He said, "You have got to do something. You can't get in the shower every time he calls."

Confronting the Abuser

Finally, it got so bad, I wanted to do something, but I was terribly frightened. I went back into therapy and my therapist helped me. I went to my father and told him what he had done to me and what had happened to me as a result of it. Just by fate or by luck, he agreed to go into therapy to deal with his own problems as a neglected child. He was emotionally and physically abused as a child, and what it means is that he never dealt with his problems. What that means to me is that it ruined my life. It devastated my life.

When I talked to my dad about the incest and what it had done to me, he was very, very defensive. He called me one night, very upset, saying, "I really did only do it one time, I'll even take a lie detector test to prove it." I wasn't in a funny mood that night, but when I think of it now, the way he said it was so absurd. And I said to him,

"I'm not going to sue you. You don't have to take a lie detector test. But the truth is, the abuse lasted two years."

I told him that he didn't remember because he didn't want to remember. I did not back down. He sincerely believes that what he thinks is true, and that if it was only once, that lessens the pain, or lessens his responsibility. He also said once, "I didn't really have sex with you, so it is not really incest." And he would say, "I didn't hurt you. I don't understand why you say it hurt you." That is why he had to go into therapy with me, because I couldn't make him understand by myself. This way, maybe he'll see what he did.

Going to Therapy With the Abuser

The first couple times my dad and I were in therapy together, it was pretty difficult, because I felt like I was the only one going through any trauma. Being in therapy with him was extremely painful for me. It would have been less painful for me could I have seen the pain in my father, but I couldn't. He's so terribly bad at expressing himself and his emotions. He's really very bad at that considering he's such a well-educated man. He can't even speak about his own emotions. He has no words for them. I guess it does make me feel better in a way to realize what a bad past my father had, what a difficult life he had.

That helped me to realize that it's his problem projected onto me. It's his problems and inabilities to cope with life and the tragedy of my mother dying that caused him to project his pain onto me. That's very difficult for me, to realize that my father is human. I guess my mother, too—they were just humans, human beings, and they made mistakes, and a lot of their own problems were brought on because of their past lives. Not that my mother was abusive at all, not at all. She was full of denial and closed, didn't talk about pain.

Dealing with my father in therapy was pretty difficult. Monique wanted me to be real angry at him and I couldn't. I don't know why. I don't know if I was protecting him because he is a weak man, he is an old man, he has this horrible heart condition. He has every illness you could think of, and he doesn't hesitate to let you know that. So, I guess, in a way I was protecting him. I don't really know. At this point in time he doesn't seem to me to be the same man who abused me. I'm not the same person either. In some respects I feel as though I'm the stronger one; I know I'm the stronger one.

He Had Never Learned to Be Honest About His Emotions

He couldn't deal with his emotions; he was having a difficult time. When Monique would ask him something, he could answer with some small things about himself. But if he had to think of something on his own, tell her something about himself, it was not possible. He is just not used to being honest about his emotions. He never learned.

I used to wonder if he went home and thought about what he had done, and why he did it, and did he try to see how it was his problem? He would go home and tell my stepmother that it was my problem, something that Didi's going through. Didi has these problems.

I told him I really resented that. It was very painful to me that he did that. I don't appreciate being the one to have to bear the responsibility for this any longer. It's not my fault, and it's not just *my* problem. It affects my whole family—my immediate family and my brothers and sisters—and it also affects my husband and my children, and I'm not going to take all the responsibility for it anymore. I told him that I didn't like being the reason that he was in therapy, and he had to come to terms with it and realize that he needs to be in therapy, first, for himself and for his own problems that I don't have anything to do with.

I Put It All in a Letter—Anger, Hurt, Pain

When we started therapy together, Monique asked me to write out in a letter what I felt, and I did. I wrote a long letter; it was six pages or something. It was really very detailed, and I said a lot about the pain that I felt and the pain he had caused in my life. It was real strong. Danny was helping me write it, and, at one point, he wanted me to say something. It was very small, a very, very tiny thing, but to me, when I read it, it sounded like I was taking responsibility, and I told him, "In this letter, I'm not taking responsibility for anything. I'm going to lay it on thick and heavy. I'm going to tell him what happened to me and what hurts me and how it affected my life."

I guess I had reached a point where I didn't care anymore about looking out for his feelings or protecting him from the truth. So I wrote a very honest, strong letter, telling him what he had done to me. I feel that I have done all I should do for him, in terms of trying to do what is right. Right now I am saying, "I've done enough," even if he never comes around, even if therapy never works for him, even if our relationship is never mended. I just don't care anymore.

I used to be so upset at the prospect of losing my father, but I've never had a father, not since I was ten years old. So except that it is painful, there's nothing for me to lose by going through this with him. I don't know exactly what happened. I didn't go to that next session and so I don't know if he read it or she read it or what happened, but eventually he took the letter home, and he has the letter, which to me means a lot.

He Tried to Make Me Feel Guilty

He called me the night that he read the letter. I was really upset because I had told Monique that she could have him call me, and then, of course, I changed my mind and didn't want him to call me at all. When he called, I didn't want to talk to him, but there was really no way that I could get out of it. But I said to him from the beginning of the conversation, "I don't really have time to talk to you. I don't want to talk for a long period of time."

Then he brought out all kinds of crap and he said, "You shouldn't feel abandoned. I didn't ever abandon you." I was so fed up at that point, I was sick of the man, so I said, "You did so abandon me. What do you call it? It was abandonment. I needed a parent, you were not a parent. I had to become a parent."

Then he skipped over that, and he tried to make me feel guilty. I told him he needed to be in therapy for himself, and he said, "Oh, no, no, I just want to know what I can do to help you get over it and to get you on with your life, because you have such a full life ahead of you and I'm going to die soon," or something like that. When he said, "I don't have much longer to live," I was really almost throwing up at that point. I said, "Come on, you need to deal with this, it's your problem first, I've been dealing with this for my whole life and I've been dealing with it in therapy for two years." I said, "You're the one who needs to deal with it. You need to reconcile yourself with your own emotions about your problem."

But he couldn't see it. I mean, you lay it out plain and simple, and he could not see it. We were talking about this in group the other night, how with some people you can explain things as clear as can be, crystal clear, a-b-c, one-two-three, the easiest way, and they still act like they have no idea of what you're talking about. It just blows my mind that I could stand there and talk to him plain as day and then he'll go on to another conversation completely forgetting what I've told him, just ignoring it completely. I guess the denial is just too strong.

Then he started to tell me about how he had been verbally abused when he was a child, and later, after I had hung up, I was thinking to myself that a normal person would call it emotional abuse. But a person who doesn't see things quite that way would only consider it verbal abuse. It's only verbal abuse if they yell at you, it's not emotional abuse.

So far he's been in therapy with Monique only a couple of weeks. She said, give it some time. I don't know what that means; I don't know what is going to come out of it. But I do know that knowing he's in therapy with her, and that all I have to do is go to the group, that really just relieves me of a lot of pain.

Group Is a Big Help

Going to the group is so incredibly helpful even when I don't have a problem and I can just go and listen. The people in the group mean so much to me because, not only have they gone through the same type of thing, but they've listened to me and they've heard what I've gone through. They know more about me than any friend I've ever had, and they still love me, and that means an incredible amount to me. I feel like sometimes they loved me when they knew even more about me than even Danny did at points. I guess because he has to live with me, I have to treat him a bit more carefully. In group, I can say anything, because then I can go home!

I'm at a good point in my life now in terms of working things out with my father, but it's also very stressful when I feel as though I'm the parent making sure that he does the right thing by going into therapy. But it also helps a lot to give up some of my parentification, which I can do because my therapist is taking care of me and taking care of my dad. So I think I can start now to let go of that feeling of being responsible for him, of being his parent.

Also I have Danny to help me. He did push me to do something, but he also followed through. He didn't push me into something and then leave me high and dry with no support. He pushed, but he was there to back up whatever decision I was going to make. And he never pushed me into a specific decision, but to make a decision, period.

Therapy Issues—Children

A lot of issues came up in therapy, in group, that I've had to deal with aside from the therapy with my dad. The problems I started out addressing in therapy centered around my marriage and my sex life with my husband, but I also think that my problems affect my girls tremendously. I think that my oldest daughter has been affected by this a lot because of my own behavior. I have problems coping with children, very understandably being tense and upset and snappy, not patient, like I believe mothers should be. Then I hear my friends talking about how they yell at their children, and I think, "You've got to be a more normal mother than I am."

I don't think that I'm abusive, but I do feel that I'm not there for my oldest daughter emotionally. She needs me to play with her, but I don't want to. I crave my privacy and I crave my moments of solitude to do things. I have a lot of projects that I'm always working on, which I enjoy doing. It gives me some self-satisfaction when I complete something. But it's just not always possible to do what I want to do, when I want to do it, and when I feel like doing it. That's caused a lot of problems for me in my home life: wanting and needing to be selfish and not being able to. I mean, how many parents with young children can take time to soak in a bathtub or read a book? It's just not possible. It's physically impossible, but it's needed so much emotionally.

I believe that one of the reasons why I've been able to go through the therapy and deal with this has been that Danny has always considered my job at home with the girls to be a very relevant position that means a lot. He shows that to me by letting me take time for myself in the evening, on the weekends, or when he's home. He never has a problem with watching the girls, and that's been a tremendous help. I always craved my privacy, I suppose because I never had any privacy, but I crave it now and I want it, and when I really need it, it's available to me and that means a lot.

Worrying That My Children Might Be Abused

Being a mother and having been an incest victim, I worry about my children. Then I worry that I worry too much, that I overcompensate, I become too protective. And then I worry that I'm not being protective enough! Whenever my daughter goes through a bad stage— when she went through a period of nightmares, which is very common at three years old, I thought, oh my God, she's being abused. I'm going to have to watch out. I'm going to ask her these certain kinds of questions to find out.

Of course, always, in the back of my mind, I worry about them being abused. I just know that Danny would never, ever hurt the children in that way. But if I ever have a question or concern, I just don't feel I have to leave them with someone. My stepmother used to always say to me, "Some day you could leave the girls over here when you go away for the weekend or something." In the back of my mind I was screaming, "No way, lady, what do you think I am—crazy? I'm not leaving my children with you."

I wouldn't say it to her, and it's never really become a problem, but it's always been something that's haunted me, that something might happen. I don't know, I hate to even think about it. I try not to. But I think that's definitely one of the problems of being a mother is worrying so much about your child becoming abused. I worry sometimes if maybe I'm not there for her emotionally, to keep that from happening.

I always look to Danny, and I guess I'm lucky that I have him. I always look to him to help me figure out whether I'm on track or not. To know whether I'm running like a normal person or whether I'm running like an abused person. He always helps me figure things out that way. I guess I just consider him to be so normal that he helps me to figure things out.

Another thing—and I think everybody must go through this—I wonder about people that know, I wonder if they were abused as children. I run that scenario through my head all the time, about almost everyone I know. I try and figure out if there were points in their lives where something might have triggered an abuse like that, or if they were emotionally abused in other ways. To me, it's almost sickening, because so many people that I know have really strong characteristics towards having been abused as children. I don't know if it's the kind of people I know or if it's really that incredibly rampant, if that many people were abused.

Feeling a Lot of Women's Issues

Another problem that has come up in therapy recently is that I've been dealing a lot with women's issues, feeling a lot of women's issues. I am feeling as though I've let a lot of things pass me by because I was too weak to get involved. I thought the easiest way out for me would be to be married and stay home with children, which is definitely not the easiest, but I believed that it would be an outlet for me. So, the women's movement kind of passed me by, and I feel like I missed something in terms of being a woman first, missing the experience of being single as an adult and being alone. I really feel like I've missed something.

I think I'm going through a period where I really dislike Danny just because he is a man, and because men did this to women, and because men feel as though they have to have a power over a woman, whether their wife or their daughter or a sibling. That's been very painful to me. Poor Danny, he's obviously never been that way! He's not an abusive man in any sense, and power to him is not an issue. He's not a man who craves power; he's just too good for that. I'm biased towards Danny, but even so, I look at him and I'm very angry with him just for being a male. Even though he is not a man in that way—he's not an abusive man, and he's not a powerful man. But I still sometimes take him for just being a man and that's been a real hard issue to resolve.

I'm Lucky to Have Good Treatment Available

Being in group means that I can share other people's experiences, and that helps me to get a better view of myself, see my experience in perspective. I feel I've been very fortunate in my search for therapy and in the help that I've received.

ANN-MARIE

Good therapy is something we have to look for. It rarely just falls in our laps. Ann Marie is one of several people in this book who ran into denial—the vestiges of denial—in the mental health professions. Or it may have been just lack of experience. Whatever you call it, it prevented Ann-Marie from getting help when she looked for it. The lesson we can learn from this is: Don't give up. There are good therapists who can help you, but you have to find them.

Ann-Marie also discusses two important issues that come up in therapy—the changes we undergo and the stress that places on all our relationships, and the question of self-disclosure.

LOOKING FOR A THERAPIST

For years I walked around with incest, like it was some huge refrigerator I carried. It's like it's attached to you. It's invisible; nobody else sees it but you, but you always know it's there. You know it's about so big and so high, but you don't what it's for, you don't know how much it weighs, you don't know what its impact on you is. You don't know where it connects to your body. That's what it was like before I went into therapy.

I started in marriage counseling in late '77, early '78. That was the first time I saw a marriage counselor, because my first marriage was really on the skids. I brought it up with the counselor, and all she wanted to know was, "Was there any penetration?" Well, hell, I couldn't remember, and I still can't remember, if there was any actual penetration. And that was the end of the discussion.

So I went to her for a while, then broke it off with my husband, then started dating somebody. That was when I had the last serious relationship that I had in between my ex-husband and my current husband. He and I ended up going to couples' counseling, and I brought up the incest again and again, but the counselors didn't say anything. I kept saying, "Gee, do you think this has any bearing on our problems?" I finally stopped asking. I just stopped asking the question because there was no response. It wasn't like I withheld it. It wasn't like I denied it in the sense of telling myself it didn't happen.

Looking for Something to Tell Me That Something Was Wrong

I finally had what I would call concrete evidence that there was something wrong here, that this was not a normal thing. I had been looking for something to tell me that something was wrong. Finally, the newspaper had an article about incest victims and I read every word of it. What struck me was it said that we don't have to be drug addicts, prostitutes, or whatever. Everything else I had ever read, any little bits that ever came out always said, "drug addict, prostitute," whatever. But this article said that even in women who are not prostitutes and drug addicts, incest leaves emotional scars, no matter what.

And I said, "Aha! It is true; there are things that are wrong with me." I don't know how else to say this, it was like I kept looking for that. I kept trying to find people who could verify that I had a problem. I knew it was, but I kept searching for people to help me with it. I could not find anybody who understood the ramifications of it because I didn't know myself.

I mean, I suspected it caused some marital problems. My ex-husband and I had a terrible sex life. It got to the point where he claimed he never knew how to masturbate. Everyone I have ever said this to has just died laughing over this. Even though I wouldn't have sex with him, I had to masturbate him. Does that sound familiar? To bring him to climax. Oh God, I hated it. I absolutely hated it. So, I knew whatever "normal" was supposed to be, this wasn't right. Even though I had never had "normal," I knew it wasn't right. I kept trying to find help, to help me understand, where is the problem, how do I fix it? I never had any success until finally I saw that article, and I decided, "Okay, I'm going to try again."

Finally, I Started Getting Some Answers

I went to a local mental health clinic where I had gone the very first time with my first marriage, and I said, "I do not want the counselor I had before, if she is still here." So I got a counselor, but ended up dropping that one. She got me into contact with another woman, and I ended my first session with her deciding it wasn't incest.

Then I talked to two counselors who were with this counseling cen-

ter. They ran a women's support group, and I saw one of them individually. The one I saw individually did have training or knowledge
of incest or something, and she was very good. It was like a light bulb
turning on. Finally, I was getting some answers to my questions.
Like the whole issue of trust: I started to understand why my trust
mechanisms are so screwy. I also went to the group. The group itself
was more of a support group for a lot of issues with women. They
were difficult issues, but I decided it was not a place to bring up the
incest.

I was doing a fair amount of travel for my job, and I started coming
down here for a project. It turned out that I got to go home every
other weekend, so that's when I saw the counselor, when I went home
on weekends. We were still able to keep that going, even though I
had to drop out of the group during the week.

Finding a Group

I met my husband Jack when I was down here. I decided to move
here, decided to move in with him, get married, and all that. Well, I
had been living here full time for about a year when I wanted to go
back to a support group. I decided to try and find a support group
again, whatever I could find. I stumbled onto the Women's Center.
There was a notice in the newspaper business section. They called it
the "Young Professional Woman's Support Group."

I ended up getting a counselor on the phone, and I talked with her
a couple of times about what I was looking for. She was trying to put
a new group together, and we went back and forth without coming up
with any group for me. I finally just decided to see her privately. I
was also pursuing the ACOA things, but I found those group meetings to be too big for the most part. I really needed a one-on-one, intense discussion. I had so much I wanted to say, and so much I
wanted to learn from other people, to ask questions, so individual
therapy seemed best.

The first year with my therapist, I swear I probably just talked a
blue streak for the most part. She guided conversations a little bit. I
told her when I first got in there that I just needed to talk. I said, "I
have no one to talk to, I've been very isolated." I told her about the
incest right up front, and that's when she told me about the incest
group. If there's nothing else that comes out of this book, I can't urge
people enough to find a good, competent therapist and a group. The
group is necessary to recover. I don't think it's an optional thing, not
for me at least.

Getting Out of the Isolation

A group is the only way you can get out of your isolation. I heard this tape that made the comment that when you're in group, it's not such a big secret anymore. It still is, because I don't tell people what the group is for. My mother, I just assume, thinks it's an ACOA thing. But the circle has widened a little bit. I don't have to cope with it alone anymore. I can get help from people who have been there.

That's why Megan has been so valuable to me in group. From the minute I laid eyes on her, I liked her. There is a sparkle of life in her that through all this has not failed her. She's just a very loving, very caring person who's gone through a great deal on her own. She's had her own struggles. I know she has definitely served as hope for me, because I see a lot of health in her that I don't think I have yet. Anyway, that doesn't matter. Even if the group is full of people who are down in the mouth, there is nothing like being in a group and being able to laugh about it together. Believe it or not, we laugh a lot.

You are there with a group of people who understand what you went through, and you're on the same wavelength. It helps because you will all have different issues that are active at different times. Like, I'm now into family secrets, because I read a book that talked about it quite a bit, and I realized it was a big issue for me. Understanding my relationship with my mother is the other major one right now, just because I heard a tape of a talk given by someone who is pretty expert on this and because it verbalized so well for me things that I have not been able to think of myself. And in group I find the same thing. People will come up with issues and talk about them in such a way that I can identify them in myself where I couldn't before.

Changes Are Happening Fast

This time my therapy is serious. When I started with my therapist and with group, we really started hitting the issues. It has only been about two years, but it has been a rough two years.

When people start therapy, one of the scariest things is the amount of change they go through. For me, the changes are happening so fast that I'm not sure how far it's going to go, or where it's going to take me. When I started, I thought—oh, well, six weeks should do it. Go to the therapist, tell her the whole story, walk away cured. "Just hypnotize me, Doc"—right? Then I realized the extent of the process, and I had to accept the risks and really believe that I had to do it to get well. The process, as painful as it is, is a lot less painful than what life would be without it.

One of the things I've had to face—the biggest danger to my own relationship with my husband—is that if it comes down to having to give up myself or give up the marriage, the marriage is going to have to go. I cannot sell myself short anymore. I don't even have a choice now.

Talk about feeling out of control—I feel that I'm on a train. There are forces in me that are happening, and I'm not going to stop. I may lose a marriage again. We were talking about the rates of change in people—even if you have a relatively healthy marriage, the rate of change can be so different between the two partners that one of them may not be able to keep pace. The process can just explode you apart.

Is It Easier Alone?

I've looked with envy at people who are going through this alone. Their progress is much faster, easier, simpler. I'm even considering separation just so I won't have to deal with the relationship—just put it aside for a while. If I have some basic needs in the relationship and if they are not being satisfied, then it's just another painful thing I have to deal with while I'm trying to heal myself.

In therapy, some needs are surfacing. These are needs I have to have met in a relationship. If they aren't, then what is the point of it? Something has got to give. I cry all the time about it; I've got to say something to him, and it starts the emotional appeals to him all over again. But we get nowhere.

So, there is a lot of risk associated with this process. But I've gone so far that I don't have any choice anymore. I've got to go on with it.

Pressure on the Marriage

I try to get my husband Jack to understand that concept, and he's slowly coming around. It's very slow, but I think he is finally showing progress. A couple of months ago, I issued, not an ultimatum, but more of a statement of despair. I said to him, "I need some *emotional* support from you. Whether you're helpful around the house, or whatever, it's not enough. I'd get that from a roommate." All I was asking for him to do was periodically, knowing that I'm grappling with these issues, to check in with me, ask me how I'm doing, or if he sees me upset, to respond. He didn't.

About a month or so ago, we had a real crisis. It was around our anniversary. We had a terrible anniversary weekend. We came home on that Sunday, and I ended up crying out, I had such pain that night. I finally said, "I need some emotional connection. I'm tired of feeling so separated from people around me."

I told him that if he wants to be my roommate, I can't have that. It's got to be more than that. I said, "I've told you, time and time again, just the little things you can do. I'm not asking you to be my therapist; just let me know you care. This is one time you've got to do it my way. I know there are other ways you can let me know you care that *you're* more comfortable with, but this is the bottom line. There is no choice, you have got to do it this way. I just need you to ask me once in a while how things are going." And I said, "If it comes down to it, if it means me or the marriage, I'll have to tell you right now, it's going to be me."

I was crying just very softly, and I said, "Jack, I'm not threatening you. I don't want to leave the marriage. I think you know that I've been through this before, and if I really felt badly, I would leave. I've done it before. I know what's involved, and I know I can survive."

Self-Disclosure

Another issue I've been confronting in therapy is self-disclosing—who can I tell? I have a friend I've known since high school—only one of two links I have back to that time. I desperately want to tell her about what happened. This is a friendship I've had 20 years! But I'm afraid. She has this one image of me, and it doesn't include incest. We've established a deeper friendship recently. We started talking about what we meant to each other as kids; we felt accepted by each other. I really wanted to tell her—she *knows* me. She knew me right at the time all the incest happened, and there are some things I'd like to ask her about, what I was like back then. But I'm afraid to tell her, because I'm afraid she's going to suddenly change her whole perception of me, that it will wipe out all the good things about me and she'll think of me only in terms of the incest.

Since being in group, I've really intensified my therapy. I have cut my contact with my family back to a very minimum, because I can't stand being there. The incest is very much on my mind now, and when I'm around even close friends who don't know, it's a burden on me, because this is a big part of me, it's a very important issue to me right now. Yet I'm very afraid to tell the people who don't know, because then I'm afraid I will lose them. I have lost friendships before, friendships that have died within a year after I told someone. I have an impression that I will lose the people I tell.

I didn't tell a soul about the incest that I can remember until I graduated from college. I told my ex-husband at some point; I don't remember how early in the marriage it was. I also told my first boss at my company, who is now a very good friend of mine. But until then, for all those years, I kept it in and never told a soul.

I Want to Get the Secret Out

The feeling I have today is I very much want to get the secret out. I think my brother and my mother were both very jealous of me in the family. In a lot of ways, I was bright, I got my father's good words, I got his love. Supposedly, I got all these great things. They never realized what the misery was. Imagine you see a stranger on the street who looks like she has it all, wealth, fame, whatever, but inside, she's got a child dying from cancer or something absolutely horrible. That's the way I felt. They resented me for things I never really had.

My mother's always said that she's loved me, but I've never really felt accepted by my own family, because they never knew the truth about it. I'm scared to tell my mother right now, and my brother, because I'm afraid of alienating what family I have left. I mean, my dad's gone. I don't know what their reaction will be, but I think that will be the worst to me. The day I know that I can cope with the possibility, for whatever reason, that they will say, "That's it. We don't want to talk to you. We don't even want to pursue those memories," if I think I can cope with that, then I'll tell them. But if I can't, then I won't. I can't do it, because I can't alienate myself from the family.

Facing the Issues Now

I feel that I need my family, although now I am feeling more anger to my mother for allowing it to happen than I do for my father for doing it to begin with. I feel guilty about that. It makes it very difficult. I run hot and cold. We had our last phone conversation, oh, weeks ago. I called her to thank her because she sent us this thing, it's a little thing with a ruffle, and it says, "Bless This Home," just a real pretty wall plaque. So I called her to thank her for it, which was real nice. I came out with such a warm feeling from that conversation. It was just nice to talk to Mom.

She's always so glad to hear from me. As soon as she knows who it is on the phone, you can hear the warmth flooding in her voice. When I go home to see her, I get a big hug, and when I leave, she always has tears in her eyes. It's not fake stuff, she really, sincerely believes it.

She's always talking about what good kids we are. Every once in a while, she'll be sitting at the breakfast table drinking her cup of coffee in the morning, and she'll just grab a piece of paper and she'll just write. I wish I would have saved some of them because they were a recurring thing, almost word for word each time.

Sometimes she'd get to reminiscing about the things that have happened, and then she thanks God for two such wonderful kids. Not quite that she couldn't have made it through without us, but kind of a general flavor that we were there, and all this wonderful stuff. I guess I've always taken it as love.

But underneath it all, I realize she didn't do the same thing for me. She wasn't there for me when I needed her. She didn't listen to me the way I needed to be listened to. You know, all those things. It's a real love/hate relationship with her. Well, not hate. It hasn't gotten quite as strong as hate yet, just a real love/annoyed relationship with her, or something. Maybe love/hate is more like it. It is something I'm working on.

Gradually, I'm discovering the issues. I'm facing them. I'm working them out. Not necessarily finding what I would like to find, but facing what I have to face. I can't stop now, I can't go back. It is frightening sometimes to see how far this process can take me, but I'd rather do it than not do it.

BRENDA

It took Brenda years to find a therapist who could help her. She had to reach a crisis point that compelled her not just to look for but to demand help. Brenda's progress in five years of therapy is evident in her clear assessment of her problems and the feeling that she is moving forward in her life rather than looking backward. Brenda is learning to take care of herself—not just survive, but to actually nurture herself and to allow other people to care for her. This is really what therapy is about—it doesn't make the incest go away; it helps us grow beyond it.

THERAPY

A Therapy Sideshow

As I said earlier, I'd made several attempts in my twenties to get counseling and found myself being a sideshow, a freak show, to doctors who had never heard this kind of story before. I was told that when you are married you have to do what your husband says. You don't have a choice; you have to have sex. "You're making a big deal out of a sexual abuse from when you were a child. You're not a child anymore, you're an adult." Basically I heard, "Get your act together and get on with your life. Why do you keep dwelling in the past?" Feeling that I had no right—my God, I was an adult, why couldn't I take care of this? So I dropped the therapy. I didn't want to be a sideshow anymore, and if I was supposed to be able to take care of myself, well then I would take care of myself. And what I did is, I locked the door. I didn't think about it anymore.

The Problems Didn't Go Away

I remember I had dated a gentleman for a number of years, and one evening we were horsing around with the kids in the living room, wrestling around. He pinned me on the floor, and, all of a sudden, I started crying. I had to get away, and he didn't understand. He thought he had hurt me; the children were upset.

I went outside and I walked around and I realized it was the same kind of position, the same strength, the same helplessness I'd experienced as a child, not being able to move. I was horrified that it was coming back to haunt me again. Even at this point, it took me a few weeks to get over that. I locked it up again and gave it no credence. After all, I was an adult. I should be able to take care of myself.

But from then on out, the sex life went down the tubes. I wasn't able to have sex; when I did, it was a functionary thing. I did it because I thought I had to. I did it because I wanted to please. I did it for all the wrong reasons. Eventually, of course, that relationship dissolved. That was the first relationship I had after my first marriage failed.

When I met my second husband, he had just finished a divorce, too. He was looking for someone to help him, and, of course, I was an adult; I could take care of myself, I was used to taking care of other people. I'm comfortable with that, so I took care of him, helped him get through his divorce and deal with matters with his children.

Another Treatment Fiasco

Then my son went into a psychiatric hospital. Once again, I was subjected to telling about myself because, as the doctors explained, they needed history so that they could help Robert. So I volunteered everything. Again and again, I would walk away, drive back from Baltimore an hour-and-a-half, being overwhelmed with these open emotions again, thinking of all the things that happened to me and not knowing how to deal with them, not getting any assistance, no one there to help me.

After a year-and-a-half of this constantly, two, three, four times a week at the hospital with my son at night and going through therapy sessions with him, things started to come apart. My second husband sat through some of the sessions, hearing the horrors. He got wrapped up in it to the point where he treated me as an invalid, as if I couldn't take care of myself, as if this poor thing who had suffered all these years had to be taken care of. And, of course, he couldn't take care of me. I was the only one who could have done it.

By this point I was in a state of exhaustion, just from the sheer physical drain of working all day and driving to Baltimore to be in therapy and driving back late at night, trying to be a wife, and a mother to my other son.

Finally, Effective Treatment

I reached a point, probably my all-time low (it was toward the end of the marriage as a matter of fact), when I walked into the Women's Crisis Center, and I knew that if I left there without help, I would kill myself. I told them that. Thank God, they turned my case over to one of the best psychologists I'd ever met; she was a woman from Argentina. I didn't know it at that time. Because I didn't know what a great experience this was going to be for me. Here again, I was very cautious. I would say things I thought they'd wanted to hear, make up stories, anything. Just so long as I had the safety of being there for the hour, or two hours, or whatever my appointment was, and gradually trying to get some strength back for myself.

My second husband went with me occasionally. That turned out to be a method that wasn't working for me. I was lying, I was manipulating, trying to rescind, create the picture that I could take care of myself, I could take care of him, and I was only there because, well, I had broken down temporarily. Basically I just wanted to get back on my feet so I could administer to the needs of my husband. It just didn't work.

I constantly broke down to the sexual demands my husband was placing on me for becoming phenomenally stronger and stronger. It seemed like he was healthy and he didn't know how to deal with an unhealthy person. It was a constant reminder that if our sex life was better our whole life would be better. The more this happened, the more guilt, the more shame I accepted, the more responsibility I accepted. Finally, after about a year of this, we separated. I couldn't take it anymore.

Trying to Make It on My Own

I continued in therapy, and I thought I was cresting over one of the "hills," when I moved and I could no longer go to the state crisis center. I had these grand illusions that I was healthy again. I didn't need therapy anyway, so it was fine.

When I moved I was in a relationship with a man. I had been separated from my husband for about six months, feeling stronger, and went into another relationship with a needy man who needed someone to take care of him, meaning someone to replace his mom, who had been a very forceful and strong figure in his life. She still was in his life although she lived far away in another state. But, she was still such a constant and strong influence that he needed someone to take care of him. I fulfilled the bill.

After about four months, I was again in a crisis situation with the sex thing. I'd throw up if I had sex. I felt used and abused, and I felt like I had no choices, and again I was just at a real bad mental state. I found the Women's Center and started there.

Back to Therapy

The reason I went back, of course, was because I couldn't have sex. I was still not relating back to the incest. The counselor, who I'm still seeing, also referred me to the incest group headed up by Monique. I was very apprehensive about that. I wasn't sure what that meant to me. I knew within the first three months of the group, to which I had made a six-month commitment, that I was going to live up to my six-month commitment. But I didn't say much. I listened. I asked a lot of questions. I was trying to figure out where I was.

Now I've been in the group for over a year, and I'm finally really starting to like myself. I'm feeling confident about my work. I've been promoted to vice president of my company, and I'm really starting to take that seriously. It's a pride thing. I used to always think that I was a token, that they're trying to appease me. I'm starting to look seriously at the compliments I receive when people say they respect my work, my judgment. I'm starting to look at that differently. I used to think, "They're just saying something to be nice." Now I'm starting to believe it.

A Real Turning Point

My second husband, Dave, at Christmas time, gave me a most wonderful Christmas gift. He had continued in therapy after our separation, and he came back at Christmas time. By this time we'd been separated for a year-and-a-half. We sat down and talked. He expressed to me that he had not heard what I said to him, that he had not recognized my feelings, and after being in therapy for the additional year, he realized the things he had done wrong, the ways he had hurt me, even though unintentionally.

This was something totally new to me. It was new in several ways. One is, someone was actually validating my feelings, someone was actually saying, "You were right. Your instincts were right. Your perceptions were right. Your feelings were right." That was so important to me; it was a real turning point. I was ready to hear that.

Also, we've established some sort of a friendship, which is an unusual behavior for me. Ever since I can remember, when something happened, someone got angry, or for some reason they moved away, I immediately cut them out of my life. It was like they never existed prior to that. It's a wonderful experience to know that something went wrong, but you can recapture goodness that you both have. It doesn't mean you're both bad people forever. It's a wonderful feeling. It's something I've not felt before. I'm starting to experience what I feel is a sense of peace and freedom. I know I still have a long way to go with the sexual aspects, and maybe that will never be right for me, but I'm coming to peace with myself.

When my mother died three years ago, I was so relieved. I was literally happy that she was dead and she couldn't harass me anymore. I never had any feelings of sadness for her. I always hated her so much, I just wanted desperately for her to die. When she died, I was glad. However, it took me months, even in therapy, to realize that she was dead and that this wasn't another horrible trick, that she wasn't going to come back and do something else that was cruel and make me feel guilty, make me feel cheap, make me feel ugly. She really was dead, and I didn't have to fear her anymore. I didn't have to take responsibility for her. I could get on with my own life, start developing who I was.

Another Challenge

In the last few months, right before Thanksgiving, a young woman came to me and said that she was my sister. She's one of the children my mother sold. It was most shocking, of course. I didn't know what to do with that. Here again, I felt I had to take care of her. She's a younger sister, but she was adopted by a very wealthy family in Virginia.

She has her own set of problems, it's true, but there were so many things going through me. Why did she get chosen? Why did she live such a normal life? Why did she have all the things I never had? What made my mother allow her to continue her life in a normal fashion by selling her, while keeping me and torturing me? There was anger, jealousy, and now I'm dealing with all of that.

She wants to be a sister and I don't know how to be a sister, but Monique's going to help me work on that one. I'm really trying to define family structures, what people's roles are in a family, as a mother, as a sister, as a friend, whatever the role is. I'm so confused about that, so used to being the caretaker. That was my only function.

Letting Go of My Mother

So a lot of things are happening. Good things. I've finally come to have some understanding of my mother after reading all the records that I'd received from the government on my mother and realizing what a horrible life she had, coming from an abusive family. A father who used to shoot at the children, beat them; they were hungry, sexually abused. Just a horrible poverty.

She was a young woman growing up with children, not having the resources that I have today nor the acceptance of society, where it's okay to be a single mother, it's okay for women to work, it's okay for a woman to say no. In those days, I know that women were dependent on men for their livelihood. To be a divorced woman—the loneliness she must have experienced, the destitution, being a mother and not knowing what that meant. I'm sure not knowing how to love her children, not knowing how to protect them.

I could feel sorry for her now. I can feel sad for her. But I'll never forgive her. It's been with Monique's help and Joanna's help (my therapists) that I've learned that it is okay not to forgive her. For a long time I thought the only way to handle it was to hate her, and I felt guilty about hating her because part of me wanted to feel sorry for her and wanted to feel her sadness. But now I can talk about it. I feel fine. I feel like everything's okay somehow between her and me.

Lately, I've thought about her. Would she be in heaven or would she be in hell? I hope she's not in heaven—although part of me hopes she's not in hell, because she had her hell. I guess the best thing I could hope for her now is that she is somewhere between heaven and hell with a therapist as good as the ones I have. That certainly is a major step in my life.

I never thought I'd reach a point where I could say anything decent about the woman. I feel good knowing that it's okay for me not to ever forgive her. Because the things she did were wrong. The way she treated us was wrong. But there are reasons, and that's a side of me I like to see. I tend to be a very black-and-white person in so many ways. I like being able to think I'm developing some grey areas.

A Good Relationship With My Children

I'm a lot more honest with my children. For years, they never knew the kind of mother they had. I lied about who I was, how I grew up. Now I can sit down and I can talk to them. I can tell them, yes, I was an incest victim. I don't go into details, but, yes, I had a terrible childhood, and I don't know a lot of the skills that I need to know, to be a good mother to them, and I regret that. But, in every way possible, I'm working to be a good mother now. And I hope they understand how much I love them, how much I want to provide for them. I will always be, as long as I'm alive, I will be here for them.

These are all so new for me, to be able to say these things to them. I am reaping some of the benefits from it. I know that they are protective of me. In their own ways they want to be there for me, and I'm trying to let them. I remember the times when they wanted to be there, and I couldn't let them, because I had to take care of everybody else. Now I'm trying, when they want to take care of me, when they want to help, when they want to assist, I'm trying to let them do that, because it makes them feel good.

All the times that I remember back over the years of taking care of them, protecting them, and doing things with them, I realize now that it lowered their self-esteem. I didn't give them a chance to grow, develop skills, and accept responsibility and also to receive the accolades that went along with it, the good feelings of success, the good feelings of accomplishing something, overcoming something, defeating fears. All those things that I thought I was protecting them from, I should have allowed them to experience. We can talk about that now.

I Have Choices Now

I can look at the relationship I'm in now with a man. Yes, I know that this is another relationship going bad, although now I can look at it and I can say it wasn't a healthy relationship from the beginning. If I can walk out of this with self-respect and an understanding of why it failed, then I'm that much healthier than I thought I was.

I am reaching a point where I do have choices. I'm not afraid to say no. If that's not okay with someone else, that's their problem. I've learned through this group therapy that everybody has problems, and I'm a good person and a caring person, and I'll do everything I can to make life easy and happy for someone. But now I need to be happy. Now I need to be cared for, and I want to care for me. I don't want to be afraid anymore. I want to recognize that I have the right to have needs.

ELLEN

After many years of unsuccessful treatment, Ellen keeps going back. We can be encouraged by this persistence rather than discouraged by years without progress. You will notice that her experience with shock treatments and mental hospitals in the 1950's is not included in this therapy chapter. That is because I don't think that experience can properly be called "therapy" as we understand it today.

Ellen still struggles with denial and is still not sure she wants to know what happened to her. She will make some progress in therapy, but she won't go very far until she herself makes the commitment. This is a reminder to all of us that we are individually responsible for our own recovery. Even the best therapist cannot make us go any faster than we are willing or ready to go. Only we can do it. But we also have to respect our own needs and trust the inner time-clock that tells us when we are ready to work in therapy. Ellen's progress in therapy is paced by an inner necessity which we all learn to respect, and trust.

THERAPY

"Therapy" Felt Like Punishment

My experiences with shock treatments, mental hospitals where I was drugged, woman-hating Freudian psychiatrists—all of it taught me one thing—they can't help me. I don't think any of it was "therapy." It felt more like punishment, like, "Oh, yeah, I'm bad, and I deserve this."

Only by turning away from it and pulling myself together was I able to have a life. But I kept trying to get help. The tape playing in my head saying, "Quit feeling sorry for yourself, there is nothing wrong with you," it didn't always work.

When Brett, towards the end of our relationship, told me I hadn't dealt with the rape that happened when I was 8, I was willing to go for help just for his sake. I didn't expect much. I was still wondering,

"What *did* happen with my grandfather?" I remembered the "playing around," the fondling of my genitals. Why did I always feel there was more? But no—can't have those thoughts: they're crazy.

Trying Therapy Again

So I went for an interview at the Women's Counseling Center, and I told them, "I'm here because I feel inferior, and I'm starting to do a victim thing with the man I'm with." He was starting to do Nautilus, and he quit smoking, and I felt that he was putting me down all the time. I don't think he was, I just felt like he was, and the feeling was getting stronger and stronger all the time. Also, I wanted a commitment from him, and he wouldn't commit, so I was starting to do a victimization number.

Anyway, the woman I talked to at this center heard all this, and she said, "You know, you sound like an incest survivor." Well, that was the *first time* anyone had ever said that to me, and something in me felt a relief, a breath of cool air flowing over me. But at the same time, a voice in me said, "This is ridiculous"—like my mother saying, "You can't let yourself believe this woman because then you'll be feeling sorry for yourself."

Then she asked me if anyone tried to do anything to me when I was little. And I said, "Oh yeah, just my grandfather—he tried to get his hand under my sunsuit, and into my vagina when I was sitting in his lap. But that's all." And she said, "That's all it takes." And then I said, "Well, I was raped when I was eight, and then after the rape, my father examined me and told me that I'd done something bad." She told me that was more than enough.

Then an explosion went off in my head. Twenty-two years of "shrinking" paid off. I thought, "So that's it—*so that's it.* Now I understand, for God's sake. Now I understand.

I've Got to Face My Problems

I got into an incest group and I felt very separated from them all. I felt like I was this mature, professional scientist who had gone through all this stuff and survived—my father never made me pregnant or had intercourse with me. So I looked at the rest of the group, and I thought, "They've really got problems. I'm just here for whatever."

But now I feel I can't take that position anymore. I've got to face my problems. I tried to use the tools my mother gave me—like, you know, "Straighten up and fly right"—but that's not working anymore.

It's like I'm splitting into two parts—the one part that has always been very strong and says, "You're fine, nothing much happened to you. You just have a weakness in your psyche, in your emotions." I've been roaring down the road with that. Now, it's like that is splitting into two pieces, and there's another piece that's saying, "Things happened to you that you need to remember."

My Therapist Kept Falling Asleep

I had a male therapist for a while, and he was great. It was before I started going to the incest group. After that, I continued to see him while I was in the group. But I got to the place where one day, I guess it was because of things that were coming up in the group, I realized that I trusted him to the point that I wanted to be like a little girl, and sit on his lap, and have him hug me, but I also wanted to get angry at him and beat on his chest with my fist. I felt that I needed to do that. So I went in and I told him that this is what I felt like doing. And he said, "No, we can't do that. You just sit there and I'll sit here." And this disappointed me so much, because I felt he couldn't deal with me.

Very shortly after that, a thing happened that made me decide to leave him. I was telling him about some sexual imagery I was having to deal with, and my anger, and *he kept falling asleep!* Then, when I said something to him about it like, "Hey, can you hear me? Are you awake?"—he denied it. I know he was asleep—but he tried to pretend he wasn't. So I knew it was time to go. He was falling asleep because he could not deal with my anger, my sexual anger.

Then he told me how I would have to start thinking of myself as part of society and not just a subset of women who have been sexually abused. All I want is to go where I'll be loved. No, that's what the *little girl* wants. *I* want to go away and rest and feel proud that I've climbed all these mountains.

Then, my last day in therapy with him, I said goodbye, and he wished me luck and all that, and he gave me a hug. I could feel that he had an erection. I could feel it against me when I hugged him. That made me wonder then about how he had been treating me. I wonder if a man can handle this type of problem.

I Think My New Therapist Is Disgusted With Me

This therapist I'm working with now is really good in terms of helping me to bring images out. But just recently I started getting in touch with anger. She has a friend who does an anger workshop, so I went over and participated. I was doing an interesting thing at that point—I was allowing myself to split into two selves—one of them was my emotional self, and the other was my intellectual self. I'd argue with myself back and forth. Through this process, a lot of the anger started to come out. I did it in a therapy session, and got very angry and emotional. At the end of that session, I felt like she was disgusted with me, and that she didn't want anything to do with me.

I haven't been able to do it since. She has tried to get me to do it, but something is holding me back from really feeling those emotions. The amount of anger that's there is just really awful. I don't know what I'm going to do about that. I almost felt that she's afraid of that part of me. I don't feel like I can trust her. It's something we are working on.

The images I have—when I do have them, I'm really doing it all by myself. She says things, and I can hear her voice, and it's comforting to know she's there, but I feel that I am all alone with it. That is part of my protection. Because if I let myself get out, and climb up on her lap and trust her or something, I'd be terribly vulnerable. And then too, I hear my mother's tape saying, "Grow up. You're a big girl; you don't need all this stuff."

Therapy Issues

Thought to keep: so many of my "huge issues" are really life's issues and aren't huge. I magnify them because of the incest victim stuff.

Reply: Of course! I have given myself permission to go through this being an incest victim, which means I must go back to being a little girl and re-experience the feelings so I can put it behind me. Bury this victimized "little girl." Thus, right now, all my adult things seem overpowering.

The kicker is, I have *always* felt like a little girl! With men I must cover up my wanting to feel little and needing their care. To feel not-like-a-little girl with a man is to feel hard and masculine, or strong and efficient and not needing anything. It is so hard for me to feel feminine and safe, to have needs.

What did my therapist say? Oh, yes. The hope, it was about the hope. He said if I separate too far from the hope—none of this will work. And sometimes, I *do* hope, like right now. But sometimes, the hope is far away, out there someplace. He said when this is over I won't *be* any different—I'll just feel different about myself. That's okay with me, I know a little about that. The rest scares me. The part I know about has already happened. I've lost the inferiority. I don't seem to need it anymore—not much, anyway. Maybe once in a while—a little attack, but it's soon over—forgotten, really.

The Pain of a Newborn Baby

Sometimes I don't want to go any further. I think I was okay before this started—Brett got me into this. The rest of the group are real victims, not me. I hate my mother because I have to convince her that I'm a victim when I'm not even sure I am. I don't want to go any further, thank you. This is far enough.

Sometimes I cry. I do not feel sympathy for myself—I simply feel. Somehow that idea gives me strength to claim my pain as all mine. I feel possessive of it—almost proud of it. I have earned this pain, have worked hard for it. For fifty long years I have hidden from it, and now I can claim it, reach it, really feel it. I don't want to let go of it. It is, I am now dimly aware, the pain of a newly born baby.

CHAPTER 7—FOOTNOTES

1. Gelinas, Denise J., "The Persisting Negative Effects of Incest", *Psychiatry* 46 (November 1983): 317.
2. Ibid. 315.
3. Ibid. 330.
4. Ibid. 319.

8

Healing: Growing Through the Pain

When I think of getting better, I think of an oyster spending years and years living with pain from a piece of gravel stuck in its guts. The gravel doesn't go away; the oyster grows away from it. Year after year, the oyster puts layer upon layer of its own secretions between itself and the gravel, until it doesn't feel the pain anymore. Because it now has a pearl!

Healing feels like that. It is gradual, it takes a long time. In an almost imperceptible progression, we grow past the pain. It takes a long time, but in the end you have produced something; you have a pearl. It is all yours, too. It is not just that you used to feel lousy and now you feel okay. You actually feel a sense of accomplishment, that from all the ugliness you have grown and developed a thing of beauty—you!

Healing comes from the pain. This is the paradox of recovery. Healing is a healthy, recuperative response to the pain, achieved with the guidance and wisdom we gain from therapy. Many of us went years and years with destructive responses that didn't heal us, that only disfigured us, as we saw in Chapter 4. Part of our therapy and our healing process is not only to address the incest, but also to recover from our destructive responses to it. In particular, we have to learn to let go of our guilt and shame, and to look at ourselves positively to develop the potential that is there. We learn to think good things about ourselves and to do good things for ourselves. In the end, we are people who really have something precious to give. We have our pearl—ourselves.

In the contributions to this section, you will see an emerging point of view—one that is self-accepting, more able to recognize the possibilities of the present, looking forward with hope more than looking backward with grief. For the first time, the present isn't dictated so much by the past, and we can talk about choices. The pain isn't gone, it is still there. But somehow we develop enough of ourselves that we have other places in ourselves to go where we are free of it. We can always go back to it, but we don't have to. We have a choice.

NOELLE

Noelle's healing process is evident in the way she is moving past the incest. There is a feeling of resolution in the way she talks about her mother and father, a sense that their inadequacies are still there but that they aren't a problem for her anymore. They haven't changed; she has. She is learning how to be happy.

Healing is a growth process. The incest doesn't go away. It isn't obliterated from Noelle's memory, or changed in any respect. It remains a given part of her experience. But, as Noelle says, "It changes from being a problem in my life to being something that happened to me." This doesn't come from somehow "changing" the incest experience. We know that doesn't work, because that is what denial is, an effort to rewrite history. Only it doesn't work, it just makes us feels crazy. No, we can't change what happened to us. But as Noelle says, by addressing it and responding to it in a healing way we can grow past it.

Healing—Incest Is Just Something That Happened to Me

For me, healing means that gradually incest changes from being a problem in my life to being something that happened to me. It's just a gradual change in perspective. I can feel it in the way I think about my parents, myself, and my children. Incest used to loom large over everything, dominating my emotions and contaminating every relationship. Now it is much smaller, and some weeks it is not even there. The incest didn't go away or get smaller. But I changed. I grew. I developed.

First I was an incest victim, then I was an incest survivor. Now it is just something that happened to me. My identity has developed beyond it. I'm not defining myself by incest, not so much as I used to anyway. I think that gradually I grew past it. You never forget it, but you don't have to think about it anymore.

My Mother

I spent the first five or six years of therapy addressing my anger and hatred for my father. That was resolved first. My mother's role was harder to work on, because it was less obvious. My father was easy, because everything in that relationship was so obvious. But my mother—well, I went through a lot of different stages with her. I can say now that I gave up on my mother when I was three, in terms of her ability to give me safety or security. I loved her desperately. I needed her. But she was just another hurt, abused child, frantically trying to take care of her children without the resources to do so.

I think she was scared to death. Here she was in a strange country, no family, no help after my grandma died, her husband's drinking out of control, and she had two small children. I could feel her love, but there was a desperation about it that came from her fear that she could not make us safe, because she did not feel safe. I can see her now, she was so pretty and gentle. She held me a lot.

When I had my daughter, I found my mother in myself. I had those same feelings of desperation that I would not be able to keep her safe—I had phobias about everything. I loved my daughter to distraction, but no matter how hard I tried, I could not eliminate all the dangers in the world to protect her. That was my mother's fear coming out in me. I was loving her the way I had been loved.

I have to start believing in the joy of life, for me. I remember, when I studied art, I loved the archaic Greek statues because of their little smiles. They were smiling, their faces had the joy of living on them. I saw that and I knew it came from some belief in the goodness of the universe, but I did not know how to get to that. I'm still trying. My father's abuse and my mother's fear took that away from me. But I think I now can make a claim to get it back.

Today, when I'm with my mom, I feel very happy about her love for me. I used to be angry because she didn't save me from my father. Now I can forgive that because I understand what she was going through and that she did everything she could to take care of me. I remember how she kept us fed by teaching art. This was not easy for her. She was sick a lot, and had my brother and me to care for. But she was very determined, and she set aside a room for a studio, put up ads, called the schools, and got students. She didn't make much, but I remember she made enough for us to eat and have shoes. When she went in the hospital for surgery, she resumed the classes as soon as she got home.

If I could have changed my mom, I would have had her suffer less. It was not good for me to have an image of suffering for a mother. I associate her love with suffering. I don't like to remember all the pain she had—the sickness, the exhaustion, the ragged clothes, the slavery to my father. But I've begun to see that she and my dad were a team. He was an abuser, she was the abused.

This was what they passed on to me. And I've spent most of my adult life trying to identify all the ways that it is re-enacted in my own behavior patterns and to throw it off. It's interesting how the incest is just one part of a whole system of dysfunction I have to correct. It had particular elements that I know are distinctive, but it really is part of the whole design of our family. But it doesn't have to be my design.

My Father

I made progress dealing with my father off and on in therapy. I think the hardest part was getting over the denial. For the first year after I remembered the incest, I was still blocking out a lot of things. I am still not fully aware of how it is reflected in my life. Every day brings some new revelation. But in that first year, I really struggled with some things I couldn't confront very well. One was my shame about being sexually aroused by Father's molestations. It was hard, so hard to face that. I felt that it meant I was bad, that if I were good I would not have felt any sexual sensations. It seemed that because I had felt something, it was partly my fault. I thought I was disgusting, and that was the start of my inability to have any sex. I am still working on that feeling.

The other thing I have struggled with is my feeling for my father. What came back to me when I remembered the incest was the great love I had for him at that time. I was bereft when he said they would take him away. The pain I felt at that was terrible. And yet he had done an awful thing to me. It didn't seem right that I could love him, but I did. And over time, as my childhood progressed and he abused me emotionally, the hurt and pain I had was just too much to bear, precisely because I had loved him so very much.

I feel ashamed now when I look back, and I have to admit that throughout all the abuse, I still loved my dad. I feel as if somehow my loving him made me an accomplice. I gave up on him but I still harbored some love for him. I always felt that even when he was abusive, that somewhere he had some love for me. It is strange, but I was always Daddy's special girl. I felt I was special. I felt that if something ever happened and I needed him to save my life, he would, but that I couldn't depend on him for just day-to-day kindness.

I think this is what damaged me the most. It was being loved in a abusive way. I learned that loving feels desolate, depressed, and abandoned. I learned that to love was to invite abuse. I've often wondered if, in my childish mind, I got the message that I was being punished for the sex, for my love. That love and sex had to be accompanied by rejection.

Today, I still know my father cannot love me for myself, but that he does love me the only way he can. I know that most of the time that means that he can only love me for himself. But if there are ways he can do that and still be acceptable to me, I will accept it. I cannot accept any more damaging love from him. When he responds to some fact about my life today with the statement, "How do you think it makes *me* feel?" I just cut it off right then. End of conversation. I will not let him do that number on me where I'm not allowed to hurt, feel pain, or have problems because it reflects badly on him.

I love him, but I feel sorry for him. I don't have to punish him. He has tortured himself enough. I just want to get on with my recovery now. I'm just very sorry that our family suffered so much. The real tragedy of my family was not so much that the incest and abuse happened, but that nobody knew how to come back from it. It was a tragedy to lose all those years to his rage and my mother's fears. But that is over now. It's over.

Myself

Now I am trying to rid myself of the shame, to accept that I was powerless, and that I had no responsibility for what happened to me. Then I can throw off the bad feelings about myself, the parts of me that were imposed on me by the abuse. Finally I will be able to claim me for myself—like being able to walk away from my father when he says, "How do you think that makes *me* feel?"

Healing for me is to allow myself to be happy, to take care of myself, to find a middle ground between caring only for myself and caring only for other people. It means it's okay for me to ask my daughter to play quietly in her room for half an hour while I rest, and that I can do that without being abusive to her, because I can do it before I reach the point of total desperation. It means I can allow myself time to take a shower, even if there are other obligations that will have to wait. Just little things, multiplied 100 times, adding up to me being able to take care of myself without desperation or anger. And being able to feel happy without the fear that it will be taken away from me.

My Children

My four-year-old daughter is not without problems, problems that come from my ineptitude as a parent. But as I get better and become more secure in myself, I can pass it on to her. I can have something to give to her. I still have bad periods, when the memories come back and I lose my self-possession to the past. When that happens, I see her start to come apart again. But then I get better, and I can make her better too. I have to keep faith that I will be able to do that, then the bad periods won't be so bad.

Let's say I've worked very hard at not panicking and not shouting abusively at my daughter when she refuses to do what I tell her to do. And she has become more secure, able to sleep by herself for a whole night, able to stay in a room by herself.

Then I have a bad period when I have some painful feelings come back. I backslide and feel overwhelmed, and I talk to her abusively. She starts to get up at night and come to my room. She wets her bed. She is afraid to sit at the table and color by herself.

Just a few months ago, I would hate myself, loathe myself, and want to die for this. I would make it worse for myself by losing faith, by letting myself despair. I would feel that I could never, ever make it right for her again, that I had lost her forever, that I would never feel healthy again. I would let myself fall farther and farther into hopelessness. It was a downward spiral.

I know I'm getting better now because I don't fall into that hopeless pit anymore. Not as much. When things get bad, I can just barely cling to the idea that I will pull out of it, but I can cling to it. I can see through to the other side of it, and by doing that I don't fall so far down in the pit. And I also can keep faith that I can help my daughter, that I can make it right again for her.

I have one image I keep in my mind, a cue my therapist gave me. She said, "Remember when you were very little, when somehow if you had a hurt, all it would take was to climb up on your mother's lap and she could make it better just by holding you?" And somehow that image stayed with me, that I had that power to do that for my little girl, because I believed in that power. And in a strange way, believing in that power, and being able to do that for her, makes me able to do it for myself, too.

Happiness

I want to talk about feeling happy, exactly what that is for me. Today I can be happy, and I have moments that are particularly clear to me, when I realize how lucky I am. I love to sit at my desk and work, or write letters, or whatever, and hear my little girl play.

She'll go into her playroom, where she's got a little tape recorder.

She'll turn on her tape recorder and play all these really happy, cute children's songs, stuff I didn't even know existed when I was her age. And she'll sing along with these songs, with this cute little high-pitched voice of hers, and it just makes me so happy to hear her sing her little song because there is joy there. There is the joyfulness to her that I never had as a child, that I didn't even know existed. Now I have that in my life, because of her. I hear that little voice singing a song, and I think, her life is going to be different.

I love to watch my baby boy grow and learn to crawl I especially like to watch him lie on the floor when he's surrounded by all his toys, and they're just out of reach, and he gets up on his knees and his hands, and he is grunting, and he is trying so hard to get to those toys. He knows they're there, and he knows that he can get to them, and he pushes himself, and he's trying so hard to get himself coordinated. Finally, he lunges forward and grabs the toy, and then he squeals, and he's so happy. He's learning that he can do things for himself, that he can be gratified, that life can be good, and I like to see that. I like to sit on the couch with my children and hold them on my lap and read them stories. I feel like it doesn't get any better than this; it just doesn't get any better.

MEGAN

Megan is happily embarking on her adolescence at age 36 The joy of healing can be felt in her tentative steps toward living. She is finally able to enjoy the good feelings about herself and her sexuality that she couldn't experience when they were bound up with incest. Scary and thrilling at the same time, she is starting to step out, free of fear and shame. After eight years of therapy, life is not so much something to be endured as it is an adventure to be enjoyed.

Going Through Adolescence at Age 36

I've had this feeling lately—it's like I'm going through adolescence, not again, but for the first time. I'm starting to feel that it's okay to acknowledge my sexual feelings and think of how I can deal with them. I can have them without it being a bad thing.

I've been going to the movies a lot, adolescent movies. I don't know why. I've seen one movie twice. It's a movie about a girl coming of age at the age of 18, and it just struck a cord in me. I went and saw it yesterday for the second time all by myself. Then I went out and bought the album that comes with it.

It takes place in 1963. It's actually a well-done movie, but it just struck something in me. I'm sure it has to do with this stage I'm in. This girl has her first relationship when she's on a summer vacation. She meets this guy who's a dance instructor; that's where the title comes from. I guess part of the reason that I think it struck me is that I always wonder what would it have been like to come from a healthy family. To have had a healthy adolescence, to discover, to feel good about your sexuality. I know you know what I'm talking about, every incest victim does.

The only way you can try and know those things is to try and vicariously live other people's lives through books and movies, and then try it on for yourself. That's why I'm watching this girl on the screen. She is an 18-year-old and she's having her first affair, but she's not self-conscious about her body. She's not without guilt about the fact that she is having this affair, but she's not driven by the guilt either.

Reclaiming My Dreams of a Normal Life

I would like to know what it would be like to have sex without just automatically, inherently, having the feelings I had when I was abused. I would like to know what it's like to have plain ordinary sex and an ordinary relationship that's not tainted by the past. Every relationship, in some way, conjures up those same feelings and the same fears that I had with my brother, and I would like to know what it would be like not to have that.

I feel like my brother's behavior robbed me of my dreams, the dreams to get married and have children. I've felt I can't have those things because of his behavior. And I've always lived with that anger; I've always had it.

Right now, I guess when I think about going out on a date, I don't know how to put it all together. For example, if he starts to make sexual advances, there's this part in me that would very much want the sex, but then there's this other part of me that doesn't want it right away, but I don't know how to establish boundaries. How do you do that? I was never taught how to establish boundaries; it was like an all-or-nothing-type approach. But what is new for me is that for the first time, I want to try. I want to start living, even if it means going back to adolescence at age 36.

Accepting the Past; Finding Myself

I know I can't erase the past. I accept that it happened to me—the girl from the picture-perfect, Irish Catholic family. I accept that it affected me deeply and that I am still uncovering its effects. I have gone through the anger and hatred and I know that I cannot forgive my brother—I do not want him in my life—that I resent my sisters for rejecting me and for asking me to keep the family secret. I know I may not forgive them for not being there for me. Because I do not forgive them for that, I accept that my relationship with my family will always be superficial. And I accept that that hurts.

So I am building a new life in a new city with old friends and new friends becoming my new family. I may not know where I am going or how I am going to get there, but I think I am on the right track. I believe that when I am healed, I will have the answers that elude me now. It is as if I have traveled to the center of my soul and discovered that it is my friend, rather than my enemy.

DIDI

Taking care of ourselves doesn't come naturally. We have to learn it, learn that we aren't "bad" for meeting our needs. Didi is now able to feel her needs and take care of them. She is also able to see a future for herself. She is reclaiming her life. Like Brenda, she is looking back less and is able to see the possibility of the future more, without losing the present.

I'm Going to Do Some Things for Myself

When I first went into therapy, I was very impatient. I wanted to hurry up and get on with my life, I was tired of this hanging over my head. I still am in a way, but I feel like I've come a lot farther than those days.

Right now I'm at a very good point in my life. I'm at a real stable point, where I'm happy and I'm beginning to allow myself the pleasure of looking at my future and saying, "I'm going to do some things for myself. I'm going to do some things that I've always wanted to do, and I can do them." I'm beginning to feel like I'm good enough as a person that I can do things for myself. I could do all kinds of things that I've thought of but never allowed myself the pleasure of even thinking about, because I didn't feel like I was good enough.

For example, I never thought I was smart enough to go to college. Now I feel that I am, that I could do it, and someday, probably, I will. I never even thought of college or a career when I was in high school, never considered it possible, not for me. I think now I would be different.

Taking Care of Me

I'm letting myself be selfish, selfish in terms of doing things I need to do for myself, to feel good and strong. I love my children, but I also know it's okay for me to need time for myself, for my own projects and activities. I took aerobics and when I would go to class, I would get all ready and be sitting on the front porch waiting for Danny. When he came home, I would just run to the car as soon as he drove up, jump in and wave good-bye. Let him be mom for a while; let him take responsibility. I didn't feel guilty, not a bit. I let myself have that time to myself.

I like knitting, too, and I have other little projects I do. I take care of the girls and give them so much of myself, but if I gave them all there would be nothing left unless I replenished myself. So I let myself be selfish, if that is what you call it. It is a good kind of selfish, taking care of myself.

One other idea I have for women home with children or working with children and dealing with incest, is to keep a journal. Write alone, every day. It helps cleanse feelings of all kinds. To be alone with those feelings and to dissect them is, I think, good therapy.

ANN-MARIE

Most of us were driven people until therapy helped us identify some basic choices in our lives. It was easier to let people or circumstances dictate to us, as we responded to our early programming that said, "You don't have the right . . ." Once we break away from that, we face the agonizing responsibility of choices. Ann-Marie is aware of the pain of making choices—about marriage, children, family relationships. Painful choices, but infinitely better than bondage to the past.

Coming to Terms With My Mother

I have been focusing on my mother in therapy. I believe that my mother hasn't got a mean bone in her body. I think if she consciously or unconsciously perceived that I was being abused, she could not have done anything because, although he never abused her physically, she was just as much afraid of my father as the rest of us were.

There have been a lot of undercurrents in my family that I think I'm finally starting to pick up. I think maybe, in her own way, my mother is trying to say, "I know what you went through. I'm sorry, I did the best I could, and I love you dearly." That's why I say, if I turn around and I lash out at her the way I'd like to, it could destroy her. I don't know.

I remember how important my love was to my mother. My mom was a waitress, and she worked in this very nice, very small, but very nice little restaurant in our hometown. It was a kind of place where lawyers and professionals would come to for lunch and such, and for dinner. Especially on Saturdays, if one of us kids were downtown, we'd stop in and say hi. Sometimes she'd buy us a coke or something. Out of habit, not even thinking about it, we'd kiss hello, we'd kiss good-bye. If she was waiting on a customer, we'd just give her a quick peck on the cheek when we'd walk by her, and walk out. I remember one day, my mom said, and this story stuck with me ever since, she said to me, "Mrs. So-and-So was in today" (Mom always knew everybody), and she said, "Remember when you walked by and you kissed me goodbye? Mrs. So-and-So said to me, 'I wish my kids would do that.'" I could sense my mother's sense of pride that we loved her. Even back then I was pleased for her that in public she got some recognition for the fact that we did love her.

The Pain of Making Choices

I think about all the struggle and pain my mom may have gone through, and that is why I give the other women in the group and anyone else I know who has children a tremendous amount of credit. I have a choice now, I'm still at a point where I'm discovering this legacy of pain, and I have a choice. When I look back on all my ancestors' pain, I say to myself, "You can break it." Well, there's only so much of it I can break. There are some things that I want to, but who the hell am I to go and take care of six to seven generations-worth of pain and alcoholism and incest?

I have this tremendous feeling that, knowing what I know, knowing that I'm a recipient for so much pain, how can I knowingly have a child and pass it on? How can I do that? That's the thing I'm going to have to talk about with Jack, my husband, and say, "Do you realize what we are passing on to our children? Your family's indifference, and my family's abuse and alcoholism, and this and that and the other thing."

The thing is, as much as I may want to have children, I don't want it to be a decision, I want it to just happen. Because I just can't make that decision. I had this boyfriend in college, he would almost want to shake me, he said, because he thought I was the epitome of "Ignorance is bliss." Here it is, 10 or 15 years later, I still think about that comment from him because I think, even now, I wish to God I'd never become "smart" about any of this. That ignorance, I realize now, was deliberate, because there is so much pain. It was my protection against pain.

The Pain Stops for a While More and More

I keep talking about all the pain, but there are many times in my life, even now, when it stops for a while. A couple of weeks ago, I was sitting at my desk on a Sunday night and doing the family bills. I had some music playing on the stereo that I really liked, and Jack was puttering around somewhere, watching TV or something. One of my cats came in, and when he wants attention, comes in and lies on the paper you're doing. Especially if you're sitting at the desk, he'll lie right in the middle of it. You pick him up and throw him off, he goes right back and lies on it again; he doesn't take no for an answer. Usually I do one of three things: (1) throw him off, (2) go ahead and pet him, or (3) I get up and say, "Okay, Toby," and go and lie on the bed with him for about five minutes and give him full attention, stroke him all he wants until he goes away quiet. Then he leaves me alone. Well, I took him to the bedroom and gave him some attention and felt something like, I don't know—I get this periodically—a sense of peace, contentedness. It's not necessarily a feeling of tremendous joy. It's just like, this is the way it should be. It's just kind of like, "This is good." And I know that those moments are going to be there for me, more and more.

BRENDA

Brenda is able to look back and take pride in what she has accomplished and look forward to what she has yet to enjoy. This is a healing point of view, a change from the wounded condition in which we look back with so much grief that we fail to see the good things in the present—until they too slip into the past and become yet another loss. Brenda can feel a "real sense of peace" coming to her as she lets go of the past, accepts herself, and lets herself be okay. Brenda is letting other people give her support, letting herself be cared for. She says it was a turning point in her therapy to believe that people would be there for her. It was also a turning point for her to trust enough to let other people be there for her.

A Real Sense of Peace

Finally, I can take pride in knowing that I came through a long hard life and I'm winning, I'm overcoming. I'm taking pride in that. I'm taking pride in the challenges that I've met and overcome in therapy. I'm taking pride in the fact that I feel better about myself and that, even if I have 40 years left to live or 20 years left to live, I'm not going to regret the things I've missed out on, like not starting earlier, not taking charge and trying to do something for myself. Because now I am doing something, and I've got years left that I'm going to enjoy. I'm going to be a normal person, whatever that is. Whatever is normal for me, whatever is right.

I just have a real sense of peace coming to me. I told my therapist the other day, if this is maturity, if this is becoming an adult, it's a good feeling. But more important, I'm enjoying the freedom of choice. I hope to enjoy more freedom of choice as time goes on.

One of the greatest things I think I am experiencing now from both of the counselors I see is the immense caring that comes forth to me. It took me several months in the incest group and several months in private therapy to trust, to think they really cared enough, that they would be there for me. And to believe what they said, that was really a turning point in therapy for me. I think you have to go through that anytime you start therapy, or you change therapists.

Sharing With Other Women

One of the exciting things now is when someone comes to me. Lately, it's been women who come to me and notice the changes in me. And they express concerns about things that are going on in their lives. I've had two people come to me who have had sexual abuse or incest in their lives, and I can talk about it, about myself. Obviously I don't go around flaunting it or broadcasting it, but if someone approaches me, I feel freer now to talk about it, without the shame that used to be there. I'm not proud that it happened to me, but I'm not carrying the burden of guilt and responsibility anymore, or at least a great deal less then I used to. I referred them to my therapist, and they're now getting counseling. Another friend who came to me had extreme alcohol abuse and physical abuse in her family, and is now seeing my therapist.

It's great because, when we want to, we can talk between us openly about how we feel, and we share a common denominator. None of us tries to be a professional therapist to one another but it's nice not to have the secrets anymore. It's nice to know that someone else's experiences have been similar to yours. And that another human being is going to make a life for herself, not one layered with guilt and burdened with responsibility for things that she had no responsibility for.

The Challenge of Therapy

I think if I could say anything to anyone, it would be that there are people who are just like you. Don't hesitate to seek help, you can only benefit, although it's not a process that's going to happen overnight. I know when I went into therapy, I thought, okay, six months and I'll be well. Six months, I'll have overcome this problem, whether I went for the sexual problem, or I went because I was depressed, whatever the reason. It's a long process. It's not an easy process; it's one that requires dedication. It requires you to take the challenge to become your own master, to put peace and happiness back into your life, to relieve yourself of guilt that doesn't belong to you, responsibility that doesn't belong to you, shame that should not be there.

When you make accomplishments, when you meet those challenges, the pride that you deserve, that comes to you, is just phenomenal. I feel like I'm so much healthier now. I hate to sit here and brag and sound like I'm on a bandstand, but the differences in me now, as opposed to four-and-a-half years ago when I started all this therapy, are phenomenal. I have enthusiasm for life. I have the energy to meet the challenges. I know I still have a long ways to go. I have issues I still need to deal with, but I'm ready to take the challenge. I'm ready to look at them.

I think you can only benefit from therapy, and you can only benefit if you know and trust and feel secure with your therapist. You have to shop around for a therapist. It's like applying for a job almost, you have to be comfortable with the person, or you're not going to trust them. So you have to interview them carefully. I wish there were hundreds of Moniques in the world, so that everyone could have her. She is one of the most wonderful, sensitive people I think I've ever met in my life. Such keen insight. I know I've benefited immensely from her caring, which has to be there as a part of therapy.

Getting Better Every Day

I don't have a strong desire anymore to understand why it happened. My strongest desire is to come to grips with what happened and to put the responsibilities where they belong, to get rid of the guilt, to be more self-accepting and expressing. I feel myself getting better every day.

Epilogue

In the time since we recorded our experiences for this book, each of us has continued to grow and recover. Everyone has written to me with updates on her life that I would like to share.

Noelle has finally started to confront her sexual fear, which she feels is the last and perhaps the worst level of trauma she has to work through. In doing so, she has hit "some all-time lows" and has had to fight what she describes as "compelling suicidal impulses." It has been discouraging for her to have come so far and then find herself again "at the bottom." "It is humiliating" she writes, "to be back in this condition again." But she also says, "I am hanging on to the fact that this may be my final step in my recovery. After this I may be able to recover my sexuality and take back that part of my life again."

Even though Noelle is again struggling with dissociation and self-destructive impulses, she finds that it is different now. "I know what is happening to me, and I can hang onto the knowledge that it will pass. It's like a huge tidal wave sweeping over me, but I'm not swept away completely by the fear and despair and hopeless feelings because I have a part of me, just a tiny part, that stays anchored to the ground." Noelle shows us what recovery is—that even in the worst times we can find in ourselves a part that is healthy enough to keep us in the present when the terror of the past comes flooding back into our lives. Noelle has done all the things she needs to do to take care of herself at this time. "I am in close contact with my therapist, who has made a point of calling me at intervals and has kept open the option of hospitalization if I should need it. I also have other people I can call when I start to feel hopeless, including a 24-hour suicide hotline. I'm also not making any decisions of any kind and relying on my husband to take care of things at home when I can't. I've learned to get help for myself, and I'm grateful to have my therapist and my husband there."

This is progress for Noelle—to recognize what is happening to her, to be able to take care of herself and, most important, to let other people help her. "I don't feel that I've lost any of the good things I recovered—I still feel contentment with my children, my husband, and my work. Nothing has changed regarding my parents. My feelings are still detached. What is happening is that I'm hitting some new material, but I am not losing what I had recovered of myself." This is probably the most important thing Noelle can bring to us—faith in the irreversibility of our recovery. Even though it may feel at times that we are losing again, that the old feelings are taking over, remember that these feelings are transient, and that the progress we have made is permanent. It is the solid spot we have to stand on, and once it is established it is there to stay. We may stray from it, but it will be there for us to go back to.

Megan reports a different experience since her story was recorded. She has been consolidating her recovery and trying some new things in her life. She got a promising new job and moved to a new city. After the euphoria wore off, she found herself dealing with a stressful personnel problem. One of her supervisors on the job is apparently a "borderline" personality (made famous by the movie *Fatal Attraction*), which has chaotic effects on the staff. Megan's response has been healthy and appropriate: "What disturbs me the most is to realize that running into and having to work with disturbed people is obviously just a part of life. That's one reason why I am not about to pack up and leave yet. I like working there and dearly love all my other co-workers, and who's to say any other place would be any better? That's why I chose the route of protecting myself by developing business contacts, so that should I need an escape I will have one ready."

Megan has made an appropriate response, although it didn't come right away. When her co-worker first started exhibiting irrational, angry, and paranoid behavior, Megan says, "It bothered me for a long time because I assumed, as usual, that I was doing something wrong, because why else would she treat me this way?" After a while, she recognized that "it had nothing to do with me . . ." and she was able to detach from the behavior. Even though her initial response was the typical "parentified" reaction we have seen so much, the proof of her recovery is in her ability to override that old response and use a new, more functional one.

Megan is generally learning to enjoy herself, with a visit to a younger sister, a trip to a jazz festival, a trip to see old friends, a vacation with cousins. She weathered a scare when her mammogram disclosed a "mass" that later turned out to be benign, and as a result has embarked on a healthy weight loss and exercise program, "something I can follow for the rest of my life." She has lost weight and now asks herself, "What will happen when I get into shape and know I'm attractive to men and have no more excuses to hide? I haven't a clue! I will keep you posted. I do hope it means that I will finally find a relationship; I could really use one."

Megan's positive and healthy new life is very encouraging but also very realistic—there are still problems, still peaks and troughs in her life, but she is handling them from a healthy position, with better results.

Didi is also facing new challenges in her recovery. Her father is still in therapy and she still has to deal with him. "He's learned to deal with his own self-hatred for the abuse, but he cannot yet forgive himself. He's much different now and so am I. I treat him differently, like I have more respect for myself. I have learned to set my own boundaries and make them known."

Another area Didi has faced is her image of her mother, who died when she was nine. "I have learned that my mother was an alcoholic . . . that has brought a new light to my life. I've begun to realize why my sister is the way she is. But more important, I've learned that I can only change myself. I can't change anyone in my family or anything in my past, but I can change the way I relate to and deal with them. I'm beginning to look at my child within. It hurts, but I am beginning to see the light. I'm starting to like myself and am learning how to 'play.' "

Didi has made great progress in reclaiming her life from the distortions of the past, not only by confronting her father with the reality of his abuse, but also by confronting the reality of what her mother was like. She has had to come to terms with her father. Until she did that, she could not let go of her mother or recover the child that she was. Her progress in that area is evident in her growing "self-ness."

Didi has also progressed in her marriage: "My relationship with Danny is great. We are in couples therapy, and each in individual therapy. He's learned he has some problems himself. Overall, everything is moving ahead."

Like Didi, Ann-Marie is also making progress in her relationships. She reports: "I recently told my brother about the incest. He and I were having an unusually personal and confidential phone call one evening. I was asking him some general questions about our childhood. In particular, I remembered that he had been physically abused—beaten—by my father, but it seemed to me that those beatings stopped when the incest with me started. When I asked him how long the beating continued, he replied, 'Until Dad was too weak to do them anymore due to his illness.' I really felt bad hearing that."

"As he and I talked, I had a real sense that this was probably going to be one of my best opportunities to tell him. So, I screwed up my courage and told him. Of course, he was stunned, but he turned right around and became very supportive, offering to talk any time. I was shaking but relieved. In group, several of the others have experienced all the usual reactions—blank silence, accusations of lying, and so on. I got none of that from him. I told him he was one in a million."

"Later that night I was really hit by grief for those poor two little kids, terrorized by their father and no one protecting them. I cried for them—I mean, I was only eight or nine and my brother, seven or eight. What could we have done to deserve that treatment at that age! After a while, I was able to console myself, reminding myself that, yes, all that happened, but it's in the past and has no more hold on me, and he and I are doing well now. This was significant because I healed myself there: I knew what to do for me when I felt this way, and I did it, and it worked! Parenting myself worked; taking care of that little girl inside worked."

Confronting her brother enabled Ann-Marie to feel her grief in a very immediate way, giving her the opportunity to heal. Over and over again we have seen this—the way we heal through an honest and direct confrontation with our pain.

Ann-Marie is still considering a confrontation with her mother. She is cautious, and appropriately so—she doesn't want to do it unless she is sure it will benefit her. One important step she has made is that of securing the support of her brother: "My brother was also supportive of me when I told him I may have to tell Mom about this. He didn't say I couldn't or shouldn't, just accepted that I may. In turn, I told him I would be sure to talk to him first before doing it, so he's mentally prepared for whatever might happen."

Another relationship in transition for Ann-Marie is that with her husband. They have started couples counseling, with good results. "Our third wedding anniversary is coming up shortly, and I think it will be much better than last year—much more relaxed, anyway, because the problems we have are no longer bottled up—they come out and we deal with them. Things are still tough, but our therapist really helps us to unravel the problems and find a way through."

The question of having children remains an issue in her marriage, but Ann-Marie says, "I'd like to be closer to health before I make a final decision one way or another." Her caution is evidence of her newly developing ability to take care of herself, one of the major features of recovery.

Much of her progress can be attributed to her growing self-esteem. "I am getting a good start at building self-esteem and self-worth. I stand up for myself more these days. I have a clearer idea of what I need, and I'm better at asking for it *and* at accepting it I still have a way to go, but I see new pieces of me all the time."

In recovery, we can give ourselves credit for our growth while still recognizing the areas where more work is needed. Ann-Marie explains: "I have changed a lot in the last year. I really feel very much in transition, hanging in the air. I am at a point where I recognize my behaviors—the ones that don't work for me anymore—and I'm trying to replace them with healthier ones, but the replacement hasn't occurred yet. In other words, I know what I *don't* want to do any more, but I don't yet know what I want to replace those with. Fortunately this transition phase isn't *too* painful—just confusing, frustrating, and too lengthy for my tastes! But then, so is this whole healing process."

Ann-Marie is a good example of how, in recovery, we learn to accept our limitations, to be patient, to know that change is as uneven as it is inevitable.

Our pain becomes a signal of our growth: "Pain still comes and goes. That's something else I've learned to recognize: when I'm hurting, and what I'm hurting about. I have felt emotional pain over the years—usually in a relationship with a man—but it had to be of an overwhelming intensity before I'd feel it. I'd beat out anything else. Now I can feel it earlier and know what it's about. I can get through it without a crisis."

Brenda has also made some major strides since she recorded her story for this book. She ended the relationship that she felt was based on old behavior and moved out on her own. She also "graduated" from her therapy group, but has continued individual therapy. Except for these changes she reports that things are pretty much the same as they were. She is happy with her progress, feels positive, and is making decisions now about where she wants to go with her life.

Ellen is also faced with decisions—particularly decisions about how far she can go in her therapy. Like many of us, she feels that having opened the door, she cannot turn back. But she also isn't too sure about moving forward. Her "gut feeling" is that time will bring her to the memories she has avoided. She feels that she will do it when she is ready. Ellen again reminds us of an important principle in recovery—timeliness. Until the time is right—well, she's going to enjoy her sailboat! She says she feels a new acceptance, a new peace, almost a surrender to what she feels she must face. When the time is right, she will know it. She reminds us that we have an inner necessity of our own that we must learn to respect.

The feeling I got from reading these letters is a firm sense of healing. Everyone has faced new challenges, nothing has been painless or perfect, but everyone is managing to stand on that tiny spot she established for herself, and that spot is growing larger. Even Noelle, who is going through yet another recurrence, views it not as a setback but as progress. She, and the others, are reclaiming themselves from the past.

Everyone who contributed to this book found that the sharing of their experience with others gave them more strength in their recovery. They wanted to continue to reach out to help others, even after their work on the book was completed. As a result, they decided to form a Big Sisters network for young incest victims. They hope it will help young victims to have available an adult survivor who will validate their experience, reassure them and provide the fellowship that is so desperately needed. This was the most gratifying news of all.

Their stories won't end here; they will go on. We will never know exactly what happens to each person, but that doesn't matter. The value of their stories is not in a happy ending but in what we can learn about the process of recovery. Recovery cannot guarantee our happiness, but what it can do is give us the equipment we need to be happy. The rest is up to us.

A Summary of the Recovery Process

Many survivors have asked, "How am I going to get better by feeling all this pain? How is talking about it going to help?" This book has followed the healing process from the first realization in Chapter 1 that we were powerless over our abusers to the final stages of healing in Chapter 8. The following is a step-by-step summary of the process.

The first step in getting better is to accept that we were damaged by incest and that we need to recover. An important part of this step is to accept that we were powerless over our abusers. We have to recognize that we were unwilling victims. Even if we loved our abusers, craved their attention, and experienced sexual arousal, we were unwilling victims. We could not fully understand what was happening to us but our abusers could. We didn't even have the capacity for consent, so whether we were physically coerced or emotionally manipulated, we were all equally powerless. We did not make it happen anymore than we could stop it from happening.

Until we can accept that we were powerless, we will be defensive about the problems we have suffered because at some level, conscious or sub-conscious, we will still blame ourselves and feel guilty. Once we have accepted our powerlessness and cast off our guilt and self-blame, we can start to be completely honest about what incest has done to us. We can start to do something for ourselves.

Also, when we accept our powerlessness over our abusers, we can let go of them and turn our attention away from them. They couldn't help us then and they can't help us now. It isn't fair and it isn't right that we have to face long years of struggle because of something they did, and we all experience bitter anger about that. But we have to accept that while the abuser alone is responsible for the abuse, we alone are responsible for our own recovery. Nobody else can fix it for us, especially not our abusers.

At this point in the process, many of us recognize that we have placed ourselves in abusive relationships over and over again, each time expecting the abuser to stop and to make it better for us in some way. And each time we suffered pain and resentment because they didn't stop, and it didn't get better. We were locked into these relationships and could not escape because we continued to behave as if we had some power over our abusers, that everything would be alright if we could just get them to change. We saw this pattern in many of the stories in Chapters 4 and 5.

Accepting our powerlessness over our primary abusers is to accept that we can't change them and they can't "fix" what happened. We all know this in our heads, but not until we can feel it and know it on an emotional level does it have any reality for us. When it becomes real for us, then we can turn away from our abusers, both the primary abusers and those we have acquired in our adult relationships as well. It is a gradual change, a fundamental detachment that grows and pervades all our relationships.

This detachment is accompanied by a change in emphasis. After talking for so long about what has been *done to us* and what we feel is still being done to us in many ways, we begin to hear ourselves. We get angry. Our anger is a healthy and valid response. It means we have finally placed responsibility for the abuse on the abuser. We begin to respond to it by talking more about what *we can do for ourselves*. This is a subtle change from passive (victim) to active (empowered). Ironically, we get our real power when we accept that we were powerless over our abusers and focus our powers on ourselves. This is the start of healing. In all of nature, the phenomenon of healing is the same: it is literally a new growth.

There is no shortcut to this process. The growth, the change, happens as a response to the pain and anger we experience. We must re-connect with the incest experience, and allow ourselves to feel the le-gitimate pain and anger we were denied for so long. When we can do this, we will finally reach a point where the pain becomes intolerable. At that point, we can detach from the abuser and we can change in ways that will make ourselves better.

Many survivors get stuck at this stage. This is where competent, professional help is important, because most of us don't have families or friends that can show us healing growth. If we did, we wouldn't be in the condition we are in. And societal models for female behavior aren't much help—most of them simply tell us how to be a better vic-tim. It is very easy for us to respond destructively to the anger and pain because those are the responses we learned so well and used so persistently in the past—denial; exploitative relationships; compul-sive eating; drug or alcohol use; withdrawal; isolation. These are the responses that enabled us to tolerate things that should have been in-tolerable, and hurt rather than healed us. With help, we can find new responses that are *growth* responses—problem-solving skills for life; healthy exercises for mind and body; resolution of anger; real inti-macy in honest relationships; development of our talents.

In a gradual change of emphasis, we start to concentrate less on what we feel other people have done and are doing to us, and more on what we can do for ourselves. We start to distinguish between things that are legitimately our concerns and things that are the concerns of others. This is the healthy formation of boundaries that we missed in our early development. When we can clearly distinguish between what is ours and what is theirs, we can be comfortable with other people. We no longer "lose" ourselves in a relationship, or isolate our-selves to avoid it. Our resentments start to diminish, because we are making decisions about ourselves. We begin to experience a new closeness with other people that comes when we are in possession of ourselves in a relationship.

As we concentrate more on taking care of ourselves, the fact that we can't control other people but can make choices about ourselves starts to have some reality for us. We experience our new self-posses-sion in many ways. For example, we will lose interest in or detach from people who hurt us, when before we couldn't let go of them. Rather than simmer in resentment over something, we learn to feel our anger, resolve it, and move on. Or, we find that things other peo-ple said or did that upset us actually have nothing to do with us. This is what it is to have boundaries. It happens when we accept that fun-damental difference between things we can change and things we can't change. This is when we repossess ourselves, because we know what is ours for the first time.

Healing is the new growth that occurs when we start to make choices and change the things we can change. We can't change the fact that the incest happened, but we can stop reliving that victimization in every facet of our lives. Chapter 7 describes the early stages of the healing process, and Chapter 8 shows it in its development. Megan describes "giving up" destructive relationships with siblings or friends and making choices about new relationships. Noelle finds that she can be comfortable with her parents for the first time because she has boundaries for the first time. Ann-Marie no longer resents that her business partner won't "allow" her to do things, but firmly states her position and accepts responsibility for it. Didi can make time for herself to go to aerobic dance class, and lets herself think about college and a career. Brenda leaves an exploitative relationship and gives herself credit for her accomplishments. Noelle gives herself time for a shower without first boiling over with resentment at her children's demands on her time. These are just a few of the many ways that healing is experienced. It is as minor as allowing time for a shower and as major as leaving a marriage. It is the experience of growth through the exercise of choices.

When we have a real sense of possessing ourselves, then we have something to give and we can know the joy of intimacy. We can reclaim our bodies and our sexuality and experience sex positively as something *we do* rather than something inflicted on us.

Healing is a gradual process of growing away from the incest, moving away from the old behaviors it imposed on us, and acquiring new behaviors and new ways of being ourselves. It is something we can understand very quickly on an intellectual level, but it takes time for it to become something real that is part of us. The important thing is to keep going. Don't get lost in the process. Here are a few things to remember.

THINGS TO REMEMBER

1. We are victims when we simply endure the effects of incest. We are survivors when we face it. We are free when we grow through it.

2. Growth comes through pain—when we allow ourselves to recognize our pain and respond to it appropriately for the first time with self-nurturing, self-love, self-acceptance, and self-respect. An intellectual understanding of incest is not enough for recovery.

3. Denial was the response we learned as children. Denial severed the connection between our feelings and the incest trauma, rendering us incapable of a healing response. To recover, we have to reconnect with our feelings and with the incest trauma. This will be painful.

4. To reconnect, we must listen to ourselves, find our own voices for the first time. A private journal is one way to do it. Or, try writing your own story using the format of this book as a model.

5. Accept that you were powerless over your abuser, and you will be able to let go of your feelings of shame.

6. Accept that you have been damaged by something that was not your fault, and you will be able to seek the outside help that you need for recovery.

7. Recovery requires a commitment, a good therapist, and, ideally, a support group or therapy group of other survivors. Only you can do it, but you do not have to do it alone.

8. In the process of recovery, we often feel we are getting nowhere. But remember: Once we take "I am bad" and turn it around to "something bad was done to me," we are starting on an uneven but irreversible progression, because truth is immutable. As long as you respond to the truth instead of denying it, you won't lose your gains, but you will face new challenges.

9. Self-possession comes with self-knowledge. Until we identify how our past incest trauma still controls our present lives, we are still victims, and we still "belong" to our abusers.

10. We can possess ourselves again, we can free ourselves from the destructive past, if we are willing to make the commitment, and brave enough to surrender ourselves to the pain.

11. In recovery, surrender does not mean powerlessness. It means a willing acceptance of the truth of your experience. It is the antithesis of denial, enabling you to help yourself at last.

12. You can recover. Even when it feels hopeless, when you can see no way out, when all the walls fall into place, remember the transience of all lies. Your prison today is built of lies from the past:

"It is all your fault."

"You wanted it."

"There is nothing wrong—what are you talking about?"

"I never really hurt you."

"You imagined it."

"How can you say such a thing?"

"You should feel ashamed of yourself."

These lies kept you from healing, but like all lies they will slowly evaporate under the clear light of the truth. So have faith, don't let despair make any permanent decisions for you, and you will grow.

● ● ●

We wish every survivor a good, safe recovery.

> *"Noons of dryness see you fed*
> *By the involuntary powers;*
> *Nights of insult let you pass,*
> *Watched by every human love."*
> W. H. Auden

POSTSCRIPT

Would you like to write to the author or to any member of the survivors' group?

If so, feel free to send your letter, comments or suggestions to:

Parkside Publishing Corporation

Attn: Incest Survivors Group

205 W. Touhy Avenue

Park Ridge, Illinois 60068

(All letters will be forwarded unopened and in confidence to the author. And thank you!)

INDEX

A

Alcoholics
  characteristics of, 17
  commonalities of adult-children of,
    with incest survivors, 18
Alcoholism, and incest, 17-18, 29,
    32, 33, 59, 167, 168
Anger
  in Ann-Marie, 64
  in Brenda, 73-4, 122
  and denial, 84, 86
  in Didi, 166, 256, 258, 261, 265
  in Ellen, 136, 282-3
  in Megan, 161, 249, 251, 260
  in Noelle, 97, 153, 155, 193, 195-6,
    240, 287
  and recovery, 3, 226, 305-6
Ann-Marie
  alcoholism in family of, 59, 167, 168
  between incest and therapy, 112-21
  and dissociation, 55, 59-60, 214
  and divorce, 119-20
  denial in, 56, 112-21
  and escape, 60-61
  family of, 56-57
  fears in, 213
  headaches in, 215
  healing process for, 294-96, 301-3,
    306
  incest trauma in, 212-15
  introduction to, 55-65
  marriage of, 61-62, 119, 121,
    170-71
  nightmares in, 213-14
  and parentification, 166-74
  recurrences in, 214-15
    cognitive, 213-14
    emotional, 213
    physical, 215
  relationship with brother, 301-2
  relationship with father, 56, 57,
    58-59, 61, 62, 113, 167, 168
  relationship with mother, 58, 61,
    62-63, 167-69, 272-73, 294-95
  and secretism in family, 56-57, 64
  and self-disclosure, 271-72
  and self-esteem, 173
  and stepfather, 63
  therapy for, 61, 120-21, 266-73

Artistic renderings, in Noelle,
  196-97

B

Behavioral recurrences, in Noelle,
  196-97
Brenda
  acceptance of full responsibility
    by, 121-22, 123
  between incest and therapy,
    121-29
  bitterness of, 69, 73-74
  denial in, 72-73, 121-29
  and dissociation, 68, 216
  enuresis in, 217
  fantasy life of, 121
  fears in, 217-18
  feelings of victimization, 126
  and foster father, 66-68
  and guilt, 177
  hallucinations in, 218-19
  headaches in, 216
  healing process for, 296-98,
    303
  incest trauma in, 215-19
  introduction to, 65-74
  and loss of self-possession, 121
  marriage of, 70-71, 128
  nightmares in, 219
  as parent, 125, 127, 181-85, 279
  and parentification, 174-85
  recurrences in, 216
    cognitive, 218-19
    emotional, 217-18
    physical, 216-17
  relationship with brother, 176,
    177
  relationship with mother, 72,
    175-76, 178-79, 277, 278-79
  self-image of, 122-25, 184-85
  sexual difficulties of, 71-72
  and sexual image, 126-27
  survival tools of, 70
  and taking responsibility, 180-81
  therapy for, 125-26, 128-29, 226,
    273-80